PRAISE FOR *BEWITCHI*

"Gabriela has once again cast a pow

and seasoned practitioners. This book is written in elegant prose through her own specialized wisdom, in a way that blends both elements of self-empowerment and magick into one cohesive guide. I so appreciate the unique detail and love that Gabriela has infused into each and every page. A rare and precious gift to add to any library."

—Danielle Noel, creator of the Starchild and Moonchild Tarot decks

"Next-level magick brought down to earth in the most modern, practical way. Full of rituals, meditations, tarot, astrological insights, and more, this beautifully written book will help the reader learn how to craft a personal practice that empowers. Both old and new generations of practitioners will find something valuable. I'm looking at the elements in a whole new way!"

—Theresa Reed, author of *Astrology for Real Life: A No B.S. Guide for the Astro-Curious*

"Fun, glamorous, informative, and . . . friendly! Reading *Bewitching the Elements* is like sitting in the living room of your magical bestie, sipping rose and cardamom tea, invoking the Goddess, anointing candles, and pulling cards to call in your dream life. Somehow, Herstik managed to create a comprehensive book, tool kit, and how-to that is as downright helpful as it is pleasurable to read. Grab your broomsticks, your lipstick, and your wand, because this book is taking you on the wildest, most joyful moonlight adventure that you could imagine."

—Amanda Yates Garcia, author of *Initiated: Memoir of a Witch*; host of *Between the Worlds* podcast

"An engaging and informative journey into your own soul. It will help any new or veteran magic seeker to foster a relationship with the elementals."

—Leanne Marrama, coauthor of *Reading the Leaves: An Intuitive Guide to the Ancient Art and Modern Magic of Tea Leaf Divination*

"When I was a baby witch, the four elements confused me. How do I incorporate earth, air, fire, and water into my spell work and altar? I wish I'd had a book as lovely, informative, and stylish to guide me. Whether you're looking for glamorous new ways to enhance your practice or a thorough and sensuous guide to get you started, this book is for you."

—Sophie Saint Thomas, witch; author of *Finding Your Higher Self: Your Guide to Cannabis for Self-Care*

"*Bewitching the Elements* is overflowing with magical offerings that harness earth, air, fire, water, and spirit to conjure strength and self-love, or confront challenges and trauma. Herstik reveals rituals, practices, and correspondences that are accessible for beginners, yet rich enough to explore for those with years of experience. Her witchcraft is so inspiring not because she has all the answers, but because she makes space for readers to cultivate the curiosity and self-awareness necessary to uncover what magical practice makes the most sense for them. A beautiful, (third) eye-opening guide to the elemental path of self-discovery."

—Kristen Sollee, author of *Witches, Sluts, Feminists: Conjuring the Sex Positive* and *Cat Call: Reclaiming the Feral Feminine*

"Gabriela Herstik has an energy about her that simply lures the soul to her work, and for great reason! It enchants your senses, adorns your heart, and wakes the Goddess from within your core. Her take on the elements and how to connect to them, work with them, will elevate your practice to entirely new heights. *Bewitching the Elements* is full of practical, much-needed information that every witch should have."

—Juliet Diaz, author of *Witchery: Embrace the Witch Within*

"Will enchant you into falling in love with yourself, the universe, and your own divine sacred spark that is interwoven into the greater cosmic web of all that is eternal, infinite, and limitless. Herstik's endless well of knowledge and wisdom is thoroughly comprehensive, utterly accessible to witches of all experiences, and deeply inspiring."

—Yumi Sakugawa, author of *The Little Book of Life Hacks: How to Make Your Life Happier, Healthier, and More Beautiful*

"Herstik's approach to magickal work is never elusive or intimidating, but warm and welcoming to any would-be witch who feels a call to the craft. In *Bewitching the Elements*, she teaches you the wondrous ways in which you can honor and connect with our sacred elements, so you, too, can tap into your own natural, witchy potential."

—Marie Lodi, journalist; witch

"*Bewitching the Elements* is a must-read for anyone wanting to explore or deepen their relationship with elemental magick. Gabriela Herstik masterfully weaves together astrology, tantra, crystal magick, energetics to create a comprehensive resource for the aspiring metaphysical practitioner. The care with which she selects each tradition and technique explicated in these pages shows a thorough understanding of her craft. It is a practical and inspiring guide for all who seek to work in partnership with the energy of manifestation."

—Ashley Manta, High Priestess of Pleasure and creator of CannaSexual®

"Gabriela has an ability to make the esoteric accessible, inclusive, and fun; this book is all those things."

—Jerico Mandybur, author of *Neo Tarot* and *Daily Oracle*

"Gabriela introduces a whole new generation to the essentials of using the elements to manifest their desires and improve their lives. If you've been looking for an entry point into the world of witchcraft, you'll find it between these covers."

—Damien Echols, author of *High Magick: A Guide to the Spiritual Practices That Saved My Life on Death Row*

"When it comes to modern-day witchcraft, there are charlatans and there are witches. Herstik is a witch. Her approachable style to the craft gives every human a chance at mastering the elements. This is a must read for all lovers of the occult."

—Gigi Engle, certified sexologist; author of *All the F*cking Mistakes*

"Gabriela Herstik unites the historical traditions of spell work, magick, and witchcraft with glorious practicality and accessibility. When you read her book, you will discover why Gabriela is at the forefront of today's renaissance in witchery: she is ethical, audacious, magickal, and empowering. So is this book."

—Mitch Horowitz, PEN Award–winning author of *Occult America* and *The Miracle Club*

Bewitching the Elements

Bewitching the Elements

A GUIDE TO EMPOWERING YOURSELF THROUGH EARTH, AIR, FIRE, WATER, AND SPIRIT

GABRIELA HERSTIK

A TarcherPerigee Book

tarcherperigee
an imprint of Penguin Random House LLC
penguinrandomhouse.com

Text photographs by Alexandra Herstik

Illustration credits: page 103 © Sharpner; page 142 © Shymo Svetlana; page 242 © Croisy; page 286 © Lukasz Stefanski

Most Tarcher/Penguin books are available at special quantity discounts for bulk purchase for sales promotions, premiums, fund-raising, and educational needs. Special books or book excerpts also can be created to fit specific needs. For details, write: SpecialMarkets@penguinrandomhouse.com.

ISBN: 9780593086216
ebook ISBN: 9780593085899

Printed in the United States of America
3rd Printing

Book design by Ashley Tucker

This book is dedicated to the Divine Mother

The Goddess, in all her faces,
to whom I devote myself endlessly.

To the elements and elementals

To earth, air, fire, water, and spirit.

To the faeries.

To my family, both blood and chosen,
without whom I couldn't have done this.

To the witches who have come before me,

To the witches who walk alongside me,

To the witches to come after me.

To the magick that's inside us all.

Contents

Foreword

When I met Gabriela Herstik, it was as if I stumbled upon a budding rose, or an alien entity. She was at once the kindest soul I had encountered, and yet she was also old and wise, as if she had sprung from the womb calm, grounded, with a purpose, and without much weighing her down. An old Soul with a young Spirit. We came upon each other through the work of my longtime collaborator and dear friend, author and visionary Ruby Warrington. Together we were all ushering in a new age of reclaiming traditions that we felt to be at the heart of humanity, necessary and yearned for, yet blasted out by the patriarchy's agenda.

Like Gabriela, I decided when I was quite young that this world was way out of whack and I must try to help. In college I wrote plays and told stories and was committed to understanding and studying the reasons why womxn, LGBTQ folks, indigenous peoples, had been written out of "his"story. Why we were lesser than. Why our power had been taken. And why we had been silenced. For all of my twenties I made a career as an artist, doing rituals of reclaiming on camera, in films and photos, and taking on the goddesses like Mother Mary, Persephone, and Mary Magdalene in my art. But the sentiment, the deep yearning for a reemergence of old traditions, a return to the earth, the elements, and something sacred and feminine and beyond white men was fueling my fire. Our power of sex. Voice. Heart. Story. Craft. Since then, I have created a global online community and mentorship program called Moon Club, whose mission is to create safe and accessible space for womxn to share their stories, be in their bodies, share and express the full range of their emotions, reclaim their inner mystic and priestess, and be empowered to lead circles around the cycles of the moon.

Many cultures and peoples around the world are tired of the patriarchal systems and religions and are seeking a way to connect to the innate wisdom we are beginning to remember that we all have. In this book, Gabriela provides the oldest and most potent set of tools for this radical remembrance. This reclaiming. This personal ritual of coming home.

The elements. The goddesses. The lunar cycles. The simple and yet profound ways we as a human species have connected with ourselves and the divine for thousands of years. As the religions have failed us, only promoting war and separation and supremacy, we turn away and we turn within. We look to the magic that surrounds us. Water. Fire. Air. Earth. The things that seem normal, and yet when we stop and examine water, it is a mystery; it holds a power; we cannot live without it; it can evaporate; it can pummel us in a tidal wave; it comes from our eyes as glorious soul drops. And fire ravages, raises, warms, and yet we take it for granted. It flickers and lights, pure magic happening in front of our very eyes, and yet we look elsewhere for the divine.

Gabriela teaches us to stop and see the magic that is *right here.* As a seed is planted and somehow manages to go from that tiny little speck to a full tree that reaches high into the sky! This is a re-sensitization of the Soul. And the future of this planet depends on it. The animals going extinct daily. The peoples in villages flooded by the rising tide of climate change. Indigenous peoples who are expelled from their forests and jungles ravaged by capitalism and corporations.

It is clear the planet could use each of us standing now, holding the flame in our hand, tilling the soil, tending to the waters, and working with the winds. This is our ancient magic.

We each hold the power to reawaken the magic we have always had. That has been trained out of us for millennia. The time is now, and Gabriela is going to take you on that journey. Get ready. The power is yours. How you use it is your responsibility. As someone who has dedicated her life to helping others rekindle their powers, their relationships to the lunar cycles, the cycles of nature, of the elements, and their innate power, I stand with her as an example that it is worth the time, the practice, the devotion. Come with a beginner's mind. It's not an instant iPhone, Google, fast practice. It's a courtship of something ancient. Give it time. Trust. The depth comes from doing it again and again and again. From putting your phone down. From looking to nature and how patient and yet ruthless she is. Be ruthless in your pursuit of freedom, of justice, of magic. It's within your reach to awaken from the systems of oppression and step out like a glorious light that inspires this world.

Take the leap. I am here with you. So is Gabriela. She has put her heart and soul on the front line as your fearless leader. She is ready to walk with you hand-in-hand toward a new world. Enjoy this process. It can feel so delicious to reclaim your inner witch, priestess, healer, alchemist, magician . . . enjoy every moment. For the people who can't. Who couldn't. We dedicate our practice to them.

May this book serve this planet and awaken the powers of many beings with a ripple effect that is beyond the eye's capacity to see. May hearts come alight. May roots sink deep. Waters calm. And winds blow with the powers we call forth. For our ancestors. For the trees. For the children. For the seas.

And so it is.

Big Love,
Alexandra Roxo
author, priestess, witch, and co-creator of Moon Club

INTRODUCTION

Bewitched by the Elements

So, you've been bewitched. Enchanted by the current of magick, swept out to the depths of the sea of the subconscious. You've cast your circle, practiced rituals, crafted healing spells, and read your cards. You believe in the freedom and worthiness of all living beings and you know the power of energy and intention. You honor your cycles and those of the earth and cosmos. You, by all means, are a witch, an oracle, a mystic. Or at the very least, embarking on the path to become one. But there's something lingering, waiting for you to find it. It's invisible yet all around you, a familiarity you can't name. Then you notice it, subtly at first: The way the sun sparkles, and the wind coos. How the dew on the flowers settles in the early morning, how the earth smells after the rain. The elements—earth, air, fire, water, and spirit—are all around you, waiting to take you deeper into your magick. Through meditation, breath work, embodiment practices, tarot, crystals, ritual, working with goddesses, journaling, and glamour, you will be led into the heart of each of these elements' teachings.

The tools and practices in this book will help you find a connection to magick, the universe, and your inner power. Committing to living a path that serves *you*, authentically you, is a radical act. When you decide to honor your desires and what lights you up and turns your soul on, you shift things. You place your worth back in yourself, choosing to step into yourself regardless of whether you've been given permission. And when you do this work alongside nature, by turning to her elements as guides and teachers, you find a map back into your ancient, intuitive wisdom. You find a map back into the expansive and feral and fierce. You return to a space of groundedness and presence. You return to embodiment, empowerment, and purpose, all rooted in the magick of what life has to offer.

You're powerful as hell, so feel empowered

In the eyes of the magician or witch, power isn't about controlling someone else, being driven by ego, or using your will to harm another being. When you work with power intentionally, it can be a way for you to meet yourself at your edge, a chance to learn about who you really are behind the things you're expected to be, behind what it means to play small. It's an opportunity to ask yourself where you feel like you need control and to see what you do when you're searching for this through external sources. Power is a way for you to get to know yourself, to learn about your personal relationships.

As the political climate continues to intensify, many of us are turning back to ritual, to self, to witchcraft, so we can move through this world with intention, purpose, and a semblance of peace. We're looking to find empowerment through connection to something more powerful than ourselves so we can then pay this forward. We're asking the earth to guide us in living holistically. Through the elements, you learn about yourself, your needs, and your own spirit and energy. Through the elements, you gain tools and practices that you can use to reclaim the way in which you experience life because the elements *are* life.

Nature is the most powerful bitch of all, period. Just look at the ocean: calm and collected one second, and powerful and destructive the next. Nature has the potential to cultivate and propagate as much as cleanse and kill. But to call nature "evil" or "negative" or "harmful" is dismissive of all her facets. When you see your multidimensional self with compassion and love and not with anger or judgment, you can work with the scarier, harder-to-accept aspects of yourself as guides for growth and cultivating an open heart, a compassionate spirit, and resilience.

Nature belongs to no one, but her beauty belongs to everyone. And by working with the elements you'll be guided into a spiritual practice that doesn't cost you anything.

The elements as embodiment

Both Eastern and Western traditions of magick and spirituality work with nature. In fact, nearly every form of high and low magick works with the elements in some respect. Earth, air, fire, water, and spirit make up the world around you, and they make up *you*. These same elements are seen in Hermetic or Western occultism, Chinese medicine, paganism, Tantra, and other spiritual practices around the world. In Hindu traditions, they're known as *tattvas* or *tattwas*, meaning "reality" or "truth." They're in the tarot, and astrology, too. *Earth* represents the material world, your relationships, your connection to Mother Nature. Earth grants you boundaries and a sense of purpose and grounding. Earth is the physical, your home, your relationships, where and who you come back to for food, love, and nurturing. *Air* is your thoughts, your presence, your ability to make decisions, create things from scratch, and manifest. Air is your breath, your guide in connecting to your body. Air is expansion and freedom. It's being present in your stillness, cleansing what no longer serves you, and working with your mind as an ally and not an enemy. *Fire* is your sexuality, your passion, your ability to alchemize your erotic energy into creativity, self-expression, and manifestation. Fire is action, the spark that creates new ideas, that which burns away what doesn't serve you and purifies what does. It's your ability to explore your erotic self without shame. *Water* is your emotional self, your connection

to the heart and your ability to feel deeply. Water is your intuition, your relationship to the divine feminine, your chance to embody love as something you can give to both yourself and others. *Spirit* is the thread that weaves them all together. Spirit is the act of embodying the elements through ceremony and ritual. Spirit is the divine that is reflected within you and an opportunity for you to see the divine all around. Spirit is the essence of connection that calls us to give back to the collective.

So what does it mean for you to find empowerment and embodiment through Mother Earth? It means you carry her message and essence with you, that you honor her. Through magickal practices, movement, intentional ritual, and energy work, you'll be able to learn the language of the elements, working in tune with nature to really live with her messages as a guiding force. You're not just honoring the elements but embodying them by bringing them into your life.

The elements as connection to power and pleasure

How would your life change if you committed to feeling pleasure on the regular? If you decided every day that this was the day in which you were going to experience as much joy and bliss and *magick* as possible, or at least that you were open to the idea?

The elements can help you connect to all your feelings, even inviting you to honor the harder-to-deal-with emotions like trauma and pain and sadness. They allow you to wade in these shadows so you can transmute this heaviness into light. When you hold space for the wounded part of you and your pain, you expand your capacity to feel love and happiness. You can't feel one emotion deeply without allowing yourself to feel all of them. And when you commit to showing up for all your feelings, you are able to really have a spiritual experience, one where you're not separating your spiritual and material lives, but instead inviting both to live in harmony. So many of us are told to shrink, to be "less," less sexual or less free or less fierce. You're taught to be small and shy. That pleasure is only something you feel sometimes, not all the time. But what if you were able to connect to the elements as the key? What if washing your hands with intention, or standing under the sun with bare skin, or breathing a delicious deep breath allowed you to connect to bliss? You would be in control of what makes you feel most ecstatic.

Through the practices in this book, you'll be called to step up the amount of joy you experience. At the very least, you'll be able to connect to the world around you in a new way, honoring yourself as a child of the earth and cosmos by embodying the messages the elements have to teach you.

Empowerment as activism

Working with ritual, magick, and the earth are means of resistance to the current political climate, which wants you to feel disempowered, disillusioned, and disconnected from the earth. This is also known as spiritual activism, the first step in real-life activism. Spiritual activism is when you're filling your own reserves, honoring your spirit so you maintain a well of inner strength that allows you to foment change all around. It's when you light up your own soul and then help others do the same (like an energetic or conscious version of *Put on your own oxygen mask first*). The saying *Be the change you want to see in the world*? That's pretty much it. You have to change your inner world to effectively change the world around you.

For most of us, spiritual practice outside of the framework of our capitalist society isn't 100 percent possible. But the practices in these pages doesn't rely on anything except you: your dedication, your commitment to connect with nature and self. Yes, I offer suggestions for crystals, cards, candles, and herbs, but these are tools and not necessities. Print your own tarot cards, grab rocks from outside (making sure to ask and say thank you!), go to Goodwill—expensive doesn't mean better. If you're called to this work, then nothing should stop you from pursuing it.

When you dedicate yourself to learning and leveling up your magick, you're inviting the universe in to help you evolve. And when you practice this outside of the idea that you need to buy a million things to be a modern mystic or witch, you're going back into the ancient days when humans and nature had a more intimate relationship. When the earth was *it*. She was where you found what you needed. I hope you find practices here that help you remember how delicious it feels to be human. May these pages serve as a guide in getting you back home in yourself and your body.

What you need to work with this book

All you need to work with this book is a belief that nature is multidimensional, magickal, and powerful, and that she reflects your own cycles of death and rebirth. You should believe in your own

magick and power, too, or at least be open to recognizing it. You'll also need to be open to energy, to intention, to the fact that you're a powerful-ass witch! The following are some concepts that I'll be expanding on throughout as well.

The elements: The five elements are earth, air, fire, water, and spirit (sometimes called *ether*), and they're found in the physical and astral realm around us and within us. Different cultures and traditions around the world have their own version of the elements, their own names and traditions. The Celts saw the elements as Wind Castles, or winds coming from each of the directions, and in Hinduism they were envisioned as *tattvas* or *tattwas*, or principles of truth, and although there were more than five, it is said that each one constitutes an aspect of divinity. If you're interested in how different cultures, traditions, and people connect with the elements, and their correspondences, I recommend *Elemental Magick* by D. J. Conway.

Magick: Yes, magick is real. Yes, you'll get to practice it! I describe magick as energy + action + intention. It's when you're directing your energy to an intention by working with an action to make it happen. Emotion has to be present too, since you have to feel it and believe it for the magick to work. My favorite example of magick is singing someone "Happy Birthday." The intention of the act is to wish someone happy birthday and to send them good energy as they embark on this new year. The energy is raised by singing and sending the recipient love and light, and the action is blowing out the candles on the cake (the only spell I know where you blow out a candle!).

Spells: Spells are a way to raise energy through specific acts with a desired outcome. They usually work with correspondences: specific colors, herbs, chants, crystals, cards, or whatever else that aligns with your desire. Think of lighting a candle with an intention, charging crystals, or doing blessings over yourself or an object. You'll be practicing spells and rituals throughout this book.

Rituals: Rituals are repetitive actions you take to create a separation from your normal, mundane life and as a way to invite in the holy and sublime. So although all spells are rituals in themselves, not all rituals are spells. A ritual can be something as long and involved as invoking the elements, creating a circle of protection, performing a spell and then dismissing the elements and closing the circle. A ritual can also be as simple as drinking tea every morning, or lighting some herbs before you begin work. Rituals are energetic boundaries you create to tell the universe you're doing something special, with reverence and a sense of sacredness.

Witchcraft: Witchcraft is a nature-based spiritual path that works with the cycles of the earth, the cosmos, and the self. Witchcraft works with magick to create change on this plane as well as unseen planes of existence, and often uses astrology, tarot, alchemy, herbalism, and other esoteric practices. Witches work with rituals and spells to honor cycles, to banish and manifest, and to heal and celebrate. Witches often align themselves with the seasons and holidays known as the Wheel of the Year, and many work with the phases of the moon. Witchcraft emphasizes the earth as the ultimate healer, mother, and teacher and often interacts intimately with different goddesses and archetypes of the divine feminine, as well as gods, spirit guides, ancestors, animal familiars, ascended masters, angels, or other beings.

The universe: You'll hear me talking about the universe a lot. And although the term means something to me, it may mean something else to you, and that's okay! To me, the universe is the All. It's consciousness, it's connection, it's divinity. The universe is my spiritual mama and papa, a loving force so much bigger than we are that we have to put human faces on it to understand what it's all about. The universe is god, goddess, my higher power, my consciousness. When I talk about the universe, I mean the supreme love that weaves all of existence together. It's where your soul comes from and after you've evolved all you can, where it returns to. The universe is your spiritual home, the feeling you get when you see something so beautiful it transcends words. The universe is magick incarnate, infinite bliss, perfect presence. You will never understand it, but you should never stop trying to.

Divine feminine: Also known as the Goddess, or *yin* energy in Chinese philosophy, the energy of the divine feminine is receptive, intuitive, psychic, and nurturing. She is the universal mother, the love you feel from the earth and the ocean, and the connection you have to your own depths, shadows, and sexuality. The divine feminine is worshipped around the world with many names: Isis, Aphrodite, Hekate, Mother Mary, Oshun, Lakshmi. When you work with this energy, you're working with divine love. Witchcraft and other earth-based spiritual practices emphasize the divine feminine, since we see the earth as the embodiment of this energy that allows one to grow and thrive. For many of us who grew up in patriarchal religions, we never had the chance to see ourselves reflected in God. Working with goddesses allows you to witness yourself as holy, as a celestial reflection of the cosmos, which is one of the most powerful experiences in this life. Throughout this book, you'll find guided practices in connecting to different goddesses and archetypes of the divine feminine rooted in the elements, so you too can see yourself through her eyes.

Divine masculine: Also known as *yang* energy in Chinese philosophy, divine masculine energy is powerful, action oriented, structured, and caring. The antithesis of toxic masculinity, the divine masculine is "god" without all the patriarchal conditioning that comes with it. This is the energy of the sun, allowing you to sustain and grow what's lingering beneath the soil, waiting to surface. Divine masculine energy is the energy of potential, of strength with conviction and integrity. It complements the divine feminine, it is the riverbanks that allow the river of the feminine to flow.

Higher power: When I mention a higher power, I'm not talking about some superintelligent alien out in the cosmos. I'm talking about *you*: your essence and wisdom, yourself, your soul. Your higher power is the purest version of yourself, that which outlives this life. It's you in your dynamic, potent, activated, highest vibration. It's the most divine version of you. And it's not separate from who you are, it's just buried under layers of conditioning, karma, and life. Connecting to your higher power means peeling back the layers that keep you from shining your light as fully as you can. It means honoring your wisdom and knowing that you already have all the answers you seek. Your higher power is a mirror to the universe and an opportunity to know your truest self.

The directions: Each element is associated with a different direction, and although this isn't the same across every culture or tradition, in our work and for the most part, the following is standard.

North—Earth
East—Air
South—Fire
West—Water
Up—Spirit

Energy: Energy is neither created nor destroyed; everything is energy. Energy is the thread that connects the physical world and magick, and by learning how to direct it with intention, you can create tangible changes both on this realm and on the astral, or energetic, one. Matter is simply atoms vibrating so fast you can't see it; even that which feels physical is simply energy.

Astral realm: If you think of the world like an onion, then you're at the center. The whole thing is *dense*; it's the material plane! This is what you can see, feel, and touch. But when you're meditating, working ritual, or practicing magick, not only are you affecting this level of reality, but you're creating changes on other realms. The astral realm is where you receive visions, where you travel to in meditations and visualizations. It's where the faeries, or nature spirits/ancestors of nature, live. This is where you can meet your guides, elementals, and higher self. It's where you go when you lucid dream, another layer of existence that you can access through your mind. It's a dimension parallel to our own, but not one we can access in the physical. As the layers of the onion move from the center out, the dimensions of reality are more energetic and not so materially based. The astral is an energetic parallel to the world we're living in, and this is where magick takes place before you see it manifest and impact the physical realm.

The chakras: In Hinduism and yogic traditions, the energy centers of the body are located along the spine and are known as chakras, which means "wheel" or "wheel of light" in Sanskrit. There are seven chakras: the root chakra at the base of the spine, the sacral chakra at the pelvis, the solar plexus chakra right above the navel, the heart chakra between the breastbones, the throat chakra at the middle of the throat, the third eye chakra between the eyebrows, and the crown chakra at the top of the head. These are our main energy points, though there are many, many more. Each chakra has its own symbol and Sanskrit name, as well as its own energetic properties and correspondences. Each rules over something different, and when they are balanced and aligned, you're at your energetic healthiest. Every spiritual path has its own version of the energy points of the subtle body, with five or seven main centers being the most common. I go more into depth on chakras in my book *Inner Witch: A Modern Guide to the Ancient Craft*.

Elementals: The energetic archetypes of the elements, elementals are the beings that represent earth, air, fire, and water. Earth is represented by gnomes, like the garden gnomes you all know and love. They are the protectors of the flora and fauna and can assist in healing magick with animals or the earth. Air is represented by the sylphs, who can bless you with creativity, inspiration, and effervescence. These winged beings are what you probably think of when you hear the word *faery*. Fire is represented by the salamanders, the energetic equivalent of the lizard with the same name. They are intense and can help you gaze into your passions and banish what you no longer need. Water is represented by the undine, an umbrella term for beings like mermaids and sirens, who can help you connect to your emotional nature, sensuality, and femininity.

Preparing for a ritual

You'll notice that the first step before you begin any ritual is to prepare the space. This is when you will turn your phone off or on silent, go to the bathroom, take care of any pets, and let any partners or roommates know not to disturb you. This is also when you set up the space. You'll gather your supplies, light any incense or candles you wish, dim the lights, and get yourself ready to be in the liminal space of a ritual. You may wish to change into a certain piece of clothing, something you'll be comfortable in that's not restricting, or you can work skyclad (naked). When you and your space are set, you'll be ready to begin the ritual.

Working with the nondominant versus dominant hand

When working with crystals or talismans, I'll often say to hold the item in your nondominant hand. It is said that this is the hand that receives energy, while your dominant hand (the one you use to write/exist) is the one that sends out energy. When you are receiving the energy of the crystal, you can hold it in your nondominant hand. When you are charging a talisman or a crystal with an intention, you can hold it in your dominant hand to send energy into it. Try both and see what works for you; even though this is a guideline, if you feel more connected sending energy out with your receptive hand and receiving energy with your dominant hand, then so be it!

When working with affirmations or rituals where you gaze into your own eye in the mirror, I'll say to look at your nondominant eye. This is for the same reason, but also because it's easier to focus on one eye than both. Always remember that you're in charge! So you may gaze at whatever eye feels the most comfortable.

🜃 🜄 🜂 🜁

What this book is and isn't

This book is a reclamation of earth-based spirituality for the modern witch. It's an invitation to say *fuck yes* to your magick, to nature, to your pleasure and passion. It's a chance for you to own your power. This book is raw, sensual, creative embodiment magick that invites you to see the world and all her mystery in a worthwhile way. It's an opportunity for you to learn about your elemental makeup and to connect with earth, air, fire, water, and spirit in a way that feeds you.

What this book isn't is a quick fix for all your problems. It's called spiritual *practice* for a reason. It's not a prescription but a recipe you can adjust per your taste. It's not a grimoire but a jumping-off point for you to deepen your own mystic journey with the world around you.

Welcome.

A note: I couldn't write this book without covering some of the same elements that I did in *Inner Witch*. If you're already familiar with some of these practices, like grounding or working with the elementals or moon phases, skip them and instead find what's juicy, new, and what resonates with you.

CHAPTER 1

Earth: Ground It

The earth is the mother of the witch. She's from where you come and to where you return. You celebrate her cycles as holidays, feed on her bounty, and connect to her when you perform magick. Mother Nature teaches about love and beauty through her flowers and creatures, inviting you to appreciate aesthetics for the sake of it. She reminds you of wonder, and many of us experience our first moments of awe and surrender in her embrace. Earth magick is when you take this into your spiritual practice; it's working with the cosmos and the cycles of the season and knowing the different properties of flowers, herbs, and roots. Earth speaks of the body, and its magick is in nourishing your body deliberately so you can bloom. Earth magick is firm and loving, supportive and inspiring, kitchen magick and energetic soul food. Earth magick is having clear boundaries so you can understand your own power; it's manifesting with clarity and intention, not ego. Earth magick is slowing down, being present, and tapping into the moment.

One of the most powerful lessons the element of earth can teach you is to work from a place of rootedness. Like the oak tree whose roots dig so deep that not even a hurricane can uproot it, you can find grounding in the chaos through ritual and spiritual practice. Through magick like grounding meditations, working with the root chakra, experimenting with gardening and herbs, and spending time in nature, you can start creating firm boundaries. Being grounded is a fun woo-woo way of saying you have a sense of spiritual security. It's like that oak tree; when you're grounded, you've created your own safety net. No matter what's going on in the world, you know you can handle it because you know you're safe. Your needs are being met. You're confident in yourself and your power. You have boundaries in place that help you communicate your needs while also honoring the space you take up. Being grounded is an imitation game with nature. It's not so much thinking that storms won't come, but being ready and knowing that it will be okay when they do.

One of the biggest lessons I hope you take away from this book is the importance of intention and mindfulness. Mindfulness, which means bringing your awareness to the present, is a way of being thoughtful. This can take many forms, many of which will naturally be woven into our conversation here. Mindfulness can look like yoga, journaling, meditation, masturbation, or art. It can look like working out, or punching a pillow, or being stuck in traffic and breathing through the agitation. Anything can be mindful. This pertains to rituals as well; creating ritual by carving out a dedicated time for this work is mindfulness, and it's immensely powerful. It can also be incredibly transformative, not to mention grounding.

When you combine mindfulness with grounding, you get the chance to create practices that consciously honor your needs. What makes you feel safe? What makes you feel supported? What makes you feel powerful? These questions provoke different reactions from different people, and that's necessary. What matters is what works for *you*. Maybe five deep breaths helps you feel grounded; maybe it's a long stretch, or a run, or a visualization. It's not what other people are doing that matters, but knowing what resonates with you. In a spiritual practice, grounding exercises literally help you connect to the earth around and below you. This can be through breath work or meditation. This can be through movement and working ritualistically with sacred herbs. This can be working with the tarot, or feeling sensations or emotions in your body, or sitting outside with your feet placed directly onto the earth. Maybe drinking a cup of nettle tea does it, or taking a long shower and then lying on the floor does. What matters is that something helps draw you back into your present, into your power, into yourself.

Having healthy boundaries is a big part of this work, too. This doesn't mean putting walls in place so no one can see you, help you, or love you. Quite the opposite; healthy emotional boundaries help you communicate your needs and express yourself when you don't feel seen or respected. They allow you to form loving, supportive relationships that are consensual and equitable. Having these boundaries means the joy of saying yes when you mean yes and no when you mean anything less.

The exercises in this chapter are written to help you engage with the earth in a new way. They ask you to see that tree in your backyard as more than a tree, but a soulful ally. They ask you to feel the earth beneath you when you sit in meditation, to honor the leaves of the tea before you drink it, to come back to your body when you need to be reminded of your magick. The earth's majesty is all around you. When you see yourself as part of her and actively work on remembering this, you too embody her power.

With this power comes responsibility. It is the witch's job to be aware of how she treats the earth, and advocating for Gaia is a huge part of this and can also help us connect to her. Climate change is real. We live with fear tactics and fearmongering as greed destroys the earth. When you volunteer, donate money, send positive energy, pick up trash, recycle, or whatever else you can do, you're practicing the ancient ritual of living in tandem to the earth. You honor her by protecting her, just as she protects and provides for you. It is the witch's job to leave the earth better than she found it. Dedicating yourself to this is a noble intention, one that creates a mutually beneficial relationship with the earth.

Creating a ritual practice

One of the ways you can connect to each element is through ritual. Rituals can take many forms, and what feels right to you is going to be unique. It's also important to remember that there's no such thing as the "right" ritual. There's only right *for you.*

When you create a consistent practice, whether it's something you do every day, every week, every full or new moon, or whenever else, you're committing to your magick and your higher self. You're dedicating yourself to this, and you're also reaffirming this connection. Through ritual you embrace your personal style of magick, hone your skills, practice divination, connect to the natural world, and really recognize where you are on this human journey! And when you are consistent with your rituals, you're able to track your progress and tweak what needs to be tweaked so you can dive even more deeply into the experience. Spirituality, discipline, magick, and occultism . . . what's the point if they don't help your evolution and growth, and, you know, hopefully help you find a deeper appreciation for life? Through ritual you get to be intentional about this; this is when practice is put into play.

I urge you to start a daily practice, even if it's for five or ten minutes. But any sort of ritual you can do regularly is great. It takes time to create consistent rituals and to find ones that fit, and

getting angry at yourself for "not doing enough" or "not being dedicated enough" when you have a full and busy life is not helpful. Be compassionate with yourself as you do what you can. Take it one step at a time, remembering not to overcommit just to wind up overwhelmed.

WHAT'S IN A RITUAL?

A ritual practice can look like many things, and you'll be using earth, air, fire, water, and spirit as your cornerstones in creating one. Each chapter addresses a piece of this puzzle, and at the end there is a worksheet to help customize your own ritual practice with all of the elements. I've also included specific rituals for each of the elements throughout to help you relate to their messages and properties.

THE RITUAL OF GROUNDING

The first step in any ritual should be grounding, even if it's short. Grounding is when you connect to the earth, to your breath, to the present. It's when you find an energetic tether back to yourself. When you ground, you call back your precious energy and take a moment to return to your body and find some stillness before beginning your ritual work, divination practice, spell, sex magick . . . and so on.

There are many different ways to ground: breathing techniques, physical postures, visualizations, sounds. Exploring is one of the most exciting parts of magick, so if my suggestions don't speak to you, please do some research and experiment to find something that does!

Once you find a grounding technique that works for you, come back to it whenever you feel chaotic or overwhelmed. Rituals are support systems. They guide you home and help you find balance in the often overwhelming world around you. When you use practices inspired by the earth, whose resilience is outmatched, then you can find the space to keep going no matter how tumultuous everything feels. You create an eye in the storm, a space of peace that is there whenever you need it, just like the earth beneath your feet.

Ways to connect to the earth

I'll be going in depth about meditation, tarot, crystals, embodiment, and goddesses, but I wanted to share some other ways you can connect to the energy of the elements—in this case, basically, anything that helps you connect with nature and return to your body and to the present. Keep this list handy for whenever you're feeling spacey, and add to it when you find your own practices that feel worthy.

» Close your eyes and take deep breaths while visualizing roots from the base of your spine growing deep into the earth, feeding you warm golden light

» Spend time outside, in nature, disconnected from your phone and present. Stand in the grass without shoes on, pressing your feet firmly into the earth, or visualize this in your mind's eye.

» Press your forehead into the ground (if you're familiar with yoga, this position should be child's pose) and imagine any excess energy returning to the earth through your third eye.

» Burn sacred smoke from frankincense, mugwort, cedar, sandalwood, copal, pine, juniper, and others.

» Spend time gardening, or buy yourself flowers. Adopt a plant; care for it regularly, feeding it love. Say thank you to flowers as you see them.

- Drink some herbal tea, taking the time to connect with each herb.
- Stomp your feet, letting energy release and vibrate through your soles, releasing any stuck or pent-up energy.
- Hug a tree and connect to its spirit, feeling its specific energetic vibration, acknowledging its wisdom and taking in its message.
- Give yourself a tight hug, or hug someone else, enjoying the pressure of flesh on flesh.
- Stretch or practice yoga, moving your body as you also work with your breath to release tension and worries and revitalize your spirit.
- Exercise, and see working out as a way to get to know your body and as a ritual dedicated to strength, intensity, or whatever else you need.
- Practice kitchen witchcraft, blessing your food, connecting with ingredients, feeding yourself literally and figuratively.
- Have sex or masturbate as a way to feel intense sensation and emotion throughout your body.

A grounding meditation to find your roots

This simple meditation was inspired by feminist neopagan Starhawk, and you can practice it to get grounded before performing any rituals or magick. It is my go-to visualization before doing any other kind of magickal work, as a way to help me connect with the earth. Adapt it as you wish.

Read this and then practice the meditation or record yourself reading it and play that as a guided meditation until you get the hang of it.

Before you begin, prepare yourself and your space, following the instructions on page 15. Then find a comfortable position, seated or lying down, and close your eyes. Start to come back to your breath, taking a few deep breaths in and out, finding a natural pace. Focus your gaze inward and start to notice where your body is making contact with the earth, feeling yourself being supported by the seat or the ground beneath you. Start to breathe into this space, imagining your spine extending like golden tree roots into the earth. These roots find their way through the floor, through the concrete, through the ground, deep, deep into the earth. Once they dig as deep as they can, begin to feel a warmth moving up the roots, up the base of your spine, up your spine and throat and heart and out the crown of your head. These golden roots can keep growing out through your crown like a beam of healing light that connects to the cosmos above, or you can imagine that from your crown they grow into luscious

tree branches that are either fed by the energy of the cosmos above or that cascade into the ground, creating an energetic circuit. Either feel this connection to the heavens above or feel the energy circling through you and the earth. Try both and see which works better for you. Stay here as long as you need, breathing in this warm, cleansing, and supportive golden light.

To finish the meditation, imagine the roots moving back up through the layers of the earth, through the cement and dirt and back to you, where they'll melt back into your body. Then visualize the light from the cosmos or the tree branches above moving back into your crown or dissolving into thin air.

I love pressing my forehead into the earth after this meditation, imagining any energy I don't need returning to the earth through my third eye while in child's pose.

GROUNDING AFTER A RITUAL

If you do this visualization at the beginning of a ritual, then you'll want to "reverse" it when you're done with the ritual, practicing the last section again. That is, if you imagined roots growing from your spine into the earth, when you're done and ready to close the ritual, you would visualize the roots and branches moving from the earth beneath you back into your spine, or you could imagine them dissolving.

Earth as healthy boundaries

Besides helping you find your way into the present, into your fortitude, earth is also a valuable teacher when it comes to boundaries. The earth's natural boundaries, like rivers and mountains, remind you that you also have limits. Earth, in all its stability and steadfastness, reminds you that boundaries aren't only important but *necessary*. The earth only grows and changes if the conditions are right—and you must only accept that which feels right for you. Although this is not always 100 percent possible, you can work on the muscle of saying no to things that don't feel right and yes to things that do.

Having boundaries doesn't mean you're stuck, and it doesn't mean you don't grow. It doesn't mean you *only* say no, or that you aren't flexible enough to help others. When you have healthy boundaries, you honor where you are, what you're feeling, and what you need before committing to something (or someone) else. How many times have you said yes to something you don't have time for only to end up resentful and angry? When you create healthy boundaries, whether emotionally, physically, mentally, sexually, or spiritually, you're taking the time to value your own needs and reinforce what makes you feel safe and cared for. Maybe this means using social media less, maybe it's saying no to any events or work you don't get paid for, maybe it's deciding to spend more or less time alone. Regardless, when you really assess and give space to what feels aligned, you forge stronger relationships with others by reminding them of what you need to be a better friend, partner, or lover. Just as the earth isn't afraid to grow where the conditions are right, knowing when to say no can allow you to grow and thrive within a space that truly suits your needs.

The witch's foundation between worlds: casting the circle

In your day-to-day life, your boundaries are etheric, not tangible like the element they're connected to. You use your voice, and maybe even your body, to enforce these boundaries and create this intention. In magick, you use your body *and energy* to create this boundary, and you do so by casting a circle. The witch's circle is one of the many tools she keeps in her toolbox to overthrow the patriarchy, helping her slip between time and space to enact her spells and magick. The circle is always one of the first steps in the ritual; you ground, cast the circle, perform the ritual, and then take down the circle at the end. The circle acts as a meeting place between worlds, a place neither here nor there, an energetic crossroads; liminal spaces are where magick is born. In this way the circle helps you access your unconscious mind and the astral realm, which exists everywhere and nowhere. The circle is even more importantly a place of protection and safety, spiritual sunblock to keep out all the low vibrations or stale energies. When you cast a circle, you're saying, "Only that which I invite into this space is welcome." Even though you don't need to spend time being scared of negative energy, it does exist, and it does manifest in unwelcome forms as psychic vampires, parasites, feelings, and dis-ease manifested as sickness. Like anything else, though, if you take care of yourself and take precautions like locking your doors or casting a circle, there's no need to feel stressed. The circle acts as insurance, as protection, especially when you invoke or invite energies like elementals into your rituals (see page 48 for a ritual). You also cast a circle as a way to raise energy, to act as a container for it until you're ready to release it. That way, when you're at the peak of your energy raising, you can send the intention through the crown of your head, beaming into the cosmos in a cone known as a *cone of power*. It is said that you must come to the circle with perfect love and perfect trust. You enter the circle as a priestess of the earth and as a son of the gods of wisdom, and here you create a container to raise your magick. When you've set up the space, prepared the ritual, and taken a moment to ground, you're ready to exist in the liminal.

CASTING THE CIRCLE

Begin facing north. If you don't actually know where north is and don't have any way of figuring it out, you can claim a direction that is "energetically north" instead, stating this out loud or through your mind's eye.

Using a wand, an athame (a black-handled ritual knife), a crystal point, or your finger to direct the energy, point to the floor beside you and *walk deosil or clockwise in a circle* as you envision vibrant blue flames or white light moving out of whatever you're pointing with to create a boundary. As you walk, envision this creating a sphere that meets above your head and below your feet, encircling you. *Walk your circle three times*, ending again in the north.

Then you may wish to say something like the following

As a meeting place between the worlds
I have cast this sacred circle
With perfect love and perfect trust
It is cast and it is done.

Now you may perform whatever ritual or magick you want.

IF YOU HAVE TO LEAVE THE CIRCLE

If you're going to be gone from the circle for more than five or ten minutes, it's worth recasting it once you're back to reinforce the boundary. If you just need to grab something or do something quickly, you can trace a door on the edge of your circle using whatever you used to cast it, and then you can step through it. I also like to use my hands to split imaginary curtains as I step through the door I just drew, another way of splitting the veil and stepping back to the physical from the liminal.

CLOSING THE CIRCLE

Once your working is complete and it's time to close the circle, you will begin once again facing north. This time you will be *walking widdershins or counterclockwise* around the edge of your circle, using what you used to cast it to visualize drawing the blue flames or white light up your arm, through your body, and through your feet into the earth beneath you, grounding the energy. Do this once, returning to where you started as you say something like the following:

The circle is open; may it never be broken.
The boundary is dissolved, but the magick still lives on.
And so it is!

And so it is! You've just cast and closed your circle, creating an energetic boundary. You got this, witch.

VISUALIZATION ALTERNATIVE

An alternative to casting the circle physically is through visualization. After grounding, you'll begin to draw in white light from the cosmos above you, down your crown chakra, and into your heart. Breathe into this space, visualizing a growing ball of light here, expanding with each inhale. This ball of light grows and grows until it encompasses you, above your head and below your feet, creating a sphere of protection around you. Breathe into this and declare the boundary sealed when you've grown the circle to its fullest.

When you're ready to close the circle, you'll do the same visualization in reverse, feeling the circle shrink and shrink with each breath, until it dissolves into your heart. When it's closed, declare it closed. You may wish to clap, stomp your feet, take a deep breath like you're breathing into a straw, or press your forehead into the earth and exhale any energy back into the ground to really close the boundary.

Earth as the first step of growth

It is from the earth that you can grow and bloom like the most radiant of flora. It is through the domain of the physical that you get to see the gifts this earth gives you. When earth is in harmony with air, water, fire, and spirit, you see dynamism. You see the new. You see abundance and beauty, all the joys of a new season. Yes, earth is grounding, but that's only the first step you take before you flower. Whenever you feel stuck in habits and cycles, you can remember that growth is always around the corner—that just like spring's rebirth after a long and grueling winter, with enough compassion and care, water and sunshine, you too can unfold and thrive.

Tarot: reading the cards

In each chapter, I'll be talking about the tarot as a tool to explore the elements and what they have to teach. Tarot is an ancient method of divination that was originally played as a card game, probably starting in Italy in the fifteenth century. The deck of seventy-eight cards is broken into two parts, the major and minor arcana (*arcana* meaning "secret"). The major arcana hold images like the Tower, Death, and the Lovers; they represent life changes, karmic lessons, and big-picture situations. They tell the story of the hero's journey, explaining the cycles of humanity's spirit from growth and self-realization to that of connection with karma and the divine. The minor arcana are broken up into four parts, called suits: Pentacles or Coins (earth), Wands or Rods (fire), Cups or Chalices (Water), and Swords or Daggers (air). They talk of your day-to-day life, of the smaller battles you face and what they can teach you. The tarot uses numerology, symbolism, and more than anything archetypes, to convey its messages.

But don't fret; your future isn't set in stone; you have free will. I like to think of tarot as a map to parts of yourself you're unfamiliar with. It's a mirror, reflecting your current situation back to you in a new way. Tarot is an energetic guide that you get to have a conversation or reading with. Although it can tell you what's to come, it can also help you reawaken your intuition, guide you to new conclusions, or help you see valuable insight or perspectives you may have missed.

Although the classic deck is the Rider-Waite, my suggestion is to invest in a deck that you really love and connect with. And while there is a myth that someone else has to buy your first tarot deck for you, this is totally not true. *You* are the one who's reading the cards, and it's your voice that's the most important when picking out a deck. Finding a deck that resonates in its imagery and feeling is vital. Check out your local bookstore or metaphysical shop and don't forget to use the Internet! I go more deeply into the tarot, interpretations, and how to read cards in my first book, *Inner Witch*, but I've included some easy steps in this section.

As far as working with the individual cards I've selected for each element, these are for you to explore in whatever capacity speaks to you. You may wish to pull these cards out of your deck and place them on your altar, dedicating the altar to a specific element or elements. You may wish to meditate with a specific card to be guided further into its landscape and messages, or you may wish to dress like one, wearing its colors or an outfit that feels attuned to its energy. Perhaps you might journal or write poetry or free write around a card, spending time digging into the character of the card or what it brings up in you. You may use the cards in your deck for spells and rituals, to represent what you're banishing, healing, drawing to you, or whatever else. Ask the spirit of the deck you're using what it wants to reveal to you, and then ask the cards, too. Give yourself permission to get it "wrong" and then enjoy the psychedelic journey into the unconscious.

READING THE CARDS

1. **Cleanse the cards**
   Use sacred smoke from herbs like yerba santa, mugwort, sweetgrass, cedar, dragonsblood, or lavender. You can also use resin like copal or frankincense. Light a few pieces of the herbs until they're aflame and then blow them out so they're just smoldering, making sure to hold them in a fireproof dish or abalone shell. If you're using resin, light a charcoal, wait until it's sparked all the way through, put it in a fire-safe dish, and place the resin on top of that. Move the cards through this smoke as you ask for them to be cleansed and cleared of any energy. You may also wish to use the sacred smoke to cleanse yourself: your palms, limbs, torso, between your legs, the crown of your head, and the bottoms of your feet.

2. **Prepare yourself**
   Before you begin to read, take a few minutes to ground and breathe. You can do the grounding visualization on page 25, connecting to the heavens above and the earth below. You can ask whatever gods, goddesses, spirit guides, deities, ancestors, or beings you work with for their blessing. If you're reading for

someone else, you may wish to breathe into their presence and ask to connect with them so you can deliver messages in the highest good of all involved.

3. **Pick a spread**
   There are many different spreads, from simple one-card pulls to three-card pulls for past/present/future, to the classic Celtic cross. I've included a different spread for each element but feel free to make your own, or look online or in books for more ideas. Each spread assigns a different card a question/position. One card may be "you" while another may be "what you should let go of." The spread impacts how you interpret the cards.

4. **Think of the question and shuffle the cards**
   Now is the time to ask the question you want answered. It's better if this is not a yes-or-no question, but try to be specific. If you're reading your own cards (if you're asking the question), you shuffle. If you're reading someone else's cards (if they're asking the question), they shuffle. Focus on the query as you shuffle in the way most comfortable for you. Stop when you feel ready.

5. **Read the cards**
   When you're ready and done shuffling, pull cards and interpret them. I've listed some tarot resources in "Further Reading" on page 330 to help. Pay attention to your intuition, to what you're feeling, and use the Internet and books and the booklet from your tarot deck to help you get started with translating what the cards mean. It takes time! Be patient and remember that your best is good enough.

6. **Close and ground**
   When you're done, I suggest taking notes in a journal dedicated to this practice. You may record any insight, interpretations, and relevant information here. Then close your eyes, connect to your breath, and do a grounding visualization to help you end this ritual and return to the physical realm. Thank yourself or whoever you're reading with and voilà: you've just read the tarot.

Earth in the tarot: the pentacles

The earth, like the body, creates containers for you to experience life in—your home and what you fill it with; lovers and friends who inhabit your life and encompass unconditional love and lessons; your job, which teaches you about value and what you will and won't accept. The earth itself is the ultimate etheric enclosure or sacred container, a floating orb of gas and water and matter that allows you to inhabit life and all its dimensions. In the tarot, earth is represented by the pentacles, which rule over the material world. Pentacles are that which you touch and feel, that which grants you security and safety. Pentacle energy is your sense of home, where you feel like you belong, and it also speaks of your health. This suit tells us of your relationship to money, your job, the work you do that brings you happiness, or abundance, or a sense of self. The pentacles speak of the life you've manifested, and all the ups and downs that come with it, and of how you're treating yourself. Pentacles remind you of balance; when you have to be focused entirely outward, you're not living, only surviving. Pentacles are the foundation, and they're often where you must put your energy first.

But when you only focus on the material, when you create a sense of value based on the amount of money you have, or if your ego is solely identified with how you look or your social status, then this suit speaks of loss, greed, and ego death.

As the earth, the pentacles speak of creating boundaries, of grounding, of abundance. The earth wants you to have enough and then pay it forward. Pentacle energy asks you to celebrate, bask in, and share your abundance; this energy reminds you you're not meant to do life alone, and it's much better when you share your good fortune with others.

THE ENERGY OF OPPORTUNITY AND GROWTH: THE ACE OF PENTACLES

At the beginning of each suit in the tarot deck, you're greeted with the Ace—the omen of new opportunities. Ace energy is that of beginnings—those chances and meet-cutes that seem to be gifts from the heavens themselves—but the Aces speak of the moments before this, when the seed is about to germinate. This is postconception, and prebirth, the manifestation of infinite possibilities. Aces remind you of your ability to create, and in the case of the Pentacles, the Ace is all about manifesting in this corporeal realm. The Ace of Pentacles can be a reminder you're on the right path, through synchronicities, omens, messages, or opportunities. This can mean that you keep receiving words of confirmation for something you're working on, you meet a new partner, you start a healthy new habit, you upgrade or change your living space, you create healthy boundaries, you land a new job. The opportunities are limitless. You can tap into Ace of Pentacles energy when you're working with grounding, boundaries, or manifestation. When you want something to change, when you want to make something happen, when you see what must be done and know how to get there (even though you may not know *why*), this is the energy of the Ace of Pentacles. This is a reminder that you already have what you need to make something happen. At this point, it's up to you to keep yourself planted, present, and ready for whatever this materialization is. The Aces speak of something that's in process, so keep your eyes and heart open. The hard part is over, the work is finished, and now is the time to receive the opportunities you've been longing for.

THE ENERGY OF FEELING STUCK: THE FIVE OF PENTACLES

If the Ace of Pentacles is the energy of new beginnings, of claiming our desires on the material plane, then the Five of Pentacles is the energy of feeling stuck, defeated, and like you can't change your circumstances. This can manifest as feeling like a victim or needing help but not knowing how to ask for it. In this card, you see two people who seem to be struggling in front of a building that shines brightly inside. This card is about being deep in it, and since it's pentacles, this struggle is probably real as hell: with a job, home, health, or a serious relationship. But even as they're knee high in the shit, these two are so close to help. A key point that the Five of Pentacles can teach us is to ask. ASK FOR HELP! Ask for assistance. Have compassion for yourself, but also enough courage and discipline to see when things aren't working and need to change. When you feel stuck, keep moving. Keep going. Keep doing what you can. Remember that if you want to get different results, you have to make different choices. Changing how you handle the situation can change the situation itself.

Pentacles energy thrives when you feel safe and secure. Think of the earth herself; though she can survive a lot (hello, global warming), she is happiest when she is well taken care of and tended to, like a garden, or like any human being. Remember that Ace is the beginning of each suit in the tarot deck, and ten is the end. That means five is smack-dab in the middle, a space that can feel unpredictable, like you're lost. It can be hard to believe there's anything next; because of this, five represents big changes or decisions. When you're in the midst of struggle, or in the midst of this intense Five of Pentacles whirlwind, remember that you'll get out if you persevere. You're allowed to ask for help and say no to what's depleting you. You're allowed to have hope. Until then, self-compassion and tending to your own garden is key. Nurture and water yourself as much as you can, and remember that everything is cyclical and you *will* be okay.

THE ENERGY OF MOTHER EARTH: THE QUEEN OF PENTACLES

One of the most beautiful gifts of the Pentacles is abundance; growing, flowering, and birthing. Mother Earth blesses you with all you need to survive, and then she blesses you with even more. When you are basking in your own abundance, when you are witnessing the miracles of nature, when you are connected to pleasure in your body, the Queen of Pentacles thrives. This queen is as regal as she is grounded, and she is both flexible and rooted. When you are living with the archetype of the Queen of Pentacles, you are intimately connected to the cycles of the earth and yourself. You are also basking in sensual experiences: eating well, surrounded by luxurious people, seeing glamorous things. The Queen of Pentacles thrives with aesthetic experiences, à la Dionysus.

This is the card of the intuitive manifestress; when you feel called to step it up and bask in the wealth and security you deserve, this is who you can call on. When you work with this queen, you are connected to your sensuality, whatever that looks like, and are channeling this energy toward something meaningful. You can call upon this queen when you need to create from a supported but heart-centered place. This is the gardener who is gentle but unafraid to pull up weeds or create protection for the plants that need it. The Queen of Pentacles can help you enforce boundaries with compassion. She can be your guide when you're doing something scary for the first time, or going through a milestone where you need help. The Queen of Pentacles is expansive, strong, and unapologetic. She is firm but not rigid, and she can help you stand tall and claim your value whenever you need her.

In a reading, this queen can ask you to own and celebrate how you've worked hard to flourish. It can also be a challenge to step up your abundance mind-set and to seek more situations that challenge you and remind you of your value.

A TAROT SPREAD TO TEND TO YOUR SOUL'S INNER GARDEN

Using the analogy of a garden, this spread will help you get clear about what in your life needs some extra care. You can work this spread with a specific question on an issue (*Is taking this job the right choice?*) or just to ask for any guidance you need in the moment. You are your own worst critic and sometimes it can be hard to see where you need some more care in your life. Healthy boundaries, remember? This spread will, hopefully, help you see this with some objectivity. Before you begin, you may wish to take a second to set up your space, lighting candles or incense, dimming the lights, performing any rituals you wish. You may wish to perform the grounding visualization on page 25 before you begin. Then shuffle your cards as you focus on your question, breathing into any sensations you feel. Pull whenever you feel ready, and then record any insight and findings you have in a journal for further review and to track your growth.

Card 1: *My roots (what's keeping me grounded)*
Card 2: *Beneath the surface (what information I can't see)*
Card 3: *The plant (where I am currently in my growth)*
Card 4: *What nourishes me*
Card 5: *What depletes me*
Card 6: *What I need moving forward*
Card 7: *Where I need to reinforce my boundaries*

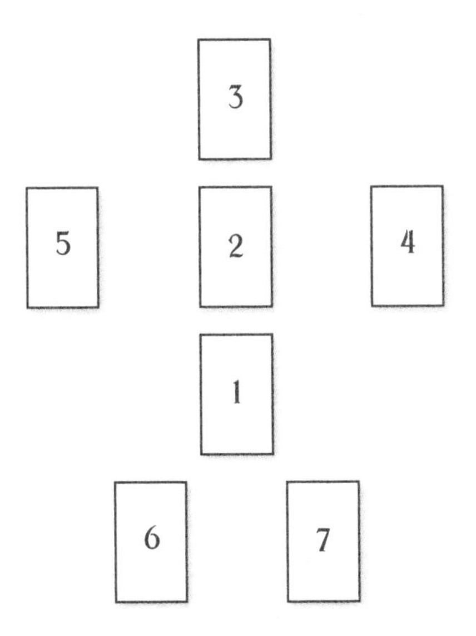

Crystals and the earth

Crystals are everywhere; whether you're reading a magazine, making your way through a metaphysical store, hanging out at your best friend's witchy palace, or paying attention to the earth, you're certain to be spellbound by these gems. Also known as gemstones and minerals, crystals are ancient parts of the earth that can take thousands of years to grow. Because of this, and the fact that crystals are perfect geometric structures, they're said to hold ancient wisdom as well as the healing vibration of the earth itself. These miracle workers are evolved beings with their own energies that you get to learn about and work with, all through the lens of their powerful beauty.

Just look at a crystal to witness its power. Not only are these formations stunning and mesmerizing, but their beauty is sacred, too. Crystals help you tune up your vibration and tune into pleasure; they're like the sirens singing a song to bring you back to the mystical, diamond-bright radiance that you were born from. When you work with crystals, you're working with the soul of the earth. You're working with revered energies used by different cultures for thousands of years. Crystals are like the tarot, guiding you into forgotten realms and caverns, eerie in familiarity since they can also act as timekeepers, storing energy. Each crystal will have its own correspondences, which are its sacred associations. Some will open your heart, some will help ground you, some will help you find protection. Their color, shape, and density (whether it's opaque or translucent) will also tell the quality of the stone. There are many books on this subject, and I've listed a few of my favorites in "Further Reading" (page 330) if you want to learn more. I'll be sharing a few different crystals that can help you get in touch with each element. And since crystals are intricately connected to the earth element, I've also shared a meditation with some stones in this chapter.

Crystals for the element of earth

Since crystals are from the earth, you could argue that all crystals are related to that element. However, some stones have more grounded, stable, flexible, and protective properties than others. Smoky quartz and tourmaline can help you experience these states of being; they help you understand the energy of the earth through the way they interact with your subtle body and energy systems.

A note: If you don't have a physical version of these stones to work with, you can always print out photos or download them as your phone background.

FOR CHANNELING THE ELEMENT OF EARTH: BLACK TOURMALINE

Black tourmaline does not mess around. If you're looking to balance your aura, clear away any energy that's no longer serving you and ground, ground, *ground*, this stone is for you. It harmonizes the energy centers of the body while healing any holes or gaps you may have in your energetic field. Like the earth beneath you, black tourmaline gives you something to physically plug into, helping you live in this realm more fully by clearing away fear and negative programming and protecting you. This stone can help you integrate your shadow side (more on this in the water chapter) by allowing you to see the value in both light and dark, encouraging self-compassion so you can accept all and grow with all parts of yourself. If you feel scared, anxious, or paranoid about being unsafe, this stone can help you feel sheltered and free from danger.

Carry it with you if you need protection, and place it at the base of your spine, also known as the root chakra in Sanskrit (*chakra* meaning "wheel of light"), when you're meditating to help clear energy and ground you to this plane. You can also place black tourmaline near the entrance and exit of your house for protection.

FOR BALANCE WHEN YOU'RE OVERWHELMED WITH EARTH ENERGY: SMOKY QUARTZ

Smoky quartz is a clear, grayish stone and a cousin to the super versatile clear quartz, but with a more stabilizing energy. Smoky quartz can help you find your footing in the moment, transmuting feelings of worry and unease into a grounded calm. It is great for anxiety and can help you clear the fog out of your head for a more centered sense of self. If you're feeling overwhelmed with earth energy, like you're so close to bursting through the surface but need a little push, work with smoky quartz.

By helping you tap into the present, smoky quartz allows you to find more space in the moment to feel your feelings without feeling stuck or overcome by them. This stone is also clearing and energizing, allowing you to move stagnant energy out of your energetic (or auric) field, transmuting this heavy earth energy into fertile soil. Smoky quartz is compassionate as hell, helping you to internalize the power of earth so you can flourish.

If you live with anxiety, try carrying a small smoky quartz around to hold whenever you need it. You can also meditate and place the crystal near the base of your spine or on your pelvis, which is the sacral chakra. Smoky quartz can also alleviate pain, so place it on top of any uncomfortable spots when you meditate to work with its sedative and healing effects.

A MEDITATION TO HELP YOU GROUND AND CONNECT WITH THE ENERGY OF YOUR STONES

This meditation can be adapted using any crystals you want, corresponding to whatever you want to feel. For this meditation specifically, I recommend grounding crystals like smoky quartz and black tourmaline. You may wish to read the meditation a few times to get familiar with it, or you can record yourself reading it and play it back as guided meditation.

Find a comfortable seat and gather your crystals. You're going to be lying down and placing your black tourmaline on the floor between your legs at or near the base of your spine, near your root chakra. Your smoky quartz will go right above that at your pelvis, or sacral chakra. Lie down and start to connect to your breath. If you can't lie down, just find a comfortable position and hold these stones in your hand, or have them close to you. Breathe in and out for equal counts (start with four or five seconds), feeling your mind start to settle. Continue to breathe steadily as you feel your body melt into the floor. As you inhale, imagine a golden light filling your body; as you exhale, imagine yourself melting deeper into the earth beneath you. Notice any tension or worry in your body and send gold light there as you inhale. Imagine the black tourmaline absorbing any negative or stuck energy as you exhale. Continue inhaling golden light and exhaling all your worries, anxieties, and fears into the tourmaline. Bask in this as long as you need.

Now move on to the smoky quartz. Breathe in the protective energy of this stone by imagining a silver, cleansing light moving up from the base of your spine through your body and out the crown of your head. Keep breathing this energy up your spine until it's surrounding you like a cloud of support and reassurance. Feel any anxieties and tension melt away. Release what no longer serves you as you exhale.

Spend as long as you need with these crystals, and with either visualization if you need more of that energy. When you're finished, imagine the golden light from the beginning filling your body, and any negative energy dissolving away. Then open your eyes, sit up slowly, and thank your crystals!

Record your feelings, visions, or images in a grimoire or journal, repeating this meditation whenever you need it.

Earth and embodiment

Although some spiritual practices focus on dissociating you from the material world and separating you from your body to find enlightenment, witchcraft aims to unite both the body and spirit *in this life*. Witchcraft, along with other spiritual practices like Tantra and western paths of occultism, asks for your spiritual practice to be based *here* because it's in this realm that you live and do the work of evolving and growing.

You strive for embodiment, or taking your spiritual practice all the way through the physical realm, so you can feel and enjoy this life to the fullest. Instead of scurrying off to a cave to meditate for hours to attain nirvana (which is dope in its own way), you create rituals that allow you to connect with your spiritual practice in your day-to-day. You internalize this magick, using it as a tool to feel your feelings and know your body and spirit. Instead of leaving this realm, you make a commitment to live in it as fully as possible, as a human who fucks up and makes mistakes and is trying to grow and be as connected to the universe as they can. You stay here so you can help others here as well: enlightenment for all beings. You may still feel anxious or nervous or depressed—you're human. But when you have an embodied practice, you're also able to recognize the feelings that lie deeper than that. You remember that you contain multitudes; even when you're feeling anxious you can still be in a state of intense presence. Even when you're sad, you can find things to be grateful for. Even when your life is chaotic, you have the tools and rituals to find your roots, to find safety. Or to ask for help when you need it.

When I write about embodiment, I'm talking about two things. One of them is practices that use breath, movement, sound, and the senses to anchor you in this realm and get in touch with yourself. The other is glamour, or curating your look and embodying the elements through what you wear, which can include makeup, clothing, perfume, color, and talismans. We'll be exploring both aspects.

EMBODIMENT PRACTICE: A SLOW MOVEMENT RITUAL TO EMBODY THE ENERGY OF EARTH

This exercise is meant to help you feel like the earth itself and can be performed inside or outside in nature. Wear something you can move in comfortably, following instructions on page 15 to set up the space.

Lie down on the floor or ground with a straight spine, arms and legs slightly spread—what's known as corpse pose or Savasana in yoga. Or find any comfortable position where you feel supported by something under you. Start to connect to your breath, breathing evenly in and out for four or five counts each. Breathe in through your nose and out through your mouth, making any sounds you need as you exhale. Do this for at least five breaths and then imagine the base of your spine, your feet, and your hands growing roots that reach deep into the core of the earth. These roots feed you delicious energy that feels warm and soothing. Feel this golden energy as you slowly move and stretch your body, feeling the roots in your hands, feet, and spine. Stretch your arms above your head, move your hips, ask for the energy of the earth to guide you. Continue to breathe! What feels good in your body? How do you need to move to feel more supported by the earth? Do what feels right but try not to go too high, physically; stay low and supported. Try swiveling your hips and torso, stretching one arm long and then the other. Breathe into your connection to the earth and then imagine expanding like your body is giant, like your soul is bigger than your body. Continue moving for five to ten minutes, taking time to pause and think about what your body wants. When you're ready, thank the earth and imagine the roots dissolving or moving back into your body. Take notes of anything you noticed and felt.

Rituals to help you get in touch with the earth

In each section, you'll be guided through different magickal practices inspired by whatever element you'll be studying. In this chapter, you'll be exploring rituals inspired by the element of earth.

GREEN WITCHCRAFT

The earth is the witch's heart. It is the earth to whom you return. It is the earth who provides you a home, who provides you power as you ground before a ritual, and it is the earth who shares an abundance of food, medicine, flowers, beauty, and love. It is through the earth that you witness the shifting seasons, the witch's holidays celebrated as the Wheel of the Year, taking time to honor Gaia in all her sacredness.

Each witch will work with the earth in her own way. Those of you who find yourselves enamored with this element may be drawn to green witchcraft, which works with the earth and nature as the focal point of the craft. If you have a stellar green thumb, love nothing more than spending time in nature, and are a sucker for working with herbs, taking care of your plant children, or tending to gardens, this is a path you are probably already living! Green witchcraft is just witchcraft. But it shifts the gaze primarily on the element of earth through work like gardening, creating herbal medicines and teas, working with earth elementals (like dryads or tree spirits), and enchanting and infusing food with energy through kitchen witchery.

If you feel called to this path but don't know where to start, just start where you are! Is there nature anywhere around you, even a small garden or a tree? Start connecting with those spirits, either in real life or through meditation. Tend to or care for a plant if you can. Start connecting with the food you're eating, thanking the earth for its abundance, practicing kitchen witchcraft. Infuse your food with white light, sending this energy from the cosmos, down the crown of your head, through your body, and out of your palms. Meditate with the earth, practicing the meditation with Gaia on page 63 or meditating on any natural space that makes you feel connected to her. Do something to help the earth, like picking up trash or planting some trees or other oxygen-increasing plants. Drink tea and pour this herbal infusion into your bath so you can absorb the herbs' messages. Spend time outside, unplugged, performing grounding rituals or earthing (see page 56). Leave libations of honey, wine, sweet cakes, mead, menstrual blood, or whatever else for the earth. Let the earth guide you, sharing her secrets and wishes with you as you continue learning this path. There are many books and resources on this subject as well, so if you feel inspired to learn more, I urge you to follow that calling!

THE RITUAL OF TEA

Tea rituals have been used for thousands of years, from New Zealand to China, to India and the United States, as a way to connect to the earth. Drinking sacred herbs is an easy way to adopt their healing properties and connect to the spirit of the plants. Even if you're not a kitchen witch, drinking tea can be a powerful ritual of warmth and healing. The key here, as with anything else, is intention. How can you bring mindfulness to your tea? You prepare and sip consciously. You know the properties of the herbs you choose, and you pick them for a reason. You visualize and connect with your tea as you sip it. In other words, as in all rituals, the act of drinking tea becomes something sacred.

Following is a list of different herbs and a little bit about their properties. There are way too many to list, so these are some of my favorites. Each is ruled over by a different planet, but since all herbs come from the earth, I decided to place them in this chapter. Tea rituals can connect you with other elements as well, like water, so get

creative and ask yourself, and the herbs, what you need before planning your ritual.

Chamomile: An herb of the sun, chamomile is healing and helps with insomnia and stress. Chamomile also helps you embrace the energy of success and tap into your sacral chakra for confidence, warmth, and light.

Dandelion: Connected to Hekate, the Greek goddess of witchcraft, necromancy, and the crossroads, dandelion is a powerful and healing herb that is associated with the passage of time and feeling comfortable with change. This herb is grounding and wonderful for the liver.

Ginger: Associated with the tarot card of the High Priestess, ginger is a grounding root with protective properties. This clearing herb can help you bring awareness to your body, find your inner fire, and heal what needs to be healed. It's great for stomachaches too.

Lavender: Lavender is an immensely healing herb that connects you to your intuition while fostering relaxation. Lavender can aid with fertility as well as helping you view the world through a more spiritual and holistic lens. More than anything, lavender can help you destress and heal in times of darkness, while also helping you manifest your desires for the future.

Mint: Although different forms of mint, like spearmint and peppermint, have their own specific properties, they are all herbs of abundance and success. Used to help attract wealth, mint also helps protect you and is wonderful to use when you need to feel refreshed and cleansed.

Mugwort: One of the most psychic herbs, mugwort can connect you to your intuition, aid in accessing insight from your third eye and crown chakras, and allow your inner psychic to flourish. One of the most common herbs used for lucid dreaming and visions, mugwort can also help those of us who bleed monthly with cramps.

Rose: An herb of Venus, roses are the flowers of love, devotion, and the heart. You can work with roses to connect to the energy of unconditional love, pleasure, and beauty. This is also a fantastic herb for healing and helping you cultivate self-love.

Vervain: One of the witches' herbs, vervain is affiliated with Venus and is used in home blessings and to consecrate ritual items. Vervain empowers any magick and can help you manifest and draw on the properties of love. It inspires you and can prepare you for magical work.

A TEA RITUAL TO HELP YOU FEEL GROUNDED IN YOUR BODY

This simple ritual uses whatever type of herb you choose alongside simple visualization and breath work to help you feel grounded. This is super useful if you're dealing with anxiety, are nervous about something, or just need a hug of warmth and light from the universe.

The wonderful thing about tea is that you can drink it even in a nonritual setting and still create a ritual with it. So even though this is written for the comfort of your own space, you can do the whole thing in your head when you're at work, waiting in line, at Starbucks, or wherever else. No one has to know! Just close your eyes and breathe.

You'll need: herbs of your choice (start with the preceding list), a tea bag or infuser *or* prebagged herbal tea, a mug of your choice, a teapot if you have one, hot water, honey, and milk if you take it, a spoon, any crystals you want to hold (such as black tourmaline or smoky quartz), a quiet space to sit and reflect.

Step 1: Set the space and make the tea

It's time to set the space. Turn off your phone, put on some ambient music, let any roomies know not to disturb you, and gather your supplies. Grab your mug and herbs and put the water to boil. As you do, start to ground and connect to your breath, releasing any tension or worry with each exhale. When you're grounded, thank whatever herbs you're working with. If you're using loose herbs, put them in the infuser or bag. If you're using a tea bag, put it in your mug—ideally one you love. Something I did to make my tea rituals more special is paint my own mug at one of those plaster painting places: I drew planetary sigils and other occult motifs, dedicating it to Venus. If you feel called, you may wish to dedicate a mug to your ritual work and use it only for tea ceremonies; ditto for your teapot.

Once the water is boiling, pour it over your tea or into your teapot, and in your mug, thanking the element of water as it cleanses and connects with the element of earth. Continue to breathe.

Step 2: Steep and breathe

The tea is made, and now you can bring some mindfulness into your practice. Grab your mug, your spoon, your teapot if you have one, and any honey, sugar, or milk and find your way over to where you'll be sitting. Set your tea down somewhere safe, grab any crystals you want to work with, place them either in front of you or in your nondominant hand, and close your eyes.

First, connect with the cosmos. Imagine a white light of pure love and consciousness moving down from the heavens to the crown of your head, down your spine, and into the earth. This white light cleanses and purifies your aura and self and helps you ground. When you're ready, start to breathe this light into your body and decide on an intention with this ritual; it can be for grounding, for healing, for presence, or whatever else. Hold this intention in your mind's eye as long as you need.

Step 3: Stir it in

When you're ready, grab your tea and take a moment to feel its warmth as you continue to breathe into your body. If you wish to add any honey or milk, now is the time. Stir it in *clockwise*, or deosil, to bring in and manifest warmth, grounding, and prosperity. You may wish to stir in multiples of three, a sacred number.

Step 4: Gratitude and prayer

Now comes time for gratitude and prayer. Imagine that same white light moving down your spine, through your hands, and into the tea. Send gratitude to this tea alongside the light and take a second to thank these herbs for their magick and support as you reconnect to your intention. You also may wish to say a simple prayer like the following:

> *Element of earth, I thank you now for this sweet offering to help me connect to your energy. May I receive the healing properties of [the herb you're drinking] as they're meant for me at this moment, in my highest favor. And so it is.*

Step 5: Enjoy

Once you feel connected to your tea, now it's time to drink it! Relish every sip. Take your time here, basking in gratitude for this offering. When you feel satisfied, thank the tea and imagine the white light returning to the heavens above you. Take a few deep breaths and continue on your day.

AN EARTHING RITUAL AND WALKING MEDITATION TO HELP YOU CONNECT WITH NATURE

Earthing is a fancy way of saying walking on the earth with no shoes on. Studies suggest that pressing your bare feet into the dirt and grass can help you sleep better, feel less pain, and be more well grounded. The idea is that electrons from the earth are drawn in through your feet, which help neutralize some damage in your body. Whether this is legit or not, the idea makes intuitive sense: the earth is a healer. Every witch knows this. You know that when you're in nature you're more connected to your own wild nature; you remember that you come from the earth. She's your mother, like she is the mother of every other living being on this planet. When you die, you will return to her.

This ritual helps you remember that through your body. When you become conscious of the way the earth feels beneath your feet, you often feel safer, more relaxed, more confident. The earth soothes you; it's a safe space. It's the feeling of coming home. And if you're in a big city or don't get to spend much time outside, you can work with this practice inside to help reconnect with nature.

You'll need: somewhere outside to walk around barefoot safely, like a backyard or park; a towel or paper towel to clean up with; a journal or notebook and pen.

You can also adapt this ritual into a walking meditation by doing it in your home and not a park. You can go through the same steps and still find grounding and connection to the earth.

Step 1: Set the space and your intention

First things first. Find somewhere you're safe and can walk around with your eyes closed (though that part isn't necessary if you're not into it). Make sure your shoes and socks are off and stowed away. You may wish to bring a friend to watch you and your stuff, just in case. Make sure there's no trash, glass, or anything harmful on the ground. You'll be pacing so you won't need a ton of space. Turn off your phone, start to connect with your breath, feel the sun shining on your skin, and then close your eyes.

Feel your feet on the earth, how they're supported. Feel the way gravity is securing you and holding you down. Breathe into this and then set an intention. It can be for presence or grounding. Maybe it's to have better boundaries, or to connect more deeply with the earth so you can live more freely. Whatever it is, send gratitude to the earth and keep this intention in your heart.

Step 2: Connect and move

Once you feel connected, either with your eyes closed or with your gaze fixed on the ground right in front of your feet, start to walk. Feel the way your whole foot presses into the earth. Feel every blade of grass and every piece of dirt press back. Pace for five to ten minutes, continually bringing your awareness to your feet and how they touch the earth. Breathe into your intention. You may wish to lift onto your toes, or dig into your heels, or dig your feet into the ground without moving for a moment. Honor what's coming up and what your body instinctively wants to do.

Step 3: Close and record

Take as long as you would like interacting with the earth beneath your feet. When you're ready, find stillness and come back to your breath. Take a few deep breaths and focus on your intention. Thank the earth for the support and take a deep breath of gratitude and open your eyes.

Record anything that came up, like feelings, smells, visions, or impressions. Then wipe off your feet, put your shoes back on, and enjoy the rest of your day!

Working with goddesses

One of the most transformative parts of my spiritual journey has been working with the divine feminine and recognizing and honoring a divinity that I see myself in. Many of us grew up in patriarchal religions that emphasize the divine as being masculine, a man. We learned that God is an old man who sits in the clouds and judges us. This is a god who is wrathful, who punishes us, who doesn't want us to partake in pleasure. Oh, and this god is most definitely not a woman.

FUCK THAT. This couldn't be further from the truth. God, the divine, the universe, whatever *it is*, is for one thing much bigger than any of us. The force you call God or the universe isn't human. It's an energy, something so much more than you are that you can't even conceptualize it. So what do humans do when they don't understand something? They create it in their own image. We have created a god, and gods and goddesses, to act as bite-size chunks of the divine because the divine is too much for us to handle. It's like staring directly at the sun—you just can't do it.

God isn't an old man in the clouds. He's not judging you. God isn't even a he or a she, for that matter; god just is. The universe just is. While I personify god as goddess, and refer to the universe as *she*, gender doesn't exist for the divine the same way it does for us. Just as everyone has both masculine and feminine, or active and receptive parts of themselves, so does the divine. But the divine is pure light, pure love, pure consciousness of presence. Although you can't comprehend the divine, you can work with goddesses and gods from different pantheons to help you form relationships with it.

I'll be talking about different goddesses in relation to different elements. Although there are just as many gods, I am particularly passionate about goddess worship and the divine feminine to help bring the masculine/feminine polarity into balance. It is for the Goddess and through the Goddess that I am of service with this work. For those of you who grew up believing God was a man, worshipping and working with the feminine energies of the universe can feel like a radical reclamation. You get to see yourself reflected in something heavenly; you get to form a relationship with the divine mother through the different masks she wears. You get to witness the Goddess in yourself through this work and you can even embody different elements through intentional relationships with the goddesses they're associated with. At first, this may feel uncomfortable and nerve-racking. That's okay! Take it slow and remember to honor what doesn't feel right. Breathe into the discomfort and honor it if it means "stop!"

GETTING STARTED

Something important to remember when starting a relationship with a goddess or deity is that it's just that: a relationship. Respect doesn't just go out the window 'cause you're working with the divine. Remember your table manners! Do your research. Learn about whatever goddess you're going to be working with. Create a space for her, like an altar. Leave an offering. Don't make any promises you can't keep, and don't demand things from her!

Creating rituals of devotion is a powerful way to form relationships with goddesses as well. This can be something you do every day or as regularly as possible: repeating a prayer, lighting a candle, leaving an offering, or singing a song. When you repeat these sacred acts, you're reaffirming your dedication to this goddess and deepening your connection with her while you're at it. You'll be exploring how to create a devotional ritual in the spirit chapter of this book.

Gaia: Greek goddess of the earth

Before there was Zeus and Aphrodite, before there were the Titans, before any of it, there was chaos and then there was Gaia. Gaia is the primordial earth goddess, worshipped as the earth personified. She is where all life comes from, and where life returns to. Gaia is the mother of the sky, also known as Urania, and she is the one who gave birth to the Titans, the giants, and the sea.

When you think of Gaia, think of the most overwhelmingly beautiful, natural space you have been to or can imagine. Gaia *is* Mother Nature, and it is in her splendor that you can connect to her most fully. How do you feel when you're in nature? What does it feel like in your body to be present with the earth? Pay attention to this; even before you begin formally working with this goddess, you already know her.

In this same vein, Gaia is a goddess of extremes. Although nature can be loving and gentle with a harmonious breeze and sunshine, it can also be intense and volatile, sending us natural disasters like tornadoes and hurricanes. For Gaia, there is no apology for her multitudes; it's by embracing all ends of the spectrum that she can teach you what it means to accept your fullest self.

Gaia is the nurturer. She is the energy of everything you need to manifest. When you're working with this goddess, you're in a mutually beneficial relationship with the earth. You're aware of how your actions impact this planet, you're aware of your own needs and boundaries, and you're reveling in the gifts you've been given. The garden of your soul is thriving. Gaia consciousness is that of the natural realm, of the beginning and the end. She is the infinity symbol, always in balance. Gaia is loving, compassionate, tender, fierce, and unpredictable. When you need to return to the arms of Mother Earth, to connect to the natural realm, to be in touch with the flora and fauna, you can call on Gaia. She is as much the earth personified as she is all the critters and creatures that inhabit it. Through her you can start to form a relationship to the earth as more than the earth, as a living, breathing spirit. Gaia is the divine feminine because through her all things are created and born, and when you honor her, you too can flourish in an energetic ecosystem that links you to something cosmic.

Creating an altar

You can start a relationship with a goddess by creating an altar. An altar is an energetic focal point of a space and the home of your magickal working. Altars are made to honor a specific intention, whether it's a holiday or a moon phase or in dedication to your ancestors. In this case, this altar is dedicated to a goddess. You'll want a flat and secure space; however, if you're not able to do this or can't openly display your altar and magickal supplies, you can create a portable one in a wooden or plastic box.

Think of items that have special meaning to you: tarot cards, crystals, candles, talismans, love notes, a cauldron, a ritual knife, a wand, jewelry, flowers, or whatever else inspires you. These can all decorate your altar alongside photos, art, and other magickal tools dedicated to your intention. You can leave offerings to your deity of choice here as well.

A note on offerings: If you can't leave out food, sweets, or drinks overnight because of bugs or pets, you can put your offerings in the fridge overnight. If you need to throw out or dispose of your offerings, take a second and let the cosmos know the offering and energy exchange are complete and then dispose of them.

AN ALTAR FOR GAIA

Since you're honoring and working with the energy of Gaia, or Mother Earth, placing plants, flowers, herbs, and other items from nature on your altar is highly recommended. You can even go outside and gather herbs and flowers yourself. (But before you pick anything close your eyes and ask the plant how it feels about this. If you feel a yes, then pick the flowers and thank them!) You may choose to decorate with statues of the divine feminine, like the Venus of Willendorf. Think about using plants; fresh herbs and flowers; candles in deep green, white, blue, and gold; and a chalice (which represents the womb or the mother). You also may wish to have a candle or sacred herbs like mugwort, lavender, or sweetgrass to light every day.

As far as offerings, try sweets, flowers, honey and nectar, chocolate, tobacco, and anything that makes you feel grounded in the energy of the earth.

Colors: The colors of the earth: deep, forest green. Dark burgundy red. Chocolate brown. Silver and gold. Deep ocean blue. Light sky blue.
Sacred objects and correspondences: Any and all herbs and flowers; anything from the earth. Plants, succulents, animals (my fish's bowl is on my altar), crystals.
Crystals: All crystals come from the earth, so all may be used to honor her. Smoky quartz, onyx, black tourmaline.
Tarot card: The Ace of Pentacles, the Queen of Pentacles, or the Empress—the Empress *is* the mother. She embodies the energy of Gaia as a creatrix, a nurturer, and a caretaker devoted to love. Put this tarot card on your altar as an invitation to connect with this energy of growth and as an invitation to connect with Gaia.
Offerings: Honey, sweet cakes, flowers, tobacco, liquor.

A meditation to connect with Gaia

There are many reasons to meditate, and working with goddesses is one of them. In meditation, you have the chance to connect with energies that you don't normally reach on the physical realm. When you travel to the astral realm, you find your higher consciousness, human consciousness, and energetic beings and archetypes like gods and goddesses. At the very least, you have the chance to go inward and connect to yourself and your guides through introspection, silence, and stillness.

For this meditation, all you need is a quiet space to sit or lie down (though be wary if you fall asleep easily!), and a journal and pen to take any notes once you're done. Prepare yourself and the space, following instructions on page 15. You can also use sacred smoke from herbs like lavender, sweetgrass, mugwort, copal, or frankincense to cleanse yourself and the space you'll be meditating in.

I suggest reading through this meditation a few times to get comfortable with the steps. You can also record yourself reading it for a little guided meditation. I like to meditate for at least ten minutes, but aim for a minimum of three or five. Set a timer if you're worried about keeping track of time.

When you're ready, close your eyes and start to ground. Return to your breath, exhaling and inhaling evenly and slowly. Feel how the earth is supporting you and breathe into this until you feel present. Then, imagine being in a field or an open space outside that's beautiful and restorative. This place can be real or imaginary; what's important is that it's in nature and feels expansive. Feel the sun shining on your skin as you start to walk, taking in the scenery around you. There are gardens of flowers, the air smells of springtime, and there are an array of animals around. You continue walking when suddenly the space opens up for you into a beautiful meadow.

As you enter this meadow, you sense something. You feel a warmth in your heart growing stronger and stronger, like a loving presence has enveloped you. You know this is Gaia, the goddess of the earth, and you feel comforted. In that moment, you sense all the elements, all the plants and birds and trees, sending you energy and love and light. Take a moment to send deep gratitude to Gaia, and promise her that you'll keep watching out for the earth and protecting her. You may also share whatever else you want this goddess to know, and you can ask for her compassion and guidance as you continue cultivating a relationship with her.

Stay here as long as you need, enjoying the sweet exchange of this blessing and embrace. When you're ready, reach into your pocket (or where your pocket would be) and visualize grabbing a rose quartz and leaving it where you're standing as an offering. Let Gaia know that this comes from the heart, for her love and support. When you're ready, walk back toward where you came, take a few deep breaths, and open your eyes.

Use your journal and pen to record anything that came to you, as well as any feelings or visions. Return to this visualization as often as you want. You can meditate outside to deepen your connection to Gaia as well.

Embodying the earth: glamour that grounds

Glamour is everywhere, and most of us have some kind of beauty ritual that we perform each day, regardless of whether we care to admit it. This can be as simple as brushing your teeth and washing your face, or as intense as doing a full face of makeup and perfume before you head to work. Glamour is something that veils what lies beneath it; in this case, the body and face that lie beneath the clothing, jewelry, and makeup you wear. When you add intention to glamour and to the rituals of beauty and style you perform each day, you can begin to change the way you navigate the world. Not only are you in control of how you're being perceived, but you can also align yourself and your style with correspondences that serve whatever purpose you desire.

In this case, you think about what you can wear to help you feel

of this earth, to help you feel grounded, prosperous, fertile, and reborn. If you don't know where to start, picture the colors of nature: deep forest green, dark scarlet red, brown the color of the earth, sky blue, slate gray. These tones can help you feel more rooted and calm, whether you're wearing them on a shirt, in a print, or on your face with makeup. You may also wish to connect with the earth by wearing her patterns; floral or Hawaiian prints or leaf motifs are another way to embrace this element. Try a monochrome forest green look, a floral button-down, or play around with dark red eye shadow. Wear your favorite slate gray coat or emerald green eyeliner and a scarf that reminds you of a cozy winter day. Think of proportions that make you feel safe and cozy; often, the more oversized the better. Sharp shoulders, structure, and clean lines are also earthy glamour. Even your favorite faux leather jacket can be a grounding piece of fashion magick; the only person with whom this has to resonate is *you*. If you've never played with style in this way, it may feel a bit odd. Give yourself permission to feel silly and explore with weird stuff! Life is way more fun when you make it an occasion to celebrate and wear something interesting.

The key with earth-inspired glamour is to wear what makes you feel confident, powerful, and safe. This is a look that you *know* feels good. Think vintage blazer with sharp shoulders, a pair of sliders or loafers that go with anything, that vintage band tee with that one pair of denim, or that floral suit you absolutely adore.

You can also work with scent. Try an earthy perfume with musk, leather, cedar, sandalwood notes, or another aromatic scent if you're looking to tap into stillness and rootedness. If you want to connect to flowers and their beauty, try a floral perfume: rose, jasmine, or lavender. Spray or dab these perfumes behind your ears and on your wrists and chest, which you can also do with perfume oils. Perfume oils, which often contain blends of essential oils in carrier oil, also have magickal properties, and you can find different element combinations online or at your local metaphysical shop. You can also make your own using your favorite grounding herbs and oils.

To embody the energy of earth, wear talismans and pieces of jewelry that you have a special relationship with. They could be crystals, pieces of wood or bone, leather, or family heirlooms; again, the sky is the limit! Create your own talisman using clay, paint, wood, leather, or any other natural material. Write the elemental symbol for earth on it, or a word or symbol for something you want more of. You can also charge an item using the following method.

How to charge a talisman with an intention

Like any other magickal work, you'll want to set up before the ritual, following the instruction on page 15. You should also come to this ritual with an intention that you want to charge your talisman with. Find a comfortable seat, put your talisman in your dominant hand, and close your eyes. Take a few slow, deep breaths to bring you into the moment, and perform a grounding visualization, connecting to the earth below. Then start to imagine a beam of light from the cosmos coming from above, moving down to the crown of your head, down your spine, and into the earth. This white light is cleansing; it's source energy from the universe. Only that which works in your highest favor can dwell here. Breathe this white light into your heart space at the center of your chest and continue breathing it down your arms into your hands, where you hold the talisman. Continue breathing this into your talisman and tell it your intention, whether for unconditional love, protection, abundance, or whatever else. If you're not sure what you're looking for, ask and see what you feel. Continue breathing this white light into your talisman as you focus on your intention. When you feel like your talisman is charged, thank it, and then imagine the light from the cosmos moving up your spine and back into the heavens above. Close with your grounding visualization, take a few breaths, and slowly open your eyes.

Journal questions to connect with earth

At the end of every chapter, I'll leave you with a few questions to dwell on. If you don't already have one, buy a notebook or a journal that you love the feel and look of and answer these questions in it. This is your grimoire, your magickal journal, for notes and updates about your practice and rituals. Come back here to process whenever you need and use the questions from each section to guide you in returning to yourself.

Take time to create a ritual of answering these questions. Make yourself some tea (you can even do the ritual on page 53) or grab some water, turn off your phone, and let any roomies or partners know not to disturb you. Put on ambient or relaxing music, light incense, grab crystals (see page 44–46 for suggestions), and then start answering:

» In what areas of my life do I feel supported and safe?

» What does it mean for me to feel grounded?

» What does my body need to be healthy and happy at this time?

» In what areas of my life do I have healthy boundaries?

» What areas of my life could use more compassionate boundaries?

» What does abundance mean to me? How can I channel this Queen of Pentacles energy?

» What am I looking to manifest in this phase of my life?

Earth in astrology: Capricorn, Taurus, Virgo

♑ ♉ ♍

Each zodiac sign belongs to a different element based on the characteristics of that particular sign. There are three signs in each element, with the element of earth consisting of Capricorn (the goat), Taurus (the bull), and Virgo (the virgin). Even without any knowledge of astrology, and by remembering what we've been discussing in this chapter, you already have an idea of what these signs are like. They are rooted in this physical realm. They are practical, strong, hardworking; they're the structures in place that you need before you come out of the cocoon.

The zodiac wheel (imagine it as a giant circle in the night sky) is broken up into twelve houses, with a different sign ruling each. Your birth chart is a screenshot of where the planets were in this wheel; so even if you don't have any planets in the earth signs (Capricorn, Taurus, or Virgo), they're still represented in your chart through the houses ruled by these signs. Plus, each zodiac sign has its own season while the sun is in that sign, so we live in each sign's domain, regardless.

When you learn about astrology, you're able to see your own elemental makeup in a new way. You have a literal chart of where you may need more of one element and less of another. My birth chart shows plenty of water and air, but barely any fire or earth. I know that I can embrace the qualities of the signs and elements I'm missing to help myself find balance and not be swept off into the land of daydreams and feelings when I really need to be rooted and find my inner flame to get shit done.

So what can you learn from earth signs?

CAPRICORN—THE SEA-GOAT

We start off each year with Capricorn's season, and all the resolutions, goal setting, and planning that comes with it. Capricorns are meticulous and driven, and they have the vision to see their most ambitious ideas through. Not only is their symbol that of the hard-working, adaptive, and persistent goat, but it's that of the sea-goat, taking adaptability to a whole new level. These elegant creatures are brilliant at breaking down big projects into digestible steps, and they have the dedication to climb whatever mountain they desire. The key here is the patience and commitment, with a good amount of fun thrown in too. Capricorns can surprise you with how much they appreciate a good time. Work hard, play hard, anyone? Although this sign can sometimes be too wrapped up in work, at their most exalted they know the power of a good boundary and celebrating with a good time.

TAURUS—THE BULL

Ruled by the planet Venus, guardian of all things sexual, sensual, and pleasure filled, Taurus is the hedonist of the zodiac. This is the earth in spring, when things are beautiful and bountiful and everything feels ripe with possibility. Taurus wants all the luxury, to be surrounded by inspiring things, eating delicious food, wearing opulent fabrics, and enjoying life. Taurus is committed as hell, working to the bone for issues they care about. This sign expects a lot and gives a lot in return, enriching your life with Venusian flavor and loyalty like no other. Although they can be stubborn and fixed at times—they are the bull, after all—as they evolve Tauruses stand firm in their loyalty and dedication to the things, people, and ideals they love.

VIRGO—THE VIRGIN

Let me begin by reminding everyone of the historic use of the word *virgin*, which means a woman unto herself; that is, a woman who is complete *by* herself. Virgo energy is that of the nurturer, of sharing from a place of completeness. It means precision, organization, and working as hard as possible. Virgos are meticulous, known for their Type A nature that calls for decisiveness and clarity to the max. Yet Virgo is also the nurturing earth mother, allowing you to tap into your sensitivity while still finding your depths. Virgos in their lower vibration may not know how to be flexible, but when they're evolved they are adaptable and aware of the ancient wisdom in their souls. The energy of the hermit tarot card, Virgos remind you of what it means to relentlessly follow your inner voice and to honor yourself wholly.

IN THEIR LEAST EVOLVED STATE

Like the earth, these energies can manifest as guarded, noncooperative, and rigid. Earth signs can get caught up in what they perceive to be the only way, not allowing anyone to help and not adjusting to fit the situation. This energy can manifest as being lethargic, bored, lazy, and immobile, like there's something keeping you from getting up and off the ground you've made yourself comfortable on. It can also manifest as sadness, anxiety, and depression if there's a sense of being stuck without direction. In its encumbered state, earth energy is stubborn and unable to see other perspectives. Thankfully, working with the other elements is a way to balance this energy.

IN THEIR MOST EVOLVED STATE

Earth signs are grounded, practical, loyal, and diligent. They're the ones who are always early, put together, and looking fabulous, ready to take on the day. Earth signs are sensualists, helping you get in touch with the body as well as Mother Earth, teaching you the joy of caring for another living being. Earth signs teach you of loyalty, of your ability to bloom and thrive with consistency and safety. They teach you to work hard and play hard, and to enjoy life by owning the abundance that comes from it. These signs can teach you the importance of slowing down enough to enjoy life, to celebrate with friends, and to bask in the harvest of your abundance. When this energy is in its highest vibration, you can manage whatever the world throws at you. Though your trunk may sway in the wind, your roots are firmly planted, supporting you no matter what.

CHAPTER 2

Air: Breathe It

So your feet have found their way into the soil beneath you. Your foundation is set and you feel supported. You've built the groundwork and now it's time to expand, to become one with the wind and sky. Air is ever present and ever moving, the intangible curiosity that sparks your imagination and brings you into the moment. It is the breeze on your skin, the feeling of oxygen in your lungs. Air energy is the feeling of solving a riddle, the joy of learning something that shifts your worldview. Air is the mind, your ability to understand and intellectualize emotions (sometimes for the best, sometimes not), your ability to reason, to decide what constitutes truth, to analyze. The element is all around you, and it's also within you. Just as your body is your physical and personal "earth," your breath is your connection to air. Through your breath you can learn about this element that craves flexibility and expansion. Air is how your body finds space, release, and purification. Just as smoke can cleanse and clear, so can your breath, drawing you back into energetic and physical equilibrium.

Air as breath and presence

How many times have you caught yourself overwhelmed with emotion and short of breath? Maybe you were so excited you forgot to breathe, or so nervous you skipped a breath. Maybe you don't think about your breath at all until suddenly it's not there. This is totally normal. In our culture, you're taught that your emotions are overwhelming and "too much" and that womxn especially should be small: take up as little space as possible, be as quiet as possible, and shrink as much as possible. Well, witches, one of your jobs is to fight the paradigms the patriarchy has established and replace them with better, more life-affirming ones. And thankfully one of the easiest ways to reclaim your space is to reclaim your breath—the vital connection to the life force you have with you all the time. When you work intentionally with your breath, when you breathe into your emotions, your worries, your fears, your gratitude, you're able to taste these feelings and soak up these lessons with more clarity and less work. Your breath does the work for you, allowing you to process by helping you pay attention to where you're physically carrying your feelings. In moments of difficulty, your breath can help you bridge the mental and the physical, taking you out of your mind by using the breath to lead your awareness back into your body and what it's feeling at that moment.

Breath is important in an array of mystical practices. In yogic traditions of the East, breath work is known as *pranayama*, with *prana* meaning "breath" or "life force" and *ayama* meaning "to draw out." Pranayama uses different postures, breathing techniques, and hand positions known as *mudras* to help create an energetic shift in the practitioner. This can be to relax, ground, and find stillness or to energize, connect, and find vitality.

In the West, breath work is also an important part of various magickal traditions. Western occultism works with breathing techniques as part of meditation and ritual, and most witches will at the very least connect to their breath through grounding and meditation. Just as working with the earth can help you ground and design compassionate boundaries, air can connect you to your body while also helping you purify and cleanse yourself.

Let's do an experiment. Take a deep breath in through your nose for four counts, filling your belly with air. Then exhale through your mouth for four counts, making any sounds or noises you need. Now do this twice more. How do you feel? Do you feel some space in your ribs and stomach where there wasn't before? Maybe you feel more present? It's such an easy trick, but your breath can show you where you're contracting and holding on to tension, anxiety, or worry. When you're able to come back to the moment, you often see that these fears aren't living in the present but in the past or future. And it's your anxiety brain that makes you freak out, thinking something is happening *right now that you must worry about*. When you use your breath, you remind yourself that you're capable, alive, confident, able; not only do you have the skills and ability to ask for help when you need it, but you also have the element of air to help you.

Air and the mind

Air speaks of your mental abilities of processing, cognitive functioning, and communicating. The mental body is the territory of air, and so is learning. Through this connection you begin the process of alchemy, of taking something intangible like an idea or thought and turning it into something physical. Fire is the spark of the idea, and the idea that forms in your mind is the oxygen, the

air. Then you connect this with an emotion, the realm of water, and then bring it into the material, earth. Through air you begin to perceive and understand. This element speaks of your ability to discern the messages you're receiving, to know what to hold on to (what resonates) and what to let go of (everything else). Air is also the way you take in other people's messages. Air speaks of your mind's strength, of your ability to channel ideas and evaluate and analyze. Air rules over what you think, what you study, what inspires you. Air is the realm of psychology, of books, of math, of the scientist, of the revolutionary and the anarchist. Air energy is innovative and asks you to unlearn old ways of being so you can adopt new ones that work better for where you are in the present. You can work with your mind and honor all the things you think by giving space to observe without judgment. Air becomes the mirror, reflecting back what you're going and growing through. When you give yourself space to dissect and prod and poke at this, you are giving your experiences the chance to share their wisdom. You choose to see how these things help you evolve.

Inhale the good shit, exhale the bullshit

There's a reason that the saying *Inhale the good shit and exhale the bullshit* is so popular (in L.A., at least). Your breath is your spiritual cleansing system. While you breathe in oxygen and exhale carbon dioxide—whether or not you're paying attention—your energetic body is also clearing out toxins without you even noticing. When you're angry, or upset, or nervous, your breathing changes; you scream, cry, yell. Your body, whether you like it or not, finds a physical way to move through what you're feeling. And this is often linked to your breath.

When you use visualization, meditation, and breath work, you can use your breath to clear out negative energy, tension, or anxiety. This can be as easy as inhaling white, golden light and exhaling unneeded energy as gray murky light. This won't mean that you simply breathe away any problems in your life, but it does mean that you can use your breath to process difficult emotions so you have clarity with how to proceed. Your breath can help you find distance and space from your feelings, giving you a safe place to work through them and confront them without judgment.

Throughout this chapter, you'll be delving into the element of air and how you can work with it for presence and vigor. You'll also explore how you can use breath work in your regular rituals as a path for growth, clarity, and freedom.

Breath as gratitude

Through your breath, you share your world and communicate your beliefs, passions, and inner self. Through the way you shape your exhales, you tell your stories, share your wisdom, and connect with others. And through your breath, you can craft the life of your fantasies.

As you know by now, dear witch, intention is vital. And when you are intentional about your words and how you can breathe life into what you believe in, you have an opportunity to manifest. Although you could use your voice to complain all day, I'm much more interested in the antithesis of this, of how you can use your breath, and thereby your voice and self-expression, to find gratitude for the world around you. Being grateful for what you do have, even if it's for something as simple as the ability to breathe, is deeply cathartic. Letting gratitude be your guide, and using your own voice to affirm what you're thankful for, is only going to invite more of this energy into your life. In this way, gratitude acts as a magnet, inviting you to change the lens in which you see the world. When you realize you have abundance, and that there's enough for *everyone* to have abundance, you're able to lean into this mind-set and get rid of the idea of scarcity. Womxn in particular are taught that there's not enough for us, that we have to fight (one another especially) and struggle to be heard and to have enough. And guess what—that's not true. You do have enough, and you deserve to live with enough. Money isn't happiness, but in our society it is freedom and security. And you deserve to feel safe and free. One way to start believing this is by using affirmations and creating a gratitude practice.

Having a regular gratitude practice can remind you of the silver lining in almost anything, and of how valid, worthwhile, and important your voice is. It also feels delicious and can help you witness the miracles happening in your life every single day. Here are a few simple ways to create your own gratitude practice:

» Write out ten things you're grateful for every day. Even if you're not a fan of *The Secret*, this practice is a potent and fun way to condition your mind to be appreciative. Every morning, in either a specific journal, in a notes app, or on the computer, write out ten things you're thankful for. You can start with *I am so grateful for* or *I am thankful for*. The key? To *feel* it. Once you're done, read this list out loud and say thank you after each affirmation. You may wish to put a hand on your heart, feeling this loving energy permeating your auric body as you read. You can also do this with anything you want to draw into your life, whether it's a romantic relationship, more wealth, a new job, community, healing, connection, or anything else. Say that you're thankful for this thing and write it out like you already have it.

» Record voice notes of what you're grateful for. I got this from Gala Darling, my friend and author of *Radical Self-Love*. The exercise is similar to the previous one: say what you're grateful for *as if it's already happened*. Get as specific as possible, talking through the day ahead and focusing on the gratitude emanating from each step. Say what you're manifesting as if it's already happened, and how appreciative you are for it. For example, this could be something like *I am so grateful to have landed my dream job working for [x] that supports me by [y] and pays me [z],* or *I am so grateful for the healing I am going through right now that's allowing me to grow, level up, and live prosperously.* Get as specific as possible about what you want. Feel how amazing it will be to have this, and how thankful you'll be. You can also do this with friends to support one another's visions, sending your voice notes to one another and asking each other questions about what you're drawing in to continue cultivating it.

» Say thank you to the universe whenever you feel good. Walk outside and feel the sun on your skin? Thank the universe! Heard your favorite song on the radio? Thank the universe! Saw a cute dog? Thank the universe! When you say thank you and open your heart to gratitude and love, you are in the vortex, in the energy of magick. Start taking time to connect to gratitude and you'll witness the universe meet you on this level more and more.

Ways to connect with the element of air

Although I'll be talking in more detail about what you can learn from air and how you can use breath work and meditation to connect to it, there are many other ways you can use this elemental as your guide. Air is all around you and when you start thinking of it as presence, purification, and consciousness, you can get deeper with how you relate to it. Some fun ways to work with this element are by doing the following:

- Meditating and being intentional with your breath, spending time taking note of how you feel in your body and creating rituals around this activity.

- Singing, yelling, or using your voice to create change, spread joy, express yourself, or generally just transfer energy from inside your body to outside it.

- Running, jogging, or taking a walk outside and feeling the breeze on your skin.

- Driving with the windows down (even better if you turn the music up and sing along), or skateboarding or biking. Set an intention, and allow yourself to connect with the ever-moving energy of air.

- Lighting incense or sacred herbs and watching how the smoke moves through the room, cleansing yourself and your space.

- Dancing and feeling the way your body moves through the space around you. Spinning in circles is an easy way you can get into a trance, another way to embody air.

- Saying affirmations to yourself, feeling the way your voice claims your truth with efficiency and purpose.

- Journaling or connecting to your thoughts and ideas through words and language; dissecting and prodding and writing prose; creating, communing, constricting ideas and thoughts until they're different.

- » Learning something new, taking a class, going to a museum, or learning a new hobby. Air wants new patterns and modes of existing. When you expand your mind, you expand your reality.

- » Inhaling sacred smoke. You can work with sacred herbs like cannabis, lavender, chamomile, mugwort, and rose by smoking them. It is said that the priestesses of the sun god Apollo at the temple of Delphi in ancient Greece would inhale smoke and fumes before delivering their channeled messages, and the Knights Templar, a medieval Catholic military order, used cannabis in their rites. Working with sacred smoke is a ritual in itself and requires intention and honesty with yourself and your health, but it is a powerful experience.

Embodiment practice: the ritual of breath

In the last chapter, I talked about how you can access the element of earth through the ritual of grounding. This is usually the first step in any ritual, and for many of us, it's the first step in our daily practices, before movement, ritual, or visualization. Just as you work with earth to find grounding, you can work with your breath to help you find presence in your body, clear away any stagnant energy from sleep, and process or recharge for the day ahead. Although you can practice rituals at any point in the day, I find that if you can do something when you wake up it's the most impactful. Even taking five extra minutes to breathe before you go to work or school can be a game changer. The more I work with my breath, the more I find myself breathing fully without thinking about it, even if I'm overwhelmed or stressed. My birth chart is air sign and water sign heavy, which means I naturally don't breathe more than necessary and I hold my breath when I'm feeling anxious; I'm all in my head and emotions. A couple years ago, after three people in the span of a week asked me if I breathe, I decided to set alarms on my phone for five times a day (at angel numbers like 11:11 a.m., 2:22 p.m., 3:33 p.m.) to remind me to take a second for a few deep breaths. And guess what—it worked! Now I find myself taking deep intentional breaths naturally, and I feel infinitely more connected to my body because of it. You don't have to be this structured about it, but alarms can be really useful in establishing a habit of checking in with your breath if this doesn't come naturally to you.

A good rule of thumb for the length of your breath is four seconds. As you get more comfortable, you can breathe for five, six, or seven counts. (This is not true for the breath of fire!)

There are many techniques out there; these are just a few, and the main ones I'll refer to throughout this book.

TO CONNECT TO YOUR HEART— THE HEART BREATH

This breath is an inhale and exhale of equal count, with no pause in between. Inhale and exhale from the heart for equal measures, and picture a warm glowing light there. You can also visualize an infinity sign ∞ (an 8 on its side) connecting your heart with something or someone that brings you love and joy, the universe, the cosmos, or a deity you work with. As you inhale, draw heart energy from them; as you exhale, send it back, creating an infinity sign.

Inhale and exhale through your nose, inhale and exhale through your mouth, or inhale through your nose and exhale through your mouth. Play around and see what works for you.

Try this breath to connect to your heart center; send love to someone else; find empathy, compassion, and presence.

TO GROUND—THE FOURFOLD BREATH

This breath is a personal favorite and very easy to work with. Inhale, hold, exhale, and hold. Then start again. Try inhaling for four seconds, holding for four seconds, exhaling for four seconds, and holding for four seconds for a few rounds before moving to five seconds and then six (again—if you can and it feels right, not constricting).

This breath is usually practiced by inhaling and exhaling through the nose, though you can also inhale and exhale through your mouth, or inhale through your nose and exhale through your mouth. Try it a few ways and see what feels best.

Try this breath to ground; strengthen your aura; calm down; get in your body.

TO ENERGIZE—THE TRIANGLE BREATH

This breath is associated with the element of fire and is done by inhaling, holding, exhaling, and starting again. This is a threefold breath, and you don't hold after you exhale. You may wish to visualize an upside-down triangle with the base between both of your shoulders and the point at your solar plexus. Start at the tip of the triangle at the bottom of your torso, move up the edge to a shoulder as you inhale, then move to the other shoulder as you hold your breath, and back down the triangle to the point as you exhale. Inhale and begin again. Start with four seconds for each breath before moving to five or six seconds.

This breath is usually practiced by inhaling and exhaling through the nose, though you can inhale and exhale through your mouth, or inhale through your nose and exhale through your mouth.

Try this breath to energize; connect with the element of fire; ground and revitalize.

FOR PASSION—THE BREATH OF FIRE

This breath is incredibly clearing and energizing, and also intense. *This breath is only done through the nose!* Breathe in, filling your belly up with air, and then forcefully exhale sharply through your nose until you automatically breathe in again. You should feel your stomach contract after the exhale. This may feel a little funky if you've never done it before! Start with a deep inhale and then try exhaling sharply, pulling your navel to your spine and then letting the exhale come automatically, doing this as many times in a row as you can after that full breath. Start with ten times, or with however many feel comfortable, and then see if you can increase the amount of exhales after each full breath. Try it for a full minute to see how you feel. It gets easier once you get the hang of it.

Try this breath to help you build inner warmth and heat; connect with the element of fire; clear away anything that's no longer serving you.

TO PROCESS AND FIND PRESENCE—THE BELLY BREATH

Another of my favorites, the belly breath is pretty much what it sounds like. Inhale through your nose as you fill your belly with air. You may wish to visualize your belly doing the breathing to make this easier. Exhale through your mouth, making sighs or sounds as necessary as you feel your belly deflate. I like to take a few breaths with sounds and noises when I start to help clear anything that's been stuck, like fear, anxiety, or tension. Once I feel more grounded, I continue inhaling through my nose and exhaling through my mouth without sound. There is no pause between the inhale and exhale, and you can start by inhaling for four seconds and exhaling for the same.

You can also inhale and exhale through the mouth, or inhale and exhale through the nose.

Try this breath to process emotions and tension; find presence; ground and cleanse your energy.

TO CLEANSE AND CLEAR USING YOUR BREATH—THE CLEARING BREATH

Very similar to the triangle breath, the clearing breath is associated with the element of water and helps you cleanse yourself from the inside out. Inhale, exhale, and then hold. You can imagine inhaling as you move from a base of a triangle at your pelvis up to the tip at your heart, exhaling from the tip down to the base, and holding your breath as you move across the base, connecting to the other side. This breath helps you wring out the lungs of any toxins, energetic or not. In the space between the exhale and the inhale you can notice the moment before expansion and take time to reside there. This breath is also very soothing. Start with four seconds for each breath before moving to five or six seconds.

This breath is usually practiced by inhaling and exhaling through the nose, though you can inhale and exhale through your mouth, or inhale through your nose and exhale through your mouth.

Try this breath to find some calm and healing; connect to the element of water; find a sense of center.

Adding breath work to your ritual practice

My daily practice includes meditation as well as breath work. Although it varies, I usually do ten breaths before I begin my meditation since it helps me focus, slow my mind down, and feel fully in my physical body. What kind of breath I pick is dependent on the day, but often I practice a threefold or fourfold breath. I like setting alarms for my meditations, and sometimes I'll also set an alarm for breath work so I know that I can just focus on my breath and not have to worry about how many repetitions I'm doing or for how long. Again, what works for me may not work for you and that's totally okay. My suggestion is to play around with the preceding techniques and see what feels good. Then try adding them to your ritual practice, adopting what feels right on that given day.

For example, if you're anxious or stressed, you may want to try the belly breath, clearing breath, or fourfold breath to help you ground and find presence. If you're feeling sad or lethargic, you may wish to work with the heart breath, triangle breath, or breath of fire to help you clear away stagnant energy and revitalize. And just as you can change your breath to change your mood, you can also work with visualization and color to help you integrate these vibrations even more.

A meditation with color and breath

This simple meditation can be altered and adapted to serve whatever you need. You'll be working with your breath and the healing rays of the divine light spectrum as a form of meditation, envisioning your auric field surrounded by the light you'll be inhaling into your body. You'll be using the chakra system as a guide for the different breaths and breathing techniques, but you can create your own meditation using your intuition and the color correspondence chart on page 89.

Find a comfortable seat. Take a few belly breaths, in through your nose and out through your mouth. Once you're feeling settled, practice your breath of choice as you connect with your crown chakra, the energy center at the top of your head. Imagine a healing white light descending from the cosmos to the crown of your head. With each inhale, this light moves through your body, clearing anything that's not working in your highest favor. As you exhale, any negative or stuck energy is released. As you continue doing your breath with this visualization, you'll start to imagine this white light changing into whatever color coordinates with your breath or intention. Continue filling your body and lungs with this healing color. Imagine it surrounding you, as if you're glowing from the inside out. Let it penetrate your energetic core, balancing your energy, letting your breath guide the way. When you're ready, visualize exhaling this light from your lungs so it is released back into the cosmos.

Start with just five minutes, adding time as you practice more and more. Again, do what feels right. The breath for each chakra is a suggestion; go with what breath and color feel right to you, and research color magick if you really want to dive in. If you're doing the breath of fire, it may take a little more practice to get comfortable; go at your own pace and ride the wave, remembering to breathe in only through your nose.

You may also wish to incorporate crystals into this meditation by holding one in your nondominant hand. My suggestion is to pick a crystal with the same color you'll be visualizing, since the

Chakra	Color	Suggested breath	Purpose
1st: Root chakra	Red	Fourfold Breath	Ground, feel safe, secure, and rooted. For a strong foundation, establish an energetic home in yourself.
2nd: Sacral chakra	Orange	Triangle breath or breath of fire	Triangle breath: connect to sexuality, vitality, and pleasure. Breath of fire: clear away any stuck tension, energy, memories, or energetic pain.
3rd: Solar plexus chakra	Yellow	Belly breath	Find confidence, warmth, a sense of self, purpose, passion, vitality, and light.
4th: Heart chakra	Green	Heart breath	Embrace the energy of the divine, foster unconditional love and self-love. Help find your way back to your heart center.
5th: Throat chakra	Blue	Clearing breath	Clear away energetic blocks so you can speak your truth. Foster and own your voice.
6th: Third eye chakra	Violet	Heart breath	Hone your intuition, see things more clearly, honor your own insight and vision.
7th: Crown chakra	White	Heart breath	Connect with the divine, heal, cleanse, and embrace your true divine nature. Connect to other realms and energies like guides or deities.

correspondences are the same. You may also wish to pick a black stone like tourmaline or onyx for the root chakra to ground and a pink stone like rose quartz or rhodochrosite to tap into your heart and the energy of love.

Air in the tarot: the swords

There's no way around it; the energy of the swords is intense. It's sharp and piercing. Swords stab and jab and cut, and they can turn acts of precision and intention into moments of pain and wounding. Ruled by the element of air, the swords are the fiercest suit, able to both free and burden whoever is lucky enough to claim their strength. In the tarot, the swords rule your decision making, your faculty for understanding and interpreting higher knowledge, and your ability to evaluate and scrutinize information. Although the divine spark of the wands (aka the fire) may be the first step in creation, it is the sword that is the first *active* step, and it is through the sword that you start scheming and planning your vision. The sword, like air, represents your ability to hear, download, live with, and decipher information. With the swords, this can be jarring, almost biting.

The cards in this suit can feel overwhelming and even scary. But many times, the conundrums you see with these cards aren't physical but mental. It's all in your head, baby. I'm not talking unsafe physical situations, but iffy moments that you may have thought yourself into; often you aren't even actually in danger, you *think* you are. Or you're surrounding yourself with people who are telling you something that you know isn't right. There is a disconnect between what you think and what you feel. The swords can peel back the veil of security and show you where you've been lying to yourself.

There's the lesson of the sword and of the occult: your mind creates. Your body doesn't always know the difference between something that feels dangerous and something that *is* dangerous. Through this suit, you learn this discernment, the ability to understand what battles you need to pick up your sword for, and which would serve you better to walk away from. The swords demonstrate the importance of using both mind and intuition to guide you, so you don't end up in these situations at all. Through the blade, your thoughts and actions have the potential to both

penetrate and pierce the unconscious and conscious mind. The magick is in the sting.

THE ENERGY OF GROWTH AND INTELLECT: THE ACE OF SWORDS

The aces are a precious energy, the energy of something that's about to be, of a seed that's about to sprout, of an idea that is just *so close* to coming to fruition. It is through the aces that you realize your potential, and it is through the aces that you claim it. The Ace of Swords delivers a message of intention before action. This is an omen of thought, of divine intervention: an "aha" moment, if you will. The Ace of Swords is that feeling when that foolproof idea hits at the impeccable time, when the pieces come together and you realize that you know how to carry this inkling into the real world. The Swords speak more of your mental state than they do of things that are palpable, and it's in the domain of thought, of consciousness and of connection, that you can relate to the potential of this ace. This card is wisdom in its rawest form; you are being handed the sword of truth, and now you must wield it. When you are given this gift it's for a reason, and you must listen to the sword's message so you can get clear about which ideas are serving you and which aren't. Once you honor the value of your thoughts, ideas, and time, you may use this ace to help you move forward with the clarity needed to bring these ideas from the ethereal to the physical.

THE ENERGY OF FEELING VICTIMIZED AND HELPLESS: THE EIGHT OF SWORDS

Your brain is powerful, but that doesn't mean it's perfect. Your thoughts can shape the way you perceive and experience reality, and sometimes this is for the worst. In the Eight of Swords you see a woman tied up and blindfolded, surrounded by swords. She seems trapped, as if she can't make her way out of the mess, at the mercy of something or someone else. But when you know the message of the sword you're able to see another perspective, able to look beyond the danger the mind perceives. This person isn't actually stuck or in danger. The ropes are loose enough for her to move, and the swords are all pointed down into the earth. The Eight of Swords talks about feeling victimized and frozen. In a weird way, it reminds you of your own unyielding power, as if to say *You got yourself into this mess, and that means you can get yourself out of it, too.*

When this card comes up in a reading, and especially when it's pulled reversed or upside down, it's a reminder that often things are not as bad as they seem. Even though you may be bound and cornered, even though things may not be their best, there's probably another way to see things. There may be a trapdoor. This is also a reminder of how you can think yourself into a sticky situation that may not even be that big a deal. This card reminds you of sovereignty, of your ability to get out of situations where you feel depleted and taken advantage of. The Eight of Swords reminds you that you can decide to leave and then leave; you're your own captor, and it's up to you to set yourself free.

THE ENERGY OF FIERCE PRECISION AND CLARITY: THE QUEEN OF SWORDS

If she were alive, the Queen of Swords would probably be called *frigid* and *a bitch*. This is not the energy of docility, of wanting to please others, or of being submissive to the king's wishes. The Queen of Swords is an unapologetic woman who trusts in her truth and wields her sword when necessary. Led by her head, the Queen of Swords teaches you about asserting your needs and speaking up for what you believe in. She is fierce precision and clarity; she sees what needs to be done and does it. When you embody the Queen of Swords you claim your worth, imposter syndrome be damned, and trust in your skills and expertise. You become the fearless leader. At her lower vibrational form, this queen can be stubborn and unable to hold compassion for her loved ones and those she rules. Sometimes she can even be a little heartless. When you're in this space, this card can mean that you are being an icy bitch, and for once you need to step back, listen to others who have your best interest in mind, and remember that a little compassion goes a long way.

But when she's in her fullest, most high vibrational state, this queen knows what she believes in and does what's right regardless of how difficult it feels in the moment. The Queen of Swords is a reminder that your mind is the most valuable ally you have, and when you work in tandem with it, and are unashamed in claiming it, there's nothing you can't do and no one you can't lead.

In a reading this card can mean that you need to be precise with where you're getting your information and how you're sharing it. Be firm in your convictions, but as this card can also warn, don't lose your ability to feel.

A TAROT SPREAD TO HELP YOU FIND CLARITY AND TRUST

The swords are aids when you need to clear through the fog and penetrate the heart of the matter. What's *really* going on? What are you feeling? Your emotions can confuse, leaving you in a state of anxiety and fogginess. You can't actually think your way out of a situation or problem, but you can emotionally process, see the patterns you've created, and consciously learn how to not choose them in the future. Thankfully, you can use tools like your breath and the tarot in helping you to see things from a new perspective. Breathe, take time to feel in your body, shuffle your cards, ask your question, and use the following layout for extra guidance and lucidity when it comes to trusting and connecting with the sharp energy of the blade. If you have a tarot journal, you may wish to record your reading in it.

Card 1: *What am I seeing clearly?*
Card 2: *What is hidden?*
Card 3: *Where do I need to see things from a new perspective?*
Card 4: *What am I being guided to?*
Card 5: *What does the universe want me to remember?*
Card 6: *How can I connect to my higher self in times of anxiety and confusion?*
Card 7: *What's next?*

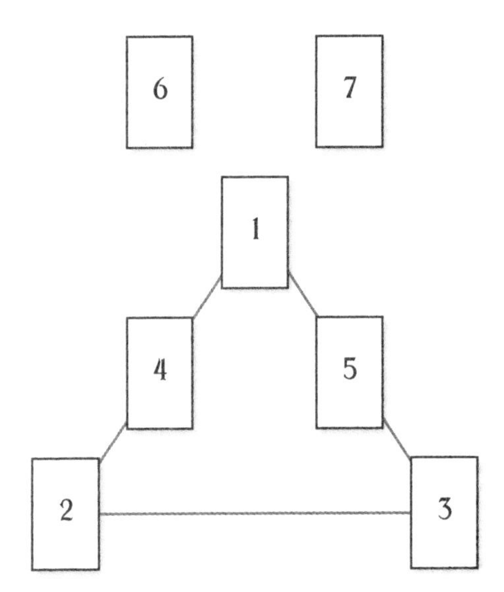

Crystals for the element of air

TO CONNECT WITH THE ELEMENT OF AIR: SELENITE

If you want to connect to the ethereal nature of air, then look no further than the heart opening and loving energy of selenite. This stone comes in a milky white color and is an incredibly high vibrational stone that can help you access your third eye and crown chakras. This stone taps into your intuitive abilities, refining your energetic body so you may hear the messages of the universe with more ease. Like air, it can help you expand and reach new limits, but it also works in this life and this body. This stone is also a stone of air because it helps you gain clarity; it opens you to intuitive messages at a soul level, giving you insight you may have missed before. Although the energy of air can feel disorienting and out of reach and not totally grounded in this reality, with selenite you can work with and embrace this without getting your head lost in the clouds. Use a selenite wand to cleanse your auric body by waving it around you as you would sacred smoke. And since this stone is self-cleansing, you can put other crystals on top of it to clear them of energy.

TO FIND GROUNDING WHEN YOU'RE TOO AIRY: BLUE LACE AGATE

If you're anything like me, you get inside your airy self too much (or just channel that energy a little too hard), so that your mind is going a million miles a minute and nothing else in your life can catch up. Yes, air in its highest form is intense presence and an element of expansion, but in its lower forms this manifests as being anywhere but here. This means fantasy, daydreaming, future tripping, thinking too hard, and not being grounded. And this is why you can work with blue lace agate to channel your vision and message with direction. Blue lace agate offers a sense of tranquility and is associated with the throat chakra. It can bring air sign energy back to earth with a sense of peace while also helping to heal the throat chakra. This crystal can reduce stress and anxiety and inspire you to speak your truth. Blue lace agate is also very therapeutic and can bring confidence and power to your story and how you channel the element of air to express yourself and your needs and desires. Work with this stone to help you release fears of asking for what you want. Meditate with it on your throat chakra while lying down to help absorb these properties.

The goddess of the sky: working with Nut

Just as Gaia is one of the primordial goddesses of the earth, so is the Egyptian goddess Nut of the sky. One of the oldest and most revered goddesses of ancient Egypt, Nut is the daughter of Tefnut (the personification of moisture) and Shu (the personification of air). Nut represents the sky in all its expansive glory, while her brother Geb represents the Earth. It was through the union of Nut and Geb that some of the most powerful Egyptian deities were born: Isis, Osiris, Set, and Nephthys, and some legends include a fifth sibling as well.

Nut is represented by a woman who stretches across the horizon and cradles the night sky, her whole body forming a bridge across the heavens. Only her fingers and toes touch the earth in each cardinal direction. The sun moves through Nut's mouth as she swallows it every night, and it exits out of her sacral chakra as she gives birth to it every morning, creating the cycles of days and nights as we know them. Through Nut we see divine order in action. Nut's sacred symbols are the cow, the sycamore tree (symbolizing protection, eternity, and divinity), the ladder (which was used by her son Osiris to enter her skies), stars, and the ankh (symbolizing eternal life), among others.

Nut is the goddess of expansion, of the cosmos, of the sky in all its grandeur. She creates a barrier between chaos and calm, acting as a shield to protect the controlled universe from that which exists outside the boundaries of her body. Nut is also a protector of the dead and a useful goddess to work with in times of grief. She can

support you in seeing transitions as a part of life, much as night and day continuously unfold and seasons transform the earth over and over again. Call on Nut for strength and protection, for she guards us against all the elements of the unknown. When your heart hurts, when someone you love has passed on, when you need a semblance of calm and peace, you may turn to Nut.

When you connect with Nut you're connecting with growth, intuition, the subtle body, and the forces inside you that are reflective of the universe at large. She can help you move beyond the energy of the here-and-now to a greater sense of freedom, as she epitomizes the ever-expanding quality of air. Like Gaia, Nut is all encompassing; she is ancient and alive in the heavens as much as she is alive in you. When you form a relationship with this goddess, you may start to see things a little differently. You walk outside and notice how clear the sky is. You feel a sense of warmth as you connect to the air and heavens. Nut is the rainbow, reaffirming that you are where you're meant to be. Nut is the clouds you watch on a beautiful day, the feeling of the wind on your cheeks as you stand under the sun. She's the energy of possibility, of growth, of stillness, of presence. Nut is the beauty of the stars in the night sky, the glowing lights that guide you, inspire you, and remind you of your inner strength. Through the immeasurable and far-reaching cosmos above us, you may better understand the message of Nut, of how she can cradle and support you whenever you need.

CREATING AN ALTAR TO NUT

As I mentioned in the previous chapter, altars can act as intergalactic gateways to a goddess. (Sign me up for whatever this ride is!) Through altars you create spaces for worship, devotion, and magick. When you're creating an altar to Nut, you're immortalizing the energy of the night sky, of the richness of air, of your ability to move and transform as the days and nights do. You may use an altar cloth that's a deep blue, silver, or gold and add candles in these shades as well as white to represent the stars in the sky. One of Nut's symbols is a small pot of water, so you may add this to her altar. Since she's associated with air, you can also have incense and herbs to burn in her honor. My suggestion for creating a relationship with a goddess is to have a ritual you can perform regularly to connect with her. Have a candle you light daily or sacred herbs you burn every day. Write her a prayer. Bring in fresh flowers, tea light candles, and statues of the goddess or of the ankh. You may wish to leave offerings like honey, wine, fresh flowers, fruit, holy water, smoke from sacred herbs, or liquor here.

Colors: The colors of the sky—deep indigo blue; rich sky blues; the white, silver, and gold of the stars. Deep, inky purple. Some Egyptians believed Nut wore a rainbow-colored robe, so images of rainbows and stars are also appropriate.

Sacred objects and correspondences: The cow, the stars, the ankh, the sycamore tree, the ladder, a water pot.

Crystals: Lapis lazuli, the deep indigo stone associated with divine knowledge and truth. Clear quartz, the master energy channel that is as clear as the air in the sky. Pyrite, the fiercely protective stone that shines like the stars.

Tarot cards: The Star. A card of destiny, of growth and vision. The Star is a part of Nut, just as she's a part of this card. You can work with this card to connect to the energy of freedom and to remember to follow your dreams. The Star reminds you that you can dissolve whatever barriers are stopping you from realizing your potential. Put this card on your altar to better recognize Nut's messages and to tap into her universal and shining wisdom.

Offerings: Honey, sweet cakes, flowers, tobacco, liquor, writing down your inspiration and sharing it with her.

A meditation to meet Nut

Before you begin this meditation, make sure your space is set. Put on some ambient music, turn off your phone, make sure pets are taken care of. Now start to think of how you can connect to Nut. Do you have some incense that makes you feel as if you were standing under a starry sky? A beautiful clear quartz that reminds you of the vastness of air? A candle dedicated to the stars and your dreams? A clear, deep breath? A view of the night sky? Do what feels right and then grab your items.

Lie down in a comfortable position, such as with your legs hip distance apart and your arms open and next to you on the floor or ground. Start to connect with your breath, sinking into the earth as you exhale, feeling the edges of your body melt. Feel your body start to soften and the boundaries between you and the world dissolve. Feel your soul and inner light expanding. Expand and expand until you're at the very edge of the sky, and you feel your body cradling the expanse of the heavens. Suddenly you notice a sun before you. It grows brighter and brighter as it moves toward you, engulfing you with its brilliance. Then you swallow the sun so it moves through your being, clearing away any worries, tension, fears, or anxieties. Continue breathing into this light, eventually imagining this sun passing through your sacral chakra, and then moving out and away from your body. You feel more luminous and effervescent than ever, and this is when you realize Nut is present. You may bask in this goddess's presence, receiving any messages, psychic visions, downloads, and feelings she wishes to share with you. You may talk to her, ask for guidance and protection, reveal that you want to know her and her wisdom. You may leave an offering, like a drop of sunshine, or a crystal, or a star. Allow yourself to feel the quality of spirit and strength of this goddess. You can repeat the solar visualization again, embodying Nut as the sun moves through your mouth and out your sacral chakra.

When you're finished with this visualization, take a few deep breaths as you feel the edges of your physical body solidifying and you return to the present. Continue to breathe as you slowly open your eyes. Record any messages, downloads, guidance, or feelings and leave an offering to Nut. So mote it be!

Etheric cording: a ritual to release and let go

Unlike the other elements, you can't see air. Air is ethereal, dancing on the line between real and imaginary, reminding you of magick, the intangible; just because you don't see something doesn't mean it doesn't exist. Air is like energy, reminding you that you perceive reality in layers; air reminds you to trust your intuition and other senses as much as your sense of sight.

Just as you breathe without having to think about it, so you create energetic connections with anyone you spend time with, without thinking twice. Even though these connections aren't visual or tactile, you still feel them. But you're human, which means that sometimes these connections you create with others aren't truly benefiting you. And that's why you perform the ritual of etheric cording.

When you interact with someone, you're seeing them in a certain light. You project an image and a vision that doesn't necessarily reflect who this person is, but who you think they are. This perceived relationship creates an energetic cord between you and them. They do the same thing for you, holding an image of who they think you are, putting more energy into this cord. Then you think about how they think of you, and of how they think of you thinking about them, which keeps energizing this cord and making it stronger. These cords, which you can imagine as thin gold ropes connecting you and someone else, get stronger and stronger the more you interact with, think of, or judge someone; this feeds energy between two people. Although they can be a source of strength and connection, let's say between you and your best friend, there are plenty of these cords that you no longer need: from ex-friends, ex-lovers, that random hater on the Internet. Many attachments serve you and can enhance your sense of well-being. But in the age of the Internet, of hyperpresence and of casual online dating, many of these energetic connections use up your energy by keeping you bonded to someone who you may no longer need in your life.

This ritual is done in meditation, so make sure you can find a quiet space where you won't be disturbed, following instructions on page 15 to set up your space. You can record yourself saying the incantation and play it to yourself as you meditate, repeating it mentally or out loud. Or feel free to adapt the following, writing something that speaks to you. Read it over before you begin to make sure you're familiar with it and then tweak it as necessary.

Lie on the floor with your legs hip distance apart and your palms face up next to you like in corpse pose. Connect with the earth beneath you as you breathe and come back to your body. Once you feel grounded and relaxed, invite any spirit guides, deities, angels, or beings that you work with for their compassion and help with this ritual. You may also wish to call on Michael, archangel of the South, who wields a fiery sword that can help cut away whatever cords aren't serving you. Take your time connecting with these guides.

Then visualize yourself surrounded by a cool, purple flame that helps remove any connections you don't need. Any etheric cords you no longer need will dissolve effortlessly in these flames. When you're ready, think or repeat the following.

Dear guides, angels, gods, goddesses, and benevolent beings, I call upon you to help remove the etheric cords that are no longer serving me. I ask you to sever these cords with healing and compassion, to remove any ties that are not in alignment with my highest good at this time. May the flaming blade of Archangel Michael help me clear out the etheric cords that aren't working for my highest evolution. May I release these ties as I'm surrounded by love and healing. And so it is.

Once you're finished, you may journal or record anything that comes up. Drink a lot of water, and remember that saying no and working with healthy boundaries is also part of this work! When you perform a ritual, you're inviting the universe to match your energy, to broaden your intention to what will serve you best. But that doesn't mean you aren't responsible for your own life or that the universe will do all the work. Cutting out toxic people, saying no to what doesn't feel right, and honoring your own needs are all ways you can match the energy of this etheric cording ritual in real life.

A smoke cleansing ritual to clear and cleanse your space

Air penetrates everything you do; it's your laugh, your scream, your breath. It's the exhale of the trees, and the oxygen they bring.

It's your ability to regenerate, refuel, and rejuvenate. Through the smoke of sacred herbs, you can release, realign, and heal your subtle body as well as your spirit. This smoke cleansing ritual can be used whenever you want to connect with the element of air in a tangible way.

This ritual will help cleanse you and your space of anything that's not in alignment with your highest good.

What you need: Herbs like yerba santa, juniper, mugwort, cedar, lavender, sweetgrass, frankincense, or copal. Something to burn them in, like a fire-safe bowl or an abalone shell. A lighter.

A note on white sage and palo santo: White sage is a plant

sacred to various indigenous peoples. Because of the mainstream use of this herb to cleanse energetically, sage has been overharvested, making it inaccessible for many indigenous people. I don't condone buying this herb or palo santo. Instead, buy another herb like sweetgrass, cedar, lavender, juniper, yerba santa, or resins like dragonsblood and frankincense. You can also grow a variety of sage that's native to your area and use that instead. The same sacredness is true of palo santo wood, which comes from the palo santo tree. Palo santo is supposed to be harvested once the tree naturally dies, after the wood has been left on the ground for five years, but because of the popularization of this herb, it's now endangered from being overharvested, and harvested incorrectly. Although it's not extinct, I don't suggest buying this wood, but rather using alternative herbs for cleansing and clearing a space.

STEP 1: SET THE SPACE AND GROUND

As in any other ritual, you're going to want to set the space, following instructions on page 15 to help. You may wish to open some windows while doing this ritual to further cleanse the space.

Before you begin, take a second to drop into your body. Close your eyes and feel the way your feet connect with the earth. Breathe and feel into your sacral chakra, the energy center at your pelvis, feeling rooted in yourself. Continue to breathe, exhaling any worries, tension, and anxieties and inhaling a clean white light. Stay here as long as you need.

STEP 2: CLEANSE THE SPACE

Once you feel deliciously present in your body, light your herbs so they're flaming, and then blow them out so they're smoking. Start at the middle of the space. Continue to breathe awhile; with your herbs, draw the symbol for air, a triangle with a line through the top. Notice the smoke and how it expands and moves; notice how this makes you feel. Once you've traced the symbol, step into it and say something like the following (which you may adapt/rewrite as you wish):

> *Element of air, I call upon you now to cleanse and consecrate myself and this space. May this sacred smoke help clear away that which does not serve me.*

Use the smoke to cleanse your body, starting at the crown of your head, moving down your torso, over and under your arms and your palms, between your legs, down your legs, and across the bottoms of your feet.

Move toward your front door, fanning the smoke as you do so and envisioning a white light emanating from it, clearing away dense and unneeded energy. At the front door, make the sign of the banishing pentagram, starting at the bottom left corner, moving up to the middle, down to the right corner, halfway up to the left, straight across to the right, and back down to the left. This acts as an energetic shield, kicking to the curb that which doesn't align with your intention. You may wish to say the following:

> *I banish, I banish, I banish thee—any energy that does not serve me.*

Then move around your space, fanning the smoke while envisioning the white light clearing away anything you don't need. Repeat the banishing pentagram and incantation at any back doors, at the entrance of your room, and anywhere else you need energetic protection.

STEP 3: CLOSE THE RITUAL

Once you feel like you've finished this ritual, put down your supplies and close your eyes. Take a second to connect again with the air. Feel the space you've created, the positive energy you've expanded to encompass both you and where you've cleansed. What does this feel like? Do you feel warm? Safe? Lighter? Take note of this! Thank the air for its support and help, finding gratitude for this ritual. Then take a few deep breaths, doing whatever else you need to finish this ritual, like pressing your forehead into the earth in child's pose and sending any energy back into the earth, where it can be transmuted into light. When you're ready, open your eyes, clap (to get you back into the here and now), go drink some water, and enjoy your newly cleansed space.

Embodying air: the glamour of self-expression

Witnessing the free-love, sprawling, larger-than-life, innovative, and present quality of air can help you think of how to start embodying these qualities in your own wardrobe. You can't experience air visually, but you can feel it viscerally and see its effects, like how the wind kisses satins and silks into floating tendrils that hum of summer days. You are already air embodied because you breathe all the time, but you can take this connection into embodied presence through glamour.

In its purest state, air allows you to embrace your fullest expression and your most creative, weird, "out there" ideas by transmuting them through clothes. Air signs are the eccentrics, the weirdos,

the trailblazers who are inventing the latest trend because they're so plugged in and invested in expressing who they are.

Air sign energy can manifest in two ways, but both hold the same doctrine: *know thyself*. On one hand, you can see air sign energy as efficient, effective, and clear in knowing what does and doesn't work for them. In glamour, this can manifest as a uniform (which can also manifest with earth energy). Why shouldn't you wear what you like if you know it works? The sharp and clean black-on-black of the writer or director or artist comes to mind as very air sign mentality. But anything that you deem "uniform worthy" can become your own signature look. In this way, knowing yourself comes from what you feel confident and powerful in. While for earth energy this may feel more like a comfort blanket, something to bring reassurance and clarity, for air energy it's all about channeled and creatively expressed energy. It's the earth sign uniform plus some DIY personalization. The black-on-black look may come with a pair of black angular glasses, or a red lip. The jeans may be the same every day, but the shoes may be couture creations every time. With air sign energy, there's always a signature or a twist, something to make the uniform *your* uniform. Personally, my Aquarius signature is my half-shaved head, which I've had since 2011. Paired with my red or orange lipstick, this is a glamour that has given back to me threefold and beyond. Having my own look, complete with gold nose and cartilage piercings, gives me an aura of confidence that has changed my life for the better. I feel like a work of art, and having the space and ability to create beauty for myself has been magick in its own right.

The other side of this *know thyself* energy is that of originality. Innovation. Inspiration and otherworldly manifestation. Air sign energy knows no bounds, and their brain (which is always on) is their best asset in creating mind-blowing looks that inspire you to see your closet in a new way. The colors of air are holographic, silver, white, clear, vinyl, metallic, anything that has you thinking, guessing, analyzing, trying to figure it out. In this same vein, since air signs themselves are so expressive and unique, bright colors, psychedelic patterns, bold patterns, animal prints, and other eye-catching colors are of this element, too.

In this form, air sign energy manifests as bold and purposeful statement looks, outfits that seem like they belong on another planet, or an ensemble so well curated, so personalized, so perfect, it has you praying to the goddess of glamour, Venus herself. The insightful and tuned-in energy of air invites you to the realm of intentional personal style that's inspired by your passions, your scholarly pursuits, and what leaves you feeling excited by life.

You can tap into air sign through glamour that is light and airy, like silks and satins and linens and cottons that feel delicious against flesh. Pieces with ruffles and layers that float and dance as you move and walk would be of this element as well. Shiny, translucent fabrics like plastic and PVC, latex, sheer laces, and anything subversive is also the realm of the sword.

You can tap into this energy by wearing things that require you to think, to solve an equation, to get imaginative with the way you dress. You can start with a bag, or shoes, or a specific piece and then work strategically around that until you have an entire look. And since swords also speak of precision and power, you can also channel this energy by wearing whatever makes you feel confident in your voice and purpose. What makes you feel like you could slay your enemies with a look that is as sharp as daggers, and an outfit to match? That is the energy of the Queen of Swords in action, and the swords in the tarot can be your guide to further embracing the power of this suit in real life.

If you want to wear talismans and crystals to connect to air, you may wish to wear pieces with selenite or other clear crystals like clear quartz. Layer with plenty of your favorite talismans, some silver eyeshadow, lots of highlighter, and a DGAF attitude, and voilà, you're one airy babe! Glitter, highlighter, lipstick, blush, jewelry, hair dye, piercings—anything that is going to help you capture *your* unique essence is of air. So go forth, let your heart and mind guide you. Indulge in what inspires you, what gets you thinking, what urges you to create and express and manifest. Allow that to guide you in what you wear; life's too exciting to wear boring outfits.

Journal questions to connect with air

More than any other element, air feels the most at home with the written word. Intellect and knowledge are the domain of this element, after all. So as with the journaling for earth, you may wish to approach these questions as their own ritual. Make yourself some tea, turn off your phone, set the space with beautiful lights and sounds and smells. Get cozy with your favorite pen and journal and dive in. Allow these questions to be a starting point, inviting you to jump into the storm of your mind, of your desires, of your unconscious. You may even pull a tarot card for each journal question if you need some extra clarity and guidance.

» What does it mean for me to be present in this moment? How does this feel in my body?

» How does it feel when I work with my breath in times of stress?

» What am I learning about right now that I'm loving?

» What's inspiring me? What are my muses?

» What does it sound like in my mind when I'm connected to my intuition?

» What are the areas of my life that could use some cleansing and clarity?

» Where can I bring some "new" into my life?

Air in astrology: Aquarius, Gemini, and Libra

As in tarot, you have each element represented in the zodiac wheel. Of course this includes our expansive and freedom-loving air signs of Aquarius (the water bearer), Gemini (the twins), and Libra (the scale). Thinking of what you've already learned about air, you can start to understand the tenacious and intense energy of this sign. Although air can be piercing in the way you think, communicate, and create in the mental realms, it also craves freedom, harmony, and growth. Air signs are the social butterflies; they're the ones who are observing as well as asking a million questions. They're quietly leading the revolution, asking you to see things from a different perspective, marching to the beat of their own drum.

So what can you learn from air signs?

AQUARIUS—THE WATER BEARER

Okay, I'm going to have to be honest. I'm biased here because I'm a triple Aquarius—Aquarius sun, Venus, and Mars—and I truly feel like an Aquarius babe. Aquarian energy is that of the collective, of turning your personal gifts into a way to be of service to the whole. Aquarius are time-traveling aliens, trendsetters and scientists that move toward new paradigms. Aquarius are intellectuals, and although they may come off as distant and unattached, it's really because they need space and freedom to flourish, and they need this on their own terms. This is a sign of communal love, unconditional love, and innovation. The water bearer teaches us how to honor and hold space for our emotions without getting lost in them. Aquarius is the container for the healing of the whole, and they can help us create a new era of love and consciousness. At the lower end of this sign's evolution they may seem aloof and distant, but once this sign learns emotional intelligence, or eventually just gets it, then they have empathy that extends to the whole of humanity.

GEMINI—THE TWINS

The only sign to have two beings as its glyph, Gemini is the twins and an air sign of depth, creativity, and collaboration. Although some are quick to judge the twins as being two-faced, in reality this just means that not only do Geminis have the ability to adapt to whatever situation they're in, their lessons also involve collaborative efforts and working with others, whether romantically, platonically, professionally, magickally, or creatively. Geminis are the mouthpiece of the zodiac, manifesting and creating ideas seemingly out of thin air, leaving us all behind as they transmute their desires to reality. Although some may see Gemini's flexible nature as a negative, calling them two-faced, in truth it means they know how to honor their own boundaries. This sign helps you think in new ways, honing your creativity in a way that feels like a message from the divine.

LIBRA—THE SCALES

One of the two Venus-ruled planets (alongside Taurus), the sign of the scales is one of justice and social sensibilities. A lover of pleasure and a sign that's deeply invested in making sure things are fair, Libra weighs things out and reminds us of the idea of peace. Deeply social and a lover of love, Libra is interested in enlightenment, in connecting to the heart of it all, of making sure that equality and equity are paired with plenty of space to shift and evolve. This compassionate sign wants us to all just get along, and it uses the powers of creation to do just that. This energy is rooted in a deep belief in the value of the individual and the individual's voice, once again reminding us that air signs aim to find the balance between the self and the collective. Although Libras can be flighty, with decisions and lovers alike, once they evolve past this, Libra brings a restoration of aesthetic and energetic harmony with them wherever they go.

IN THEIR LEAST EVOLVED STATE

In their least evolved state, air signs can become overly intellectual, creating boundaries and putting up walls with their analytical minds to create separation from their emotions. These signs like to intellectualize their feelings and experiences instead of honoring and processing them. They also tend to get lost in thought, venturing to other dimensions instead of being in the present. Air signs are sometimes off in their own world while their bodies remain here, causing them to feel distracted, disconnected, or disengaged. This can feel sharp and unnerving, their words poking and prodding and causing discomfort because of their own deep-rooted insecurities. Air sign energy in its encumbered state can also manifest as being hyperactive or scatterbrained. Thankfully, working with the other elements can balance this energy out.

IN THEIR MOST EVOLVED STATE

In their most evolved state, air signs can help you reach your potential. Like the sky, they are limitless. Like birds, they are freedom personified. They lead you to envision a future where love is the answer and expansiveness is a necessity. They're the "if you can dream it, you can be it" of the zodiac. Air signs remind you of the importance of intellectual connections, reminding you that evolution and adapting to the future and changes in technology is part of this. Air signs inspire the feeling of total vulnerability, of space, of honoring your own evolution. Through air you can hone in on your truth and use it to pierce everything around you. In short, air signs don't fuck around. They don't allow you to dwell in illusion. Through this sign's commitment to seeing through the veil, you can perceive the divine wisdom in everything. Air signs show your boundaries and then tell you to adapt around it. Your mind is the limit; since your mind creates your reality, that means you're limitless, too.

CHAPTER 3

Fire: Burn It

Warm, vibrant, cinnamon red, and hot, fire calls you to attention with its intensity and fervor. Through fire you are called back into your power, into your wild nature, into your carnal self. This is the magick of fire. This is the realm of the sensual, of spirit. Each element has its own signature. Through earth you find stillness and roots. Through air you find expansion and freedom. Through water you connect to your heart and emotional center. And through fire you can find your fullest expression of self. Out of all the elements, fire is the most dangerous, the hardest to control, the most volatile. And with it comes transformation unlike anything else.

As I work on this chapter, we're in the middle of Aries season. This is the first zodiac sign of the twelve, and we enter this season near the spring equinox, which also marks the astrological new year. This is the energy of the Ace of Wands, the spark of creation, and Aries is the fire that ignites it all. Aries is the visionary and the leader, a call for revolution, a new paradigm. You can use Aries and fellow fire signs to understand what it means for this element to be directed and harnessed with integrity. Fire has the ability to hurt—but it doesn't have to. Fire teaches us discernment: what is meant to burn and what is meant to grow.

Fire as our desires

At its most evolved state, the energy of fire is deeply alchemical; it has the opportunity to show us new ways of being, feeling, and doing. When you tap into this you see the world differently; things are aligned, like the world itself is your lover. It's not just someone that turns you on, but life itself. I like to think of fire as life force energy, known as *prana* in Hindu philosophy. This is the energy of recharging under the sun on a warm, beautiful spring day. It's illuminating, it's vibrant, it allows you to tap into a sense of peace and radiance that can become otherwise clouded. The energy of fire is forceful, since fire is action, but it is also deeply erotic, sensual, sexual, and charged. This is the energy of creation, that same prana. We live in a sex-negative and whorephobic society, where we are not taught to embrace pleasure and embody our sexual essence. Those who do embrace this, or, goddess forbid, capitalize on it, are stigmatized and shamed. This is especially true for womxn. We all have an inner fire, an inner flame that is stoked by our desires, and when we claim it and honor it in this society that wants us so badly to do the opposite, things change. Things that aren't in alignment clear away and you are led back into your rooted, sexual life force. In Kundalini yoga, this is known as Kundalini energy, which lies dormant at the base of the spine like a coiled snake. The goal is to stimulate this energy so it moves up the spine to the crown of the head, resulting in an awakening or enlightenment. You can work with your own fiery energy as a way to evolve, shed karmic baggage, and fall in love with the world around you. Even if you're asexual, you can still engage with fire in a nonsexual way.

What makes you feel charged, erotic, powerful, and transformative may be something that's not sexual at all—that's okay! Allow your intuition, and your body, to lead you. This is more about the feeling and the experience than a specific act.

Take a second to meditate on the word *desire*. What does it strike up in your body? Maybe something feels kind of warm, or electric, or maybe you're indifferent. Think about what this word means to you. How do you relate to it? And then think about what your own desires are. This is the container for the fire energy in your life; just as water needs something to hold it, fire needs something to burn through. This fuel is your desires. Whether it's for something in your

own life, or in the world at large, you can use your desires to help you create the most fulfilling life possible. Fire craves change, something to transform; when you live in this place you are charged by your inner fantasies and not burned out or harmed by them. Your desires are sacred. So are your passions. So is your inner flame.

Fire as alchemy, as transmutation

Fire is dangerous; it will burn you, and that bitch won't even care. But fire isn't worried about that; it knows that it will clear away anything unnecessary and fortify and strengthen whatever will make you stronger. This is the gift of fire. This is the gift of metamorphosis. When you work with this element with intention, reverence, and presence (when you know you may get burned, but you're willing to approach the edge with caution anyway) then you are led through some transformational experiences, coming out the other side unrecognizable even to yourself. Sometimes this is by choice; sometimes it's not. Sometimes fire is a tragedy or trauma or loss; you are forced to move through it, and you become stronger because of it. No matter how or why you approach this sacred flame, it is always an initiation. There is always the promise of something on the other side if you just keep going.

Think of a time in your own life when you went through something difficult. Often you don't believe you can survive something so intense and so painful until you have no choice. We often don't give ourselves enough credit for our resilience, for our courage, for our inner tenacity. But you are all these things, and when you choose to recognize this, you can become the most evolved version of yourself possible.

I live in Los Angeles, where there's a high chance of forest fires whenever summer hits. The summer of 2018 was the deadliest and most destructive season of wildfires in California's history, with more than a million acres on fire. Fire cleared the land and homes were lost. And yet a year later, after an intense winter and two-plus months of rain, there is more green than ever. We're out of a drought and it's been the most beautiful spring I've ever seen. After completely leveling the land, the fire made space for the soil to be fertilized. For new life to grow. For something to rise from the ashes. After the rain, everything blossomed into shades of green. There was a superbloom of poppy flowers, and with it came the biggest migration of Painted Lady butterflies since 2005. This new life is more vibrant than ever. The phoenix has to burn to rise from the ashes. There must be clearing before a new foundation is created.

Fire as the wild

Fire is the feral, untamed wildness that's rooted in the ancient aspects of your most primal self. This is lust, anger, rage, passion, strength, shadow, the undomesticated part of you. This is especially seen in womxn, those of us who bleed, those of us who know how to listen to the subtle. Fire reminds us so badly of what the patriarchy wants us to forget; the only rules that matter are your own. Nothing is worth more than your intuition, the feelings that live in your body, your ability to destroy and create and love all at once. Fire doesn't apologize for the pain it may cause. It only shrinks when it's not being fed, when it doesn't get what it needs. But give it oxygen and fire can spread with ease, causing you to leave your home and your way of life because of its uninvited invasion. When you separate yourself from the part that craves something unconventional or subversive, you're dismembering yourself. You're cutting yourself into fragments. Fire wants you to scream and growl and hiss and cry. Fire wants you to take all the pieces you've cut off and offer them to the flames. Fire wants you to burn through all the fear and old narratives that have kept you playing small. Fire wants to turn these old parts of you to ash and reinforce all the parts of yourself that are strong, divine, grounded, and ready to claim your fullest power.

EXERCISE: TAPPING INTO YOUR WILDNESS

Before you begin this exercise, take some time to journal about what the wild and feral feminine means to you. What are the subconscious messages that you've picked up from society that tell you how to act? What are the boxes you've put yourself in because it's how you were expected to act? So many of us grow up being told we are too much, too loud, too sexual, too this or that. And because of survival or pain or trauma or whatever else, many of us decided these other people were right, and because of this we shrank. Take the time to think of the ways in which you've let yourself become tamed and palpable. What does it mean to you to be unhinged, unleashed, fully free? Angry? Enraged? Are you scared of this? Do you even know what this feels like? Journal about this, using the words *desire* and *taboo* to further inspire this introspection.

Then to do this exercise, find a comfortable seat for meditation. You may wish to lie on your back or sit up; do whatever feels better for you, keeping in mind you will be moving your body and making sound. Close your eyes and ground, feeling yourself return to your body. Breathe as you start to focus your inner awareness on your wildness. You're going to be calling on your inner feral feminine and giving her a form. Maybe you see yourself, or you see an animal. I have recently connected to a black jaguar in meditation, whom I recognize as my shadow or savage self, this same untamed archetype. Find yourself in a natural setting and then call upon this inner aspect, reassuring the feral and free side of you as it comes out to mingle and flirt. You may practice breath work, chanting, mantras, or even dancing and drumming at this point, or you may also just remain in a still meditative posture.

When you're ready, start taking deep inhales through your nose, filling your belly with air. As you exhale through your mouth, make noises like growls or moans or hisses. Continue doing this, swiveling and shaking your hips and lower body as you move that energy through your body with your breath. You can inhale those pieces of your wildness that you want to cultivate more of, and as you exhale, purr and growl, releasing any tension or worries. Continue with this breathing for as long as you need, or until you feel this visualization being integrated and cleared, and a sense of peace. Thank all parts of yourself, including whatever piece of yourself you saw, including any animals, sensations, or downloads you received. Close with some grounding breaths and some gratitude and thank your inner divine feminine fire before continuing on with your day. You can continue cultivating this side of you by creating an altar, practicing meditation or visualization, trance work, dance, art, and journaling.

Ways to connect to the element of fire

Although you can connect directly with the earth, immerse yourself in water, and surround yourself with air, you cannot come directly into contact with fire. Fire requires safety; it requires distance. You must watch fire with reverence and respect or it can be damaging. Fire asks you to be present and face what you're feeling head-on; there's no shortcut for getting comfortable with this

intensity, but baby steps help. Here are a few ways you can safely connect with the element of fire.

» Light candles! It's easy to do and the ultimate vibe; work with candles to connect to fire by surrounding yourself and your space with them or by gazing at their flame and scrying (see page 244). Remember never to blow out any candles in spells or rituals (as this is said to "put out" the spell) but to fan or snuff them out. And don't leave lit candles unattended!

- Spend time under the sun, especially around high noon, when it is at peak power. If you can spend at least fifteen minutes under the sun, that will recharge and replenish you (apply sunscreen beforehand and don't spend too much time baking under the sun's supercharged rays!).

- Work with red and orange crystals like carnelian, citrine, garnet, and orange calcite to connect to your own power and a sense of passion and purpose. These crystals help balance and fortify the lower chakras, which are associated with sex, confidence, harmony, vivaciousness, and power.

- Work with warming spices like cinnamon and eat spicy foods to find heat from the inside out. This is another way in which you can embody fire without the fear of actually burning yourself.

- Write down what you want to let go of, what you're angry about, and want to transmute or release, then rip it up and set it aflame, burning it up over a pot of water.

- Work with your orgasms and sex magick as a way to direct and channel sexual energy.

- Transmute your anger through working out, creating art, singing, dancing, or something else active or creative.

- Make time to move and breathe and jump up and down as you shake and growl and hiss and scream and laugh and cry. Allow these dynamic feelings to come to the surface as you alchemize them through sound and movement.

» Work with candle magick. Carve an intention, or your name and zodiac sign, into a candle. Then dress it with herbs and oil (you can use Appendix 2 to help) to help empower it. If you're attracting or manifesting, rub the oil from each end to the middle. If you're banishing, rub the oil from the middle out to each end. Then sprinkle the herbs the same way. You can do this in ritual, in a circle, with the elements present. Light the candle and visualize your desired outcome as you raise energy through masturbation, chanting, dancing, jumping, spinning, or however else you want, sending the energy to the candle at the climax of the ritual. Let the candle burn all the way out—never blow a candle out. Use a snuffer, fan, or cup to put out the candle. If you relight it, practice the visualizing and raise energy again if you want. Once the candle is finished and the ritual is complete, you can throw out any excess wax or glass container at a garbage can at an intersection—the modern witch's crossroad. I go more in detail on how to practice candle magick in my first book, *Inner Witch*.

Ritual practice: creating mantras and affirmations for new patterns, power, and purpose

Your thoughts are the sword, but your words are the magick wand. You speak things into creation, declaring the reality around you.

Occultists and witches know the power of incantations, spells that you weave with words. This is why my morning practice includes meditation, breath work, journaling *and also* affirmations, and mantras. These are positive and empowering sayings that I write for myself, usually on the new moon or at the beginning of the week, to inspire my subconscious mind and remind myself of my intentions. I'll be sharing some of my favorite mantras in a little bit, but I also want to encourage you to create your own to serve your particular needs.

I've found that taking time in a ritual setting to focus on what I'm feeling emotionally or spiritually, especially around a new moon or full moon, is helpful for figuring out what sort of mantras I need for the coming cycle. Since I journal and meditate every day, I tend to have a good idea of what patterns I'm working through, and I can go back and see where I was last month or at the last moon cycle to help. But if you don't have this consistency, doing this in a ritual setting where you feel safe and able to melt deeply into the moment is just as powerful.

I create mantras and affirmations based on reminders I want to tell myself and things I want to happen. I create affirmations that *affirm* both my esteem and my purpose. If the swords are the words and the letters that you're vibrating aloud, then the wands and the element of fire inspire you to take these desires seriously, to believe in them, trust them, and know their truth as you repeat them. The swords are the oxygen, and with fire you are able to strike the match and bring the flame into this realm.

I really love affirmations because they can help you create new patterns and ways of relating to things, people, and situations. They can help you see your relationships in new ways, or embrace change, or find healing. They can be whatever you need them to be.

HOW AND WHEN TO SAY YOUR AFFIRMATIONS

Okay, good news: affirmations can be practiced anytime and anywhere. Whisper them to yourself on the subway, assert them to yourself when you're stuck in traffic, repeat them while gazing in the mirror after meditation. The bad news is you don't have an excuse to *not* start working with them. Aim to say your mantras at least once a day; two to three times a day is optimal, but really say them whenever you need. I recommend repeating each three times, but do what feels right.

I say my affirmations to myself, either with my eyes closed and feeling the weight of the words throughout my body, or with my eyes open and gazing at my altar. Or I practice these affirmations in the mirror as I gaze in my left (nondominant) eye (my preferred method!). Experiment with what works for you. Then think of how visceral and bright and demanding the energy of fire is. You know its presence because you feel it. This is the same for your affirmations; do what lights you up on the inside. Practice them in a way that inspires you to believe them, that makes you believe them. You have to fake it till you make it sometimes, but it does work. And following what feels right in your body and soul is always the key to doing this in the most empowered and embodied way possible.

Before you begin, think of how you want to see yourself! Claim this as if it's true. "I am, I embody, I claim." Don't affirm anything you don't want to be true; don't say "I am not this" or "I am not that"; instead say what you *are*. Embrace what you want to manifest. Ask yourself what you need and go from there.

AFFIRMATIONS AND MANTRAS TO WORK WITH

Here are some mantras I work with. Again, feel free to adapt, to create your own, and to do what inspires you. Allow fire to be your guide.

FOR POWER AND SELF-CONFIDENCE

» I am rooted in my strength and grounded in my power.

» I shine as my fullest self and nourish my inner light.

» I am radiant, confident, and empowered by my ambition and desires.

FOR GROWTH AND EVOLUTION

» I grow, bloom, and evolve with ease.

» If it doesn't serve me, I let it go.

» I surrender to the universe and trust in my evolution.

» I integrate the lessons of my evolution at the perfect time.

» I breathe into the discomfort of growth and trust it's in my highest favor.

FOR PROSPERITY AND ABUNDANCE

» I am abundance and prosperity and wealth are my birthright.

» I live in alignment and receive blessings and abundance with ease.

» I live in a state of awe and gratitude and I experience miracles every day.

» I am powerful as hell and money comes to me easily.

» I am a rich witch and I bask in my bounty, and share it with joy.

FOR HEALING

» I trust the universe and honor my healing even through the pain.

» I tend to the garden of my heart with care and compassion.

» My shadows are worthy of love and acceptance.

» I ask for help when I need it and allow myself to feel whatever it is I'm feeling.

» My healing journey does not have to be linear to be valid.

FOR PROTECTION

» I am safe, supported, protected, and aligned with the highest vibration possible.

» I listen to my intuition and trust that I am divinely guided and protected.

» I am surrounded by white light and trust in the blessing of the universe.

» I am safe, I am seen, I am held, I am protected.

FOR LOVE AND PLEASURE

» I open my heart to all possibilities of love and pleasure.

» I honor my sensuality and surrender to the erotic.

» I am surrounded by love and I follow the path of pleasure and passion.

» I follow what feels the most delicious for my heart and soul.

» I am divine love.

FOR CONNECTING WITH THE DIVINE

» I return to what feeds my purpose.

» I am of the divine; ever changing, ever growing, ever flowing.

» I surrender to the universe and know it's working in my highest favor.

» I am a conduit and reflection of the divine, and channel my higher self whenever I need to.

FOR TAPPING INTO THE ELEMENT OF FIRE

» I follow my passions and desires and allow them to feed my soul.

» My passions, purpose, and power fuel me.

» I embody the element of fire. I *am* fire.

» I embody my fullest, most radical, and authentic self.

» I'm a sex god/dess and receive love and pleasure with ease.

A lava meditation to flow with the fire

If you haven't caught on by now, meditation is essential. Not only for understanding each of the elements and their unique gifts and messages, but also in understanding yourself. Meditation doesn't just look like one thing either; although it can be done in stillness, it can also be done in motion, with breath, with dance, with song. *There is no one way to meditate.* And that's especially true when it comes to embodying the elements. The closest you can come to being immersed in flames is by spending time under the sun, but when you meditate, you embody this energy in another way, using your third eye and energetic body.

This particular elemental meditation has a prerequisite, and that's that you spend time looking at videos (and photos) of lava flowing. It's incredible and inspiring and something you should absolutely watch and enjoy. This will help you understand the energy of fire in a new way: lava is dense but can also be fast; it's ethereal and otherworldly.

Before you begin this meditation, set up the space. I like ambient music and incense burning, but do what feels right. When you're ready, find a comfortable space where you can lie down. If you can, lie on your back so your arms are at least a palm's width from your body and your legs are hip distance apart. Breathe into your body, feeling how it feels on the floor, relaxing into this support. Take deep breaths until you feel fully relaxed. Now, visualize lava moving slowly into the crown of your head. As you inhale, draw this lava in and as you exhale move it through your body, through your third eye and arms, through your torso and hips, through the tips of your fingers and down your legs. Feel this lava moving through you with a slow, intense warmth. Allow yourself to make sound and move your body if you need to. Let the lava feel however it feels; let its colors and unhurried movements talk to you. Once you feel every inch of your body consumed by this warmth, visualize yourself at the top of a volcano. Look into the crater filled with lava, and then notice the volcano itself, the mountain you're standing on. You see lava in front of you and suddenly you melt into it, becoming one with this molten version of fire. You move down the volcano, floating and reabsorbing into the lava that is holding you. Let yourself be carried, and as you breathe, feel the lava consuming anything that you don't need. If you want to moan and make sounds and move your hips, do. You may also start breathing out of your mouth as the heat of the lava intensifies. Exhale anything you want to release, anything you want to let go of. And allow the lava to transform you, to embrace you, and to hold you. Continue to breathe and move and moan as long as you need. When you're done, take a few breaths, thank the lava and volcano, wiggle your fingers and toes, and open your eyes.

Fire in the tarot: the wands

In the tarot, the wicked, wild, and impassioned element of fire is represented by the wands, or rods. This is the energy of creation. The wands are the cosmic orgasm of the universe, the climax of the four suites, and the energy of the Big Bang in an elemental symbol. In the Rider-Waite deck, the wand is phallic, which could be seen as heteronormative but can also just be taken as how interconnected fire and wands are with human sexuality and your own relationship to that as a concept—with how you're seen, how you feel, and how you choose to engage (or not) with this energy.

The wands take you on a journey through your own yearnings and longings. They ask you what you want to channel and create with this bright and expansive gift of an idea, relationship, or way of being. What are you called to manifest? What do you wish to celebrate? What do you *desire*? More than anything, this suit tells you of the actions you can take to alchemize this, bringing it to the

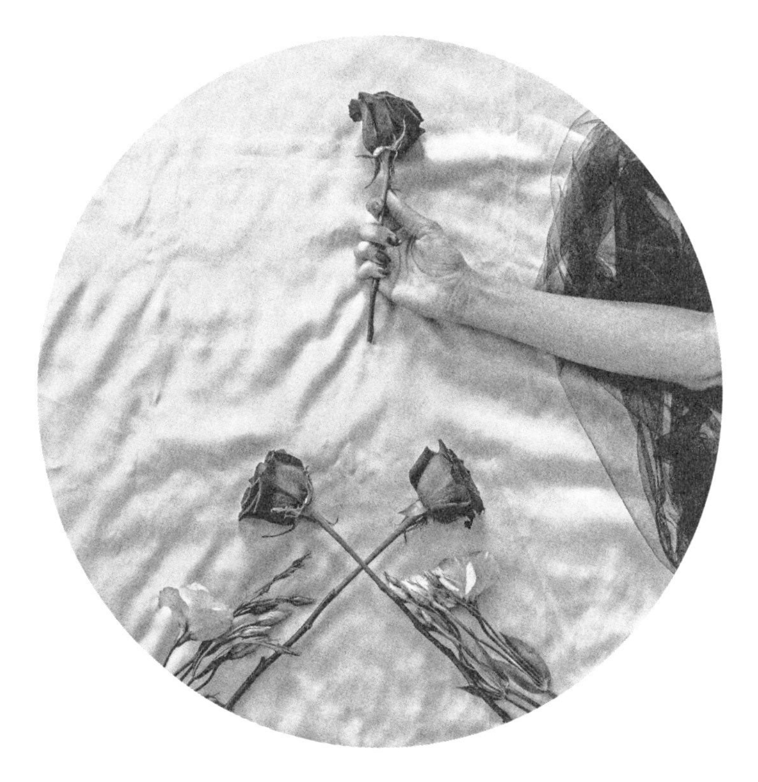

physical. The wands speak of what inspires us to create, what feeds our soul and purpose. They can speak of karma, of where we're giving up our voice and our truth to be more acceptable or respectable. The wands speak of what keep us turned on and excited. The wands also show you where you're being led deeper into the spiral path of your spirituality. They light the path of the Initiate, of the Shaman, of the Wild Woman; the wands are the catalyst for our inner revolution. This is not a path of the subtle. This is a path of intensity. This is a path of ferocity. This is the path of the fierce, of the undefinable. It's one you walk, whether you choose to or not, at various points in your life. But this is a path that can taste the most delicious.

THE ENERGY OF NEW DESIRES: THE ACE OF WANDS

The Ace of Wands is "having a new crush or lover" energy. Everything feels sticky, sweet, slow, like molasses or honey. Senses are on high. Chemicals like norepinephrine and dopamine are flooding the brain, making you feel happy and giddy, even aroused. Your palms sweat and your heart races. You're so excited about this person you can't stop thinking about them. There's something waiting just under the surface to sprout, and you're channeling your positive attention to it because you can't stop even if you wanted to.

This "crush" could be anything: a new venture or hobby, a friendship, a work project, or of course a romantic interest. That energy is about to burst forth, like it's fueled by an orgasm. There's a sense of appetite and aspiration that's deeply rooted in this card. Own it. Work with it. If it feels overwhelming, try transmuting it. Wield Kundalini, or sexual energy, into your desire, into what you will. I write about sex magick later in this chapter, and I'll talk more about harnessing those orgasms and orgasmic feelings to manifest and create. The wands represent initiation, an act that transforms. When you see the Ace of Wands, it's an omen that something big is waiting for you, something charged and transformational.

The Ace of Wands asks you to face your fears when it comes to embracing what you want. When you enter any kind of venture or partnership that is conscious or karmic, you are taught lessons that force you to grow. To step outside your comfort zone. And when you do this and decide it's worthy of your energy, you also have to face your fear of success, of getting what you want. The Ace of Wands asks you to see this—and then take a match to it to burn it to the ground and start new. The only way out is through, and you are already in the process of bringing this newness into your life.

THE ENERGY OF CELEBRATION: THE FOUR OF WANDS

Guess what? You made it! You did it! Now you can celebrate. The Four of Wands is a card of fortitude and persistence, passion and perseverance, a playful culmination of celebration. This is party energy, welcoming in the next chapter with cheer and applause energy, spring energy, the energy of the sun. Think of a memory that you hold fondly, one where you were celebrating something and truly enjoying it. What does this feel like in your body? The Four of Wands invites you to bask in this moment, to sit with what you've accomplished and the fact that no matter what, you're still here, and that's worth owning. This is a confirmation that you're making aligned choices: choices that feel good, that live in tandem with your ethics and beliefs, that are worth cheering on and honoring. You can work with this card by being grateful for your life, by celebrating what you've achieved and given and received. The Four of Wands invites in the joy, play, and bliss that come with having this corporal human form, so enjoy it. Where are you holding back because you're afraid of this? The Four of Wands suggests enough organization and structure to play, to plug back into what feels good. If you've been ignoring how things are feeling in your body, this card can be a reminder to move, dance, breathe, shake, and fuck so you can change things up and enjoy them!

THE ENERGY OF RULING WITH PASSION AND CHARISMA: THE QUEEN OF WANDS

The Queen of Wands follows the path of passion and pleasure. On her throne, in her holiest embodiment, this queen reminds us of the dynamism of intentional and affirming action, action led by the heart and the conscious and evolved carnal. She is sharp and charismatic, able to burn through the bullshit and get to the heart of the matter. The Queen of Wands is rooted in her sexuality and sensuality, and she knows what she wants, period. This is an embodied energy that comes from mindfulness, passion, and experience. In this way, her vision and appetite act as an arrow, clearing the way for her to manifest whatever she dreams of. She is unstoppable, on a level with her intuition, able to sense what feels right in any given moment. Fire demands intense presence and intention, and so does this queen. When you pull or embody this archetype, you are connecting to life energy in its purest, highest form. Prana energy. Kundalini energy. Sex magick energy. This queen is not detached from her sexual identity—no matter what that identity is. She is aware and conscious of it. She works with it intentionally, whether it's through sex magick, or creating art or music, or transmuting it through another medium. The Queen of Wands asks you to follow your lust, to sniff and poke and prod at it until it tells you its story. She asks you to find grounding in the truths you hold sacred. This queen's magnetic aura inspires everyone she knows. Her heart-centered energy is ignited by a deep need to create, transform, and embody. This is revolutionary energy. She is volatile when necessary and isn't afraid to use her burn for the cause she believes in. The Queen of Wands claims all her depths, all her multitudes, and uses them to incinerate what she deems unworthy. She is your guide in embracing life as fully as possible.

In a reading, this card can act as a signal to forcefully and intentionally take up space, daring you to claim your fullest expression. It can also be a suggestion to be soft and less volatile, to hear another side of the story.

A TAROT SPREAD FOR CLARIFYING THE LESSONS OF TRANSFORMATION

When you're in the thick of the flame, in the pit of the fire with smoke swirling and the heat growing hotter and hotter, it can be difficult to see clearly. It can be hard to concentrate; you can feel both energized and confused, not knowing what an insight or emotion means. Where you are being called to change, to shed your skin and to step into something new, when any of the elements overwhelm you, it can be hard to process what you're feeling or experiencing. Fire takes this intensity up a notch. You may be led through the embers without knowing what lies on the other side. What lesson are you being taught?

Before you go through any initiation, that moment where the fire burns through everything you thought you knew and shines light on something entirely different, you often feel fear or resistance. You see this chance to step up and alter the status quo—and you resist. It's easier to play small and stay comfortable. But the beauty of fire is that it reminds you of what lies beyond your comfort zone. Fire can be a guide for what you must do to evolve.

This tarot spread is meant to help you understand this, to gain insight on how the path before you is unfolding. It will help you get clear on your yearnings and what you're evolving toward, reminding you of the lessons that you still have to learn.

Before you begin, take a moment to set the space. Grab water, light candles, put on music. Then breathe, ground, cast your circle, connect, shuffle, and pull. May the cards guide you deeper into your own wisdom.

Card 1: *Me*
Card 2: *My current situation*
Card 3: *My desire*
Card 4: *What I'm evolving toward*
Card 5: *The lesson I'm meant to be learning right now*
Card 6: *What still needs to be alchemized and transmuted*
Card 7: *The outcome*

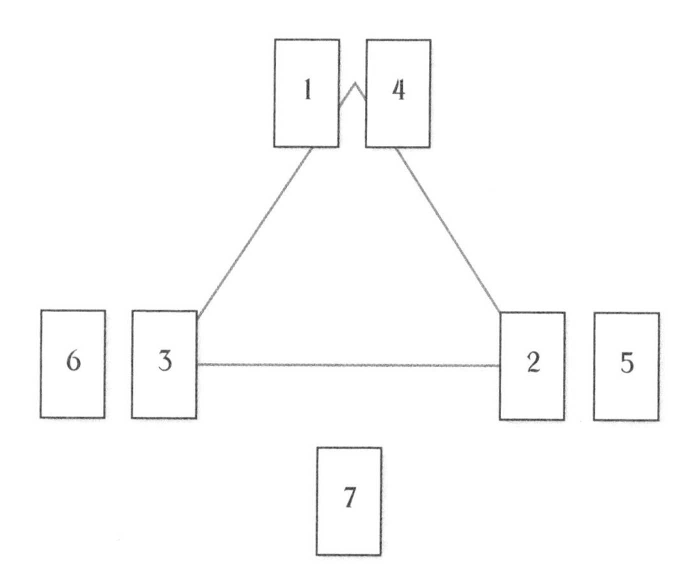

Crystals for the element of fire

Although you can't touch fire, you can work with crystals to connect to this element in a tangible way. Orange, red, and yellow crystals that reflect fire's colors carry that same energy and ignite your root, sacral, and solar plexus chakras. When you work with crystals that embody fire, you're working with stones that ignite the energy centers of your body that regulate your sexual energy, your life force energy, and how you feel inspired by the universe around you. This can be compassionate yet intense. When you embrace these uncomfortable energies, you get to see the magnificent power of fire up close, becoming the phoenix itself.

Place these crystals on your lower chakras or anywhere on your body that needs some power.

TO TAP INTO THE ELEMENT OF FIRE: CARNELIAN

Carnelian is an invigorating and bright orange-red stone associated with the sacral chakra and is deeply grounding while also creatively stimulating. This stone can help you embrace your inner vision, the spark that inspires you to follow through with intention and presence. Carnelian embodies fire in its most evolved and directed form; it is a stone of action that is also discerning. Carnelian carries wisdom, allowing you insight into your ego and how your yearnings can reveal where you may need to change habits to support your growth. It can help you understand what you're trying to generate in this realm, taking a feeling or an idea from ethereal to the physical. A great sex magick stone, carnelian can help you reconnect to pleasure and to your sensuality by instilling the clarity to know what you want and the confidence to go for it. Place this stone on your sacral chakra while meditating lying down or hold it in your nondominant hand to tap into fire and find clarity and direction.

TO WORK WITH WHEN THE FIRE IS BURNING TOO MUCH: FIRE AGATE

Fire agate is a mesmerizing stone in shades of deep red, orange, and yellow. It is stimulating and clearing, and since it's also associated with the element of earth, it has a grounding quality that facilitates healing by making you feel safe, rooted, and connected to the earth. This stone is protective, helping to shield the auric body while dispelling fear, aiding you in your journey of transformation and evolution, even when you don't know if you can handle it. This stone is fortifying, helping you believe in yourself and your pursuits and assisting you in making them happen. This stone also helps revitalize the aura, preventing energetic burnout, so you can channel and direct the intensity of fire without being overwhelmed. It can help you process, aiding you in the devotion needed for spiritual growth, especially when you're feeling discouraged. Place this stone on your sacral chakra while lying down and meditating, or anywhere on your body where you want to call your power back.

Kali: Hindu goddess of creation, destruction, transformation, and time

As I was writing this book, I had an idea of the goddesses I wanted to include. Each came to me in a different way, but when it came to fire, at first I was stumped. The goddesses associated with this element are fierce and require loyalty and dedication, and I wanted to write about one I had a special connection to. As I was brainstorming and sitting with the heat of this element, who came to mind but Kali Ma, the goddess of ego death, transformation, creation, and destruction.

Kali is not classically seen as a goddess of fire, yet one of the oldest mentions of her references her as a "tongue of fire," the most destructive of the eight tongues of Agni, the Vedic god or archetype of fire. Though there is imagery of her deep in the transformational flames, for the most part, this isn't a main aspect of her mythology. In my opinion, it's because she embodies this energy. She *is* it. Kali *is* fire. Kali's skin is midnight blue-black like the void, representing her ruling over the illusion of time, space, and form. Kali rules over the dissolution of negative ego, the divine

mother who is here to protect you and help you disconnect from anything stunting your growth. Kali embodies fire because she knows what must be consumed before new growth can emerge. She sees what she must feed on, what she must burn through, and she teaches that if your ego fights it, it will only make it worse.

Kali, like fire, is demanding. You don't approach her without respect and mindfulness. Kali consciousness is the need to protect, even when it calls for confrontation—she is the Dark Mother, after all. But she is compassionate and loving, too; the only thing she's worried about destroying is what's no longer serving you. Kali fortifies, as does her eternal wisdom, as does the eternal flame.

Kali is a dark goddess, associated with the shadows and the subversive. She wears a garland of skulls and a skirt of arms because ego arises when you identify with the body, with status, with wealth. She's not here for that. This dark goddess has skin like midnight to represent the void from which she emerges, from where you come and from what you return to. Nothingness. Consciousness. All of it and none of it. In her role as fiercely protective and devoted mother, she will not hesitate to destroy anything that threatens her children, or those who are devoted to her. You are never alone when Kali's around. And though her iconography may make her seem like a goddess of death or war, Kali is far from evil. She's a benevolent caretaker who is here for when you want to start on a path with fierce dedication. She is the channel of fire like the wand, and you can work with her to burn away your current situation so you're guided into something new and fertile.

After the fire has done its job, it creates fresh space. Kali is that eternity between destruction and creation, the sea of possibility. When you are entrenched with this energy, you grow and evolve without capitalistic or patriarchal notions of success impacting your value or worth. You know *you* are the real magick. When you are in Kali's embrace, you are taken to your edge and asked to peer into the void. Kali helps you find your way to your most evolved sense of self through this void of the impending unknown. You can work with Kali with the sigil and sex magick ritual on page 157 to help you transmute feelings of anger and pain into healing. She can help you take things from a lower vibration to a higher one, teaching what needs to be sacrificed in order to be reborn. Even though Kali asks you to detach from ego, she also asks you to be present in your body, to feel the feelings so you can work with them as power, as fuel. Kali sees the resentment and wrath and pride and envy, and she asks you to embrace and embody it, so you can see it, name it, destroy it, and grow from it.

AN ALTAR FOR KALI

If you come to Kali with the intention of cultivating a relationship with her, you will not be disappointed. She asks a lot of her children, and you must be willing to face the shit show she brings up. In many ways, Kali is a shadow goddess who asks you to confront your demons of anger and rage and chaos so you can experience transcendence through the pain.

You can create an altar dedicated to the alchemy she demonstrates. Start with candles in red and black. You may place a ritual knife (especially one of obsidian) as an offering; flowers in red, orange, and black; and any offerings of wine or menstrual blood. Kali wants you to let go so you can write letters and intentions of release and leave them on her altar. Light a candle with a heavy and fiery scent like cinnamon, sandalwood, or cedar, as well as incense like Nag Champa. You may place statues or photos of Kali on your altar, crystals dedicated to her, art you've created, and whatever else stokes the flame of your inner transformation.

Colors: Black like the void, gray like ashes, navy blue like her skin, red and orange like the colors of fire.

Sacred objects and correspondences: The sword that Kali holds in her hands is the sword of knowledge, destroying ego with one swift cut. Kali is also associated with time, or rather timelessness, like the void she comes from. Kali has three eyes to see into the past, present, and future, and she is associated with the cobra, which represents transformation and divine wisdom.

Crystals: Black tourmaline, onyx, smoky quartz, carnelian—stones that absorb negative energy, clear your aura, ground you in your sensuality, and transmute destructive chaos into creativity and organization.

Tarot card: Death

Alongside the Tower, Death is one of the cards that people resist. I have a different feeling about this card: I love it. The Death card is not the marker of anyone actually dying (though it could technically mean that, the odds are very, very, very, very low) but rather an omen of change. Kali is both the destroyer and creator; often you must demolish before you build, and Death holds this same energy. Through this card you learn of cycles, of your ability to transform, grow, die, and become reborn, emotionally, spiritually, and physically. The Death card extends the same invitation as Kali and fire; if you're willing to step through the doors of metamorphosis, if you're willing to leave your ego behind, then something even better awaits. If you trust, and even are willing to get hurt and do it anyway, then the fire of Death will fortify you through your next phase of evolution. All you have to do is follow Kali Ma. Death asks you to remember that this reality is just one way of seeing and being out of many. When you trust the path and commit to your growth, not even ego death can scare you.

Offerings: Leave fresh fruit, menstrual blood, venous blood (a prick with a sterilized needle or pin is enough!), liquor, wine, flowers, and honey. Offering up what no longer serves you, both literally and through ritual and meditation, is also a way to honor the divine mother.

A meditation to meet Kali and connect with the void

This meditation will bring you into a state of expansion and peace. You'll be calling on Kali to help you burn away anything stuck or stagnant, and then you'll find the spaciousness of the void she represents. Before you begin, set up your space, following instructions on page 15. Then find a comfortable position.

Read through this meditation a few times to get comfortable with it. You can also record yourself reading it as a self-guided meditation.

Close your eyes and connect to your breath. Practice the triangle breath, inhaling, holding, and exhaling. Do this at least ten times as you find your way into your body. Feel this breath circulating through you and then take note of anywhere you're holding tension or stuck energy and breathe into this, letting it go with each exhale. Ground and as you feel ready, call on Kali, asking her to help you embrace the void, asking her to guide your transformation. Ask her to burn away what's no longer serving you. Now imagine warm orange-red flames moving up your feet and legs, up your hips, up your torso and arms, up your head, eventually surrounding you. These flames are pleasantly warm, not painful; their gentle heat is cleansing and clearing and you feel all the stagnant points in your body start to awaken. Once the flames die into embers, continue to breathe, feeling your aura expand and expand. Visualize yourself melting into pitch black, the void, like you're melting outside the edges of your body. As you continue inhaling and exhaling, find a sense of freedom. You exist, but outside yourself. This is spaciousness and peace, a feeling of finding balance among the all. Allow yourself to stay here, connecting to Kali and talking to her if you wish. When you're finished with this meditation, thank the goddess, breathe back into your body, feel your body rematerialize, move your fingers and toes, and slowly open your eyes.

Embodiment practice: sex magick

What does it mean to hold space for the alchemical and seductive power of fire in your body? You can turn to nature to find out. Think of what it feels like to stand naked under the sun or near a bonfire (an experience I recommend highly). Imagine every inch of your skin soaking up the delicious rays of light and warmth. Now imagine this radiance starting from the core of your being, growing and glowing. With intention and breath, and a healthy dose of horniness, you can turn up this flame and work with this energy through sex magick. Though this set of practices doesn't belong to a single element (you can also practice sex magick while connecting with earth, air, water, or spirit), fire is most associated with this visceral and potent practice.

Working with sexual energy and orgasms has been practiced around the world for thousands of years. In the West, we think of it as sex magick. In the East it's known as Tantra, which works with

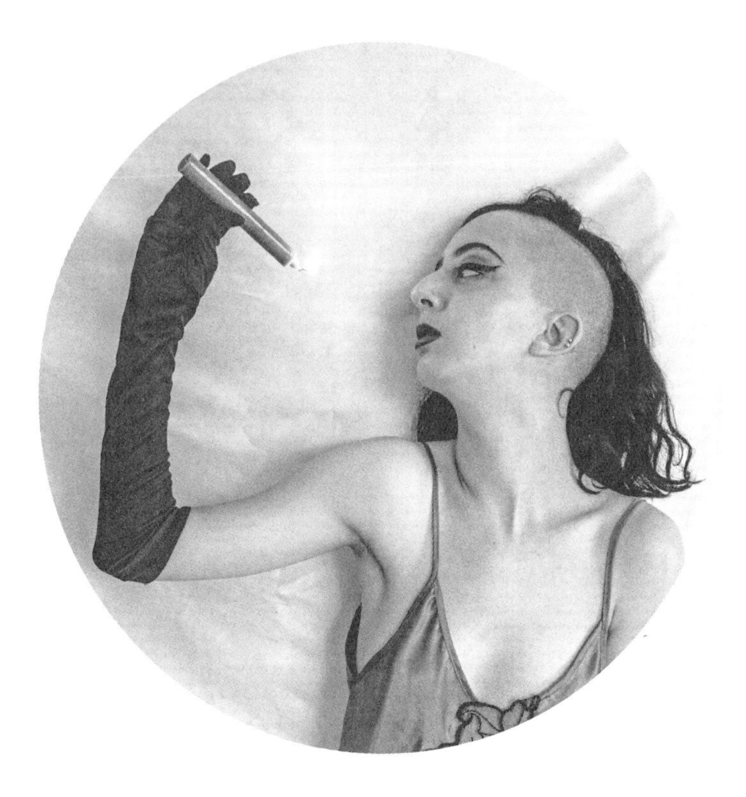

Kundalini energy. Although prana is this same energy, Kundalini in its awakened state is a form of consciousness. And this makes sense when you feel it in your own body. Think of a time when you were with a lover, or out in nature, or in a deep, deep state of peace and pleasure. It feels like everything else shifts; things look different. You're literally in an altered state of consciousness because of all the dopamine and happy chemicals in your brain, but you're also in a liminal space as in ritual, neither here nor there. You can work with sex magick not only to connect to this powerful state of transcendence but also as a way to raise energy.

Sexual energy is the energy of opportunity, of manifestation, of connection to power and possibility. It's the energy of the Magician in the tarot deck, capable of creating anything, and it's the energy of the Ace of Wands. Orgasms are called a climax for a reason; it is a vibrational peak, similar to how you raise energy during spell work. When you harness this climax and work with it intentionally, you can channel its potent force toward your desires. You can use it to rejuvenate, to attract, to transfigure, to heal, and to gain a deeper sense of bliss not just while doing this ritual but also in your day-to-day, waking, nonmagickal life. Fire transforms and it also awakens. Cultivating a sex magick practice and rituals of sensuality and self-seduction transform and heal your inner realm, and *that* shifts how you move through life. When you do this work, you wake up parts of yourself that have been dormant for months, years, generations, or even lifetimes. To allow the fire to transform you, all you have to do is trust and open yourself up to the possibility of feeling more.

ABOUT SACRED SEXUALITY

I have a lot of feelings about sacred sexuality, mostly because I believe that all sexuality is sacred. You can't disconnect one from the other. What separates sexuality from sacred sexuality, at least in my eyes and the model of this book, isn't the act itself but the intention. What do you do when something is sacred? You set aside time to honor it, to treat it with reverence and respect; you devote yourself to it. When I talk about sacred sexuality, I'm talking about what sexuality means to you, and however you return to it regularly to explore.

Sacred sexuality is the way you connect to pleasure. It means seeing the world's divinity as an erotic and charged point of inspiration. Suddenly putting on lipstick or smelling a rose ignites your sacral chakra. Kissing a lover and smelling their skin wakes up all of your senses. Walking under the midday sun with skin exposed is sensual and juicy; sacred sexuality means surrendering to how tantalizing and alive your senses and the world make you feel.

For those of us who are witchy, mystically inclined, freaks, pervs, kinky weirdos, or just willing to explore our erotic edge, sex magick and sacred sexuality can offer a deeper look into our magickal practice. By honing your desires, creating an intention and being present in your body, you can take masturbation or sex from mundane to magick. My suggestion is that if you've never worked with sex magick or using orgasms to cast spells, try it out for a while by yourself. Solo sex magick is a powerful way to arouse yourself and find what feels good in your body. You can create sacred spaces and perform rituals to dive deeper into your sensuality, too. The ritual surrounding sex magick becomes like foreplay; you seduce yourself to get into the state of mind where this magick flows.

A NOTE

Please remember the most important thing always: there's no one "right" way. For sexuality *especially*. Sexual energy is life force energy and can be worked with in so many ways to support you, your healing, and your own journey. Take things slowly. Honor your feelings and your body. Orgasm is a great way to raise energy, but if it doesn't happen or you can't orgasm, that's okay! Maybe you raise the energy that way as much as you can or you run or chant or dance instead of masturbate or have sex. That's totally cool; do whatever makes you feel the most confident and comfortable.

HOW TO START WORKING WITH SEX MAGICK

Okay, so you know you want to work with the vaguely chaotic but alluring energy of fire through sex magick. You know that you'll be using your orgasm and sexual energy to send an intention, but how do you get there? Here are some simple steps to think about, and as always, check "Further Reading" (page 330) for book recommendations.

Know your turn-ons

The old occult maxim *Know thyself* holds especially true when it comes to knowing what turns you on. This is vital information, so take time in meditation and masturbation to explore and see what you like. Think of the kinds of spaces you like to have sex in, the kinds of feelings, sensations, levels of intensity. Read! Explore! Go to your local sex shop and take a class! If you're interested in kink, the crossover between BDSM and sex magick is extensive, exciting, and fascinating. Letting yourself explore your desires and then asking for what you want are huge sex magick rituals in themselves. Knowing your desires and turn-ons is only going to make the rituals and spells you perform more potent.

Set up the space and yourself

Besides knowing what you're into and what feels good, consider your environment. Your senses play a huge part in how you're feeling. Make sure you have enough blankets and pillows, and that the lights are right. You may wish to light incense and candles, burn sacred herbs, and call in any guides, deities, or angels you work with. Get water, put on ambient music, turn off your phone. The key here is to get the temple ready, to erect an environment that is relaxing and sensuous.

Then think about what you need. If you'll be using sex toys, have them somewhere nearby. Ditto lube or condoms. If you want to wear lingerie, now is the time to slip into that something (check out the glamour guide on page 162–64 for inspiration). Wearing something that makes you feel like the sex witch you are is highly suggested, and always remember you can work skyclad or naked.

Set an intention

What's the point of this working? Maybe you're doing this under a full moon and manifesting, or under the new moon to help clear away old patterns. Even though sex magick uses sexual energy, you can set an intention around nearly anything. What are you manifesting? What kind of love are you looking for? What kind of career opportunities are you calling in? What do you need help healing? What could use some positive energy? There's so much room to play! Take the time to meditate on your intention so you *know* it feels right. Sit with this as long as you need and then record your intention and ritual in a grimoire so you can see how your spell manifests in the future.

I like getting very clear on my intention, but I also love focusing on a feeling. If you want to bring in abundance, it can be helpful to have a specific goal or set amount in mind. Or you can dedicate the ritual to calling on and embodying the *energy* of abundance. If you're aligned with the universe, and you trust that what plays out is for your highest good, then you can trust that the details will be filled in by the cosmos. When you focus on feeling the feeling instead of on the specifics, you can give yourself—and the universe—room to play.

Work with the senses

Work with your senses to level up your sex magick game. Besides the setting of the room—the music, the colors of the lights, and the smells—also think about touch, taste, and breath. What sort of sensations do you like? Maybe you want to touch a fresh rose against bare skin, or maybe you like to be spanked. Maybe you like running an ice cube on the inside of your thighs, or a feather against your neck. How about taste? Maybe you love eating bright red strawberries in bed, or drinking tea before you touch yourself. Maybe you like being blindfolded, or using a gag. Maybe you know that you just have to wear all red and have pink sheets. Create an indulgent experience for yourself, thinking about what you like to see, taste, hear, touch, and smell.

Solo or partnered?

If you've never done sex magick, then I suggest starting solo. If you're in a relationship, you may explore with a partner later on, but get to know yourself first. I don't suggest trying or practicing sex magick with anyone you don't trust deeply, and I don't suggest trying it with anyone with whom you don't want to form an energetic connection. Communicating your desires, your expectations, and how to handle the possibility of things going awry (which there always are) is vital. Listen to your gut. Don't do this with anyone who dims your light, who makes you feel less than. Whoever shares this sacred practice with you should be willing to see you in your fullest and truest power.

When you practice sex magick with a partner, your energy systems intertwine from the root chakra all the way to your crown, forming a double spiral up your spine. As you raise energy together, it moves up, up, up out of the crown of your head and out into the universe. You are intentionally weaving together your energetic centers with someone else's. If you know that you're already comfortable with a partner, it can bring you closer and open up new realms of erotic possibilities in your relationship.

Work with breath and sound

Although you can work with specific types of breathing, simply paying attention to your breath is enough to start with. You may wish to inhale through your nose and out through your mouth as you begin your solo or partnered sex session, letting your inhalations guide you deeper into your body and your exhalations deeper into pleasure. You can also use your breath to draw out your orgasms, so when you finally climax they're more powerful. Make noise. Moan! Be loud! Let your throat chakra live! As you exhale, allow any moans, hisses, or growls to come out. Always follow whatever feels right and real and primal and raw. Try experimenting with different breathing techniques (see chapter 2 for more details) and see how it affects the energy; then adjust accordingly!

Raise and dedicate the energy

Once you have your sacred space and altar set up, you're wearing something that makes you feel erotic, you're grounded in your body, and you're present, it's time to begin! If you wish, you can cast a circle at this point as well, and invite in the directions and elements (see page 28). You can also invite any deities you want to work with like Venus or Isis or another god or goddess of love. Connect with your breath and begin to come back to the present moment as you start appreciating yourself and your body, touching yourself in any way that feels good. Whisper loving things to yourself, focus on your breath, and just enjoy being in this physical realm. As you masturbate or have sex, focus on your intention. Let pleasure pave the way, and follow what turns you on, staying here as long as you need, inviting any kinky or sensory experiences in at this time if you wish. Always remember that your breath can bring you back to the present moment if your mind starts to wander.

As you get closer and closer to climax, keep your intention in your mind. As you orgasm, visualize energy moving from your sacral chakra up your spine, out the crown of your head toward the cosmos. If this is too difficult, send out that energy to the universe when you've just finished and are in the afterglow. Take time to dwell here, sending that sexual electricity toward your intention. When you're done, you'll ground and close the ritual.

Ground

Find a seat or comfortable position and remember the intention you set. Feel back into your body, breathing white light into every nook and cranny. Feel the satisfaction of the ritual coursing through you as you continue breathing deeply. If you invited any goddesses or gods, spirit guides, deities, or angels in, now is the time to thank them and let them know the ritual is over. Thank yourself and the universe for support. As you exhale, visualize any stagnant energy leaving your mouth. If you cast a circle, you'll close it, and if you invited in the elements and directions, you'll dismiss them and let them know the ritual is closed. Press your forehead into the floor as in child's pose, and send any excess energy back to the earth through your third eye. Write down insights, what steps you took, how everything felt, and then go drink some water and eat some food. So it is!

Fire as alchemy: working with anger

Hopefully by now you've taken a second to close your eyes and think about fire. About the way the flames lick, about how its intensity feels in your body. What does fire feel like when you're turned on? When you're inspired and passionate? When you're angry? You can connect to how your body feels in these discrete emotional states to learn about your relationship with this element. All your feelings are sacred, even the scary and hard-to-deal-with ones like anger.

Anger is fire in its lowest vibration, the most painful and volatile version of this element. Think of being "blind with rage" or "seeing red" to picture how far this energy can go. When anger is at its maximum, it's destructive like a wildfire; if you're in its way, you're going to get hurt. And although some of us have an easier time navigating this territory than others, you can't simply box up your anger, hide it under your bed, and call it a day—much as you can't do this with any of your emotions and feelings. Instead, you can let the anger burn clear and find the wisdom of clarity and discernment it leaves in its wake.

Anger without wisdom is just pain that doesn't know where to go. When you get angry as a way to deflect, you're taking out your pain on something else. You get angry at someone, or at yourself, or at the world, because of a thing you can't change. Anger by itself can be incredibly destructive, but with compassion and with intention it can transform into new growth. When you turn your anger into inspiration to change things, you are using the alchemy of fire to transmute from a lower vibration to a higher one. You are turning it into wisdom. When you take the time to meditate on what's making you angry and why, and what you can do to learn and grow from the situation, you're embodying the message and power of fire.

It's not that you can't or shouldn't be angry. It's that you have the chance to learn from this feeling—whether it's how you navigate a relationship, or confront a systematic injustice, or deal with the way someone treated you at work. You can take the pearl from the oyster and use ritual and fire to descend into this chamber of deep and intentional catharsis. Anger often comes with pain, and when you give yourself the chance to feel this in a space where you can safely process it, then you can create true rituals of healing.

A sigil and sex magick ritual to transmute anger and pain

Anger is one of those feelings that can be hard to figure out how to transform. You can work out, or punch a pillow, or scream into water in the tub, or jump up and down, but sometimes your anger is more deep-rooted than the physical. Ritual and sigil work can channel this anger and send it toward an intention that you release to the universe. This ritual uses meditation and breath work to connect with your anger, to witness what needs to be done. You will form an intention, create a symbol to represent it, and raise your energy through sex magick before sending that energy to this symbol. This symbol is taken in by the subconscious, where it's able to grow and manifest without our doing. Sigils are potent, especially in sex and candle magick, and they create a sacred container for transmuting your intention.

This ritual can be performed whenever you have feelings like anger and pain that you want to transmute, though during a new or waning moon rituals of release and banishment are especially supported.

Read through this a couple of times so you're familiar with the steps and have it by your side if you need it.

You'll need: a pencil or pen and paper or a grimoire, a red chime or votive candle and a holder for it, matches or a lighter, sex toys, lube.

Optional: oil to dress the candle (like olive oil or honey for healing with sweetness) and herbs to dress the candle (cinnamon to cleanse and purify or lavender to heal), a cauldron or pot of water to burn your sigil in.

STEP 1: GATHER SUPPLIES, SET UP THE SPACE, AND GROUND

Preparation is key, especially when it comes to sex magick, and now is the time to set up your altar with candles, grab your sex toys, and follow the rest of the instructions for setting up your space before ritual on page 15. The environment should be comfortable and inviting. Dim the lights, get some cozy pillows and blankets, and play music that will help you relax and get in the mood.

Take a few breaths and then cast a circle, either walking around its perimeter three times or through visualization. When you're ready, find a comfortable seat with your body in a passive and open position and close your eyes.

Start to breathe, connecting to your body and the moment. Feel whatever is arising, and with each inhale draw yourself deeper into these sensations. With every exhale, release this feeling. Perform any grounding visualization you need, or do the triangle breath to tap into the element of fire.

You also may wish to feel warm orange or cool violet flames moving up your body and cleansing and purifying you, feeding on your pain and anger and turning them into a bright healing light. These flames heal you as they form a protective cocoon, keeping you safe.

Call in the energy of fire; call on Kali or whatever deities, masters, angels, and guides you work with. Ask for their guidance, for their compassion, for their healing and help. Talk to them about your pain, about what you need. Allow yourself to open up and trust, and when you're ready, meditate on your intention.

STEP 2: MEDITATE ON YOUR INTENTION

Think about what upset you and breathe into it, feeding it energy until you feel the anger and pain in your body again. Take note of where it's located. Are your shoulders curled up toward your ears? Do you feel a tightening in your stomach, acid burning in your solar plexus or throat? Notice where this energy has settled, inhale through your nose, and send white light there; hold it, then exhale through your mouth, releasing it. Continue breathing into this pain, making any sounds and movements that you need to let it go. When you feel this tension start to leave your body, when you feel that the anger and pain have shifted, think of what it's trying to teach you. What is the lesson?

When you send energy to a sigil, you're directing it at your intention. What container do you want this energy to take? Maybe your intention is to find internal space and peace, maybe it's to create distance in an unhealthy relationship, maybe it's to find a job with a better boss or a new house. Channel fire to clear away the pain so you can see what its message is.

STEP 3: MAKE THE SIGIL

Once you've gotten mentally clear on your intention, slowly open your eyes and write it down. You can write it down as if it's already happened, as if it's happening, or as if it's going to happen. You may wish to begin your statement with *so it is* or *I will it*—the specifics aren't as important as making sure it feels right. Be as specific as you can, but remember you can also focus on a feeling. Whatever it is, record your intention. It can be something like *I forgive myself for the pain I have caused* or *I release the anger I have at ____ who hurt me* or *I heal myself with love and compassion.*

Once you have your intention down, cross out all the repeating letters. Some say you also cross out the vowels, but you decide what feels right. Then take the remaining letters and create a symbol from them, layering them on top of each other and combining them, adding swirls and dashes, until you have something that doesn't look like letters at all. Draw a circle around it.

You can carve this into the candle you'll be lighting (which we'll do in the next step), or have it in your grimoire or on a piece of paper; just make sure to keep it next to you because you'll be looking at it to raise your energy.

STEP 4: DEDICATE AND LIGHT THE CANDLE

Now you will dress your candle. Grab a pen and carve your sigil into your candle, then use the oil to dress it. To banish, rub the oil from the middle out to the ends. Then sprinkle any herbs onto your candle this same way.

Once the candle is dressed, breathe into your body, feeling what you're feeling. Focus on anywhere you have tension and perform the triangle breath if you need to anchor. State your intention, either out loud or in your head, envisioning it as truth. When you're ready, light the candle and get your sex toys to charge your sigil.

STEP 5: RAISE THE ENERGY AND CHARGE THE SIGIL

Feel into your body, breathing into your sacral chakra as you move and masturbate or have sex. Come into your physical self, appreciating how things feel. Take the time to raise your anger or pain level again, letting it fuel your desire, breathing into the tender points of your body as you feel this tension play out. Use these hard feelings to help you move more deeply into your erotic edge. Moan and make noise and exhale and feed into this magick. Let your senses guide you. Once you're about to orgasm, or as close as you can get, grab your sigil and look at it, directing the energy of this climax into this, into your intention. Afterward, take the time to enjoy any sensations in your body and any space you've created for yourself. Stay here as long as you want.

STEP 6: CLOSE AND GROUND

Once you're done basking in the afterglow and want to finish this ritual, find a comfortable seat once again and close your eyes. Notice if anything feels different in your body. It's okay if not; the ritual and sigil are still working. Breathe and visualize and perform whatever grounding practice you need. Thank whatever guides or deities you called on, on Kali or fire. Sit with the discernment and wisdom that comes from moving through the fire and not avoiding it. Remember that you are the phoenix rising from the ashes and trust that evolution is never done. If you cast the circle, now is the time to close it, declaring the boundary dissolved and the working completed. You may press your forehead into the ground as in child's pose, envisioning any unneeded or stagnant energy moving from your third eye back into the crystal core of the earth. Take a moment to sit in gratitude. Drink some water, move your body, and enjoy.

If you drew your sigil in a grimoire, that's fine! If you did it on a piece of paper, you'll want to destroy it. Tear it up and light it on fire in a cauldron or over a pot of water, flush it down the toilet, or hide it somewhere you'll never see it again. Let the candle burn all the way down, and if you need to extinguish the flame, use a snuffer or fan it out. Remember not to blow out the flame, and dispose of any excess wax in a garbage can at an intersection. Relight the candle each night until it is done. So it is!

Embodying fire: the glamour of power and desire

Fire packs an aesthetic punch. Fire energy is not subtle, it is not afraid, and it is not underdressed. This is the glamour of curation, of intentional rituals of beauty. Through the glamour of fire you get to embody your desires and create fantasies out of your makeup, wardrobe, and self. This is a gift for many reasons; first, claiming and owning who you are through self-expression safely is a privilege. Creative self-expression is also incredibly healing. When you want to harness the spirit of this element, you can dress in a way that reminds you that you already carry the flame. Second, you can return here when you feel like you've forgotten about your inner life force and need to find it again.

I relate to my sexuality through fire by wearing and embracing all her colors. As I write this deep in Aries season, I've been obsessed with wearing monochrome red outfits. I'll wear red leggings and a red crop top and a big red sweater topped with red lipstick and my red heart glasses. This warms me up from the inside out. I walk differently; I feel lighter.

Wearing red, orange, and yellow is an affirming way to connect with fire, and I can't recommend it enough if you want to feel embraced by this element. Try wearing a red top or red sweater, or red nail polish. Even wearing red lipstick is a transformational act of glamour. Fire is all about your passions and what makes you feel vibrant, so let your intuition guide you into incorporating these hues into your life and wardrobe. You may also connect to this element through wearing gold: gold eyeshadow, or gold jewelry layered to excess. The gaudier the better, so don't be afraid of your grandma or grandpa's jewelry drawer or the local thrift shop filled with costume jewelry. Rituals of self-seduction and beauty are also spells of fire sign glamour. Luxurious skincare, body butters and lotions, nice soaps, high-end fabrics, and moments of mindfulness inspired by aesthetics are all of this element.

Another way you can connect to the sensuality and sexuality of fire is through lingerie. Lingerie, while marketed to womxn, is for everyone. No matter your gender or sexual identity, you can find something that makes you feel spectacular. And let's not forget that "lingerie" means anything you wear under your clothes; I'm less worried about whether you're in boxer briefs or a thong, and more worried about how you feel in them. Wearing something daring, sexy, or beautiful under your everyday clothes connects you to your inner power. You know this when you feel it; you experience reality differently. This is the energy and alchemy of fire. If you want to connect to this glamour, you may wear red lingerie, too. Even if you're not sharing it with any lovers or partners, wearing lingerie for yourself is possibly one of the most underrated power moves there is.

Working with alluring scents like opium, smoke, musk, sandalwood, leather, citrus, cinnamon, and spice can also help us tap into this element's signature. Perfumes that smell enticing can move us into a profound state of seduction, even if it's just for ourselves (*especially* if it's just for ourselves!). Spritz perfume anywhere you want to be kissed.

The alluring thing about the glamour of fire is that it can look like anything. The key term is *heat*. If you like showing off your skin, do it. Wear whatever makes you feel like you can walk into a room and set anyone's soul aflame with a glance. I am all for the camp of dressing provocatively, and if this is something you want to explore, this is the element to guide you through it. Spend time gazing at a candle flame and then ask what you're meant to wear to embody its energy. Listen to your desires and intuition to create an outfit that sparks a renaissance in your soul. Who knows, it could be the match that sparks another person's sartorial revolution as well.

Journal questions to connect with fire

Like fire, writing is alchemical. It gives you the space to take something from your mind and transmute it into the physical, the page. We write to connect to the power of fire in all her glory, illuminating where your desires are asking you to invest. Fire is action, it's motion, it's movement; it's multifaceted, just as you are. Journaling is a way to check in and see what's smoldering beneath the surface. Give yourself space to rant, to be, to say all of the things that are festering inside asking to be let out. There is no judgment here; I truly believe that getting all the chaos out of your head and onto the page is some deep magick, especially when it comes to what you don't really enjoy thinking about. If you want to work with this element by journaling, write your feelings out on looseleaf paper and then burn them when you're done as an offering. I do think there's a lot of medicine in going back and reading old journal entries, but with some of the more difficult emotional situations, especially if you're looking to embrace and embody fire, burning it up as a release is a powerful alternative.

Before you begin journaling, set up the space! Burn some sacred herbs, grab your carnelian or fire agate, light a bunch of candles, and put on ambient music. Turn off your phone, grab your journal, take a moment to ground and enjoy the ritual. Then ask yourself:

» What does the energy of fire feel like in my body right now? Where am I feeling it?

» What are the old patterns and paradigms that fire is burning away for me right now? What is the wisdom that I can find in this new era?

» Where in my life am I holding on to anger and resentment? How can I let this go, or work constructively with it, to make room for other feelings like pleasure?

» What brings me pleasure? How can I bring more pleasure into my life?

» What are my desires for this current time in my life?

» What are the sort of feelings I'm calling into my life right now?

Fire in astrology: Aries, Leo, and Sagittarius

♈ ♌ ♐

Love them or hate them, it seems that everyone has a strong opinion about fire signs. These charismatic and outgoing zodiac signs embody the bold and forceful energy of fire, helping you evolve and own your fullest nature. These are not signs that are worried about being passive or likeable, though you're probably already drawn to them regardless. This isn't the comfort of the earth signs, or the intellectualization of the air signs, or the emotional depths of the water signs. Fire signs call on you to see the freedom of this life. They call for expansion, for anarchy; they are not interested in the mundane but the magick. Like fire, Aries (the ram), Leo (the lion), and Sagittarius (the archer) call for presence. If you don't entertain them, give them enough attention, or fan their flame, they'll leave. If you try to contain them, they'll leave. All in all, you really can't make a fire sign do something they don't want to do, and once you accept this, everything shifts. If you give this element space to burn and dance, you'll witness an illuminating ritual of light and spark, the ballet of becoming. Fire signs ignite your deepest passions and remind you of your inner realm. These signs are charismatic, they're sexy, they're alluring; they're the signs you want flirting with you, even if you don't know it quite yet. When you work with fire signs or are in a season ruled by a fire sign, you're led into the wilderness of your soul, illuminating what makes you tick.

ARIES—THE RAM

Aries is the first zodiac sign of the year, ushering in spring and all the beginnings that come with it. Represented by the glyph of the ram, Aries is a ferocious fire sign that leads the way to revolution with a bold and committed mind. This is the Ace of Wands energy, the energy of orgasmic possibility that holds you in the palm of your hands and promises that you can accomplish whatever you set your mind to. Aries are unpredictable, inspiring you with their dedication to live in each moment, and making sure you're enjoying the ride even if you don't know where you're going. They are visionaries, using their inner fire to spark change and lead us to new ways of being. Although they can have trouble being objective and seeing things from different perspectives at their unevolved state, Aries energy is that of growth. It's the first step you take in making your dreams a reality.

LEO—THE LION

Leo season hits midsummer, when flesh is out and you're feeling yourself. Represented by the lion, Leos are the self-proclaimed kings and queens of the zodiac, and they have the dramatic flair to prove it. If you want to have a good time at a party, invite a Leo; they'll have everyone smiling, dancing, and enjoying themselves. One of the gifts of the fire signs is their ability to shine their inner light so radiantly. Leos especially have this gift, charming anyone they come into contact with and, at their least evolved state, demanding attention along the way. You can learn how to enjoy your life and make the most of it from Leos, who are committed to owning what feels good and having fun. A sense of play is part of fire sign culture, and this is true for the lion as well. Though they can get caught up in ego, when Leos become unattached from this they are both protective and devoted to themselves and loved ones. Leos remind you of the balance of playing hard and being committed to those things you care about enough to enrich your life and help you find meaning in the banal.

SAGITTARIUS—THE ARCHER

One of the themes that runs throughout the fire signs, and the element of fire itself, is freedom. And Sagittarius, more than any other fire sign and possibly every other sign, needs and craves their space. The archer wants to be able to aim their bow at their vision; if they see something, they claim it. Sagittarius is a humanitarian, turning their expansive insight to the world at large. This is a sign dedicated to evolution, to knowledge and learning, to trying new things, to travel and seeing as much as possible. At their lower vibrational state, this can cause the archer to have a fear of commitment because they feel like their freedom is being restricted. But at their evolved state, this is a sign whose vision can bloom anywhere; give a Sagittarius space and they'll set your world on fire and turn it upside down. Deeply adventurous and into the taboo, this is a sign of sacred rebellion, of pushing boundaries for the sake of growth (Sagittarius are very kinky); even if it seems scary, the fun will be worth it. Sagittarius will lead you into unknown depths with arousal and anticipation.

IN THEIR LEAST EVOLVED STATE

In their least evolved state, fire signs will burn you. They'll come in, all gassed up for the party, ready to live it up and force everyone to live it up, too. Then they'll unleash their true nature, have the most fun, incinerate everything, and leave, leaving you to wonder *what the hell just happened*. The maxim *Live fast, die young* applies to these signs, who do the most, then burn out because that lifestyle is unsustainable. When led by ego, fire signs can be obstructive and destructive, not allowing room for compassion or intuition to guide them in fostering intimate connections. They can be extremely passionate lovers who can also be scared of losing their independence; a fear of pain and rejection leaves them smoldering on their own. When fire signs feel threatened by limitations or glass ceilings, they'll either run or bust. Yet even at their least evolved state, fire signs teach us the importance of committing ourselves to the space we need to move through this world intentionally. Even with ego, these signs can teach us independence and radical self-responsibility.

IN THEIR MOST EVOLVED STATE

In their most evolved state, no one can turn on your soul and show you a new route like a fire sign. If you need a solution to a problem, a fresh perspective, or just something that's going to make you feel inspired by life, then hit up your favorite Aries, Leo, or Sagittarius. When they're in their fullest embodiment, this is an energy of presence, of being able to find the joy in any situation, in an uncanny ability to bring warmth and light to whatever is at hand. Fire signs remind us of the fun of flirting, of the temptation of danger, of our limitless natures. Fire sign energy is invigorating, it's sexy, it's inspiring; some of our most revolutionary thinkers have been fire signs, leading us to new heights with their uncompromising attitude and commitment to having free rein over their lives. You can't fit these babes into a box, and even if you did, they'd burn it down anyway. These signs teach us about harnessing and embracing our desires as fuel and committing to what feels pleasurable. Fire signs teach us about persistence, about inspired action that can change everything. With this element, there is no limit to what you can do.

CHAPTER 4

Water: Feel It

When you recognize that you are held by the energy of unconditional love, by the energy of the universe, by the watery world of the self, you are being supported by your soul and by the divine feminine. You are swimming in your eternal consciousness, not succumbing to the intensity of your emotional nature but instead surrendering to it. Through water you learn about the self—past all the thoughts, all the programming, all the fear. Through water you wash away the layers of old stories, old lovers, old selves, and once again see your essence.

Although earth is a connection to the physical, air to the mental, and fire to the sexual, water is a connection to the emotional. Through this element you learn about your innermost world, about how you love, about your fears, about your shadow. Water is your connection to your intuition, to the all-knowing consciousness that's bigger than just you. When you embrace the fluidity and majesty of this element, when you recognize your own ability to flow and ebb, you are able to come back to your magick, to your mysticism, to your truth: unconditional love. A mystical being in a human suit. Through water you feel, and through water you heal.

And when you connect to this element, you can connect to the divine feminine, to the moon, to your heart center. Water needs a container, and this container is the body (which is at least 60 percent water), through which you learn about and come to understand your emotions. This container is also the chalice, the womb, the energetic center where new life is born. This is the center of the immaculate heart.

Water as healer, as a connection to the heart and self-compassion

As you work with water, I invite you to imagine the soft lapping of the ocean at your feet. I invite you to embrace the sea's energy of healing, to think of self-compassion. I am a huge believer in self-care, and in taking the time to honor your spiritual and emotional needs, and I am also a huge believer in self-compassion. Self-compassion is water in her exalted state; flowing, buoyant, reminding you that you are allowed to hold space for yourself. That you are allowed to be exactly where you are, without shame or judgment. Self-compassion means radically accepting the moment; it means giving yourself permission to not be perfect. Through water, you can have self-compassion for wherever you are, and then take the chance to heal what needs to be healed.

Have you ever floated in the ocean or in a pool, feeling totally supported by the water under you as you gaze at the sky above? In awe of your ability to be in complete surrender to the present? This element is that same energy. When you release and surrender to your feelings, your emotions, whatever you're going through, you are given the chance to transform the present moment into what you truly need. You free up the future by letting go of expectations of what your healing will look like, and then you consider what will really honor and serve you *right now* instead. This doesn't mean you heal all of your trauma in an instant, or suddenly get rid of your shame. But it means that you have the tools to understand the language of your soul and subconscious to better serve your growth.

What is it that heals you? That nurtures you? Where do you turn for support when you're in pain? Maybe you go outside and spend time in nature; maybe you take a bath. Maybe you make some tea, or go to therapy, or scream into a pillow. Maybe you spend time with a family member, blood or chosen. All of these practices are in the dreamy and curative domain of water.

Ways to connect to the element of water

Always remember that the elements are guides and that you may call on them and work with them as you wish. Although each element has its specific form, they also have energetic forms: the feelings you get when you're doing certain rituals or magick. Sometimes doing something physical can be a watery practice that helps you transmute your emotions. Sometimes burning things can be an air practice, allowing us to release old patterns of thought. The key is intention. There's no right way to start; all you have to do is start.

There are many ways to get in touch with your emotional self through water. Immersing yourself in water, meditating with or spending time around water, drinking water, or anointing yourself with blessed water can be an incredibly powerful ritual that will help you gain clarity and insight. Here are other ways to connect with this element.

» Seek out an ocean, lake, or river. Spend time in the water or near it with your phone off, breathing deeply, as you gaze at her surface. Ask the elementals and spirit of this body of water for messages and meditate, journal, or create art inspired by this.

» Take a ritual bath with Epsom salts and herbs like lavender, jasmine, mugwort, or rose. Exhale your worries away as you feel yourself embraced and healed by the water. You can also look on pages 206–9 for a bath ritual.

» Turn washing your hands into a ritual. As you run them under the faucet, visualize white light cascading with the water so you're cleaning your hands with this healing vibration. Breathe into this with gratitude.

» Drink tea and spend time connecting with the elements of earth and water as you do so.

» Cry—connect to your feelings as you cleanse and release your emotions.

» Listen to your intuition. Close your eyes and feel your gut, that numinous sense of truth in the depths of your stomach. Ask it questions and listen to its answers.

» Connect to your heart. Meditate and ask her what she needs and then take the time to give this to yourself.

» Turn your showers into a ritual. Visualize white or golden light cascading from the showerhead, cleansing your energetic field and body of any negative, stuck, or unneeded energy. Exhale any worries or anxieties as this cleansing light surrounds you. You can do this same visualization with a waterfall of golden, divine light, practicing this anywhere you need, even if it's not in the shower (and look on pages 203–5 for a shower ritual).

» Spend time under the moon. Visit her regularly, learn her cycles, and when she's full spend time under her rays. Talk to her, write poetry to her, see her as your muse.

» Use Florida Water—in a spray bottle to help clear the energy of a space, in a bowl as an offering, or as a perfume.

» Drink water! Hold your hands above or around your glass, visualizing white light from the heavens moving through your body, out your palms into the water. Feel this sacred white light moving through you as you drink.

» Dance in the rain! Next time it's raining (and warm and safe) put a bathing suit on (or go skyclad, there's no judgment) and go enjoy! Take time to dance and play, returning to a childlike sense of joy and bliss as you enjoy the rejuvenating and invigorating effects of the rain.

Water as a mirror to the moon

It is not just a popular myth that witches are obsessed with the moon. Almost all of us fawn over her in any and every phase, cooing at her pale yellow fullness or her sliver of crescent, though the full moon is a particular favorite. The moon is tied to the energy of water because of what she represents, the intuitive, the subtle, the dreamy, and also because of the tides she rules. The moon makes the ocean calm at low tide, allowing you to spend time at the beach and enjoy the tranquility she offers. But she also causes high tides, leaving you on edge, asking you to step back and proceed with caution as her waves kiss and whip the shore. In this same way, it is the moon that rules over your cycles. She reminds you to honor your own patterns of growth and stagnation. Through the moon, you are able to understand the divine and all-knowing part of yourself and dive into the ocean to touch your own divinity and your own relationship to the Goddess. Throughout the world, the moon has been worshipped as divine and immortalized as the Moon Goddess, and as the Triple Goddess representing the cycles of birth, death, and rebirth through her faces as the Maiden, Mother, and Crone. Regardless of whether you believe in a god or goddess, you can still connect with this planetary body and the messages of the liminal she represents.

The moon is the bridge to your innermost world; she rules over the unseen, the shadow, the unfamiliar, and unknown. The moon guides us to our personal underworld and the collective unconscious. The moon is the untamed but also the most holy. She is your soul truth, your ability to grasp and understand that which your eyes can't see but your soul can feel. The moon represents both your light and shadow, your emotional strength and that which needs support. This is the domain of water. This is where you transmute your pain, where you alchemize your shame and grief by creating for it and speaking to it. The moon reminds you of your ever evolving potential and shines her light (or lack of it) onto whatever needs to be exposed.

The moon can't be separated from the subtle, for she is its archetype. The moon, like the element of water herself, rules over your intuition. She is your gut feeling, your ability to sense with more than the five senses. When you tap into her, when you work with her phases, when you embrace your own inklings of the truth, you end up with more understanding of your depths, which leads to more self-compassion and self-love. Through the moon, we're guided into connection, to the realm of unconditional love. This is when our cup floweth over, when we're able to share the gifts of our hearts with the world around us. You can't work with earth, air, and fire without thinking of water; what's the point of having a body if you're not honoring your soul?

Ritual practice: working with the phases of the moon

One of my favorite ways to amplify my magick is by working with the phases of the moon. When you connect to the cycles of this celestial body, you're connecting to your own soul's never-ending dance of death and rebirth. You connect to your own cycles by understanding that the cosmos mirrors them and by working with sympathetic magick, or magick that imitates its desired outcome. As the light of the moon grows or waxes, from the new moon until the full moon, you focus on what you want to manifest and call in. Then, from the full moon to the new moon, as the light shrinks or wanes, you focus on what you want to let go and release. The halfway points between these two phases are a time to continue the work you've started at the full or new moon as well as a chance to check in so you can get clear about your direction and intention.

If you have a regular ritual practice, working with the moon can assist in taking it to the next level. When you work with her phases, you are unconsciously working with your own subtle energy and collaborating with the divine on a soul level. Even if you're not always paying attention to what sign the moon is in or what she's doing, taking notes of the new and full moon and doing magick, spells, and rituals accordingly is a potent way to upgrade your practice. And remember, your spells and rituals don't always have to be about what you're going through. You can work with the phases of the moon, especially the new and full moon, to perform rituals of healing and protection for the collective or individuals if you get their consent. You can send out golden healing light to people or groups of people at the full and new moon for example, or light a white candle for someone's healing if there's nothing in your own life that needs manifesting or banishing.

THE NEW MOON

Time for: shadow work, introspection, goal setting, manifestation, banishing, and beginning a cycle

Although the Gregorian calendar is timed by the sun, the new moon marks the beginning of the moon's cycle. Like those of us who bleed, the moon moves through her phases every twenty-eight days, giving you the chance to set your goals, manifest, and then release. When greeted with a new moon, you're able to tune into your depths with more ease. When the light of the sun isn't reflecting on la luna, your shadows are able to express themselves. This time can feel intense, inviting you to step into your soul with a clarity you may not get when the moon is full. The new moon allows deep-seated patterns to make themselves known. It's a chance for you to really see where you are, past the illusion, while alone in the dark. You can also perform banishing work at the new moon, create energetic boundaries or performing protection magick while the moon is dark and you're able to move through the astral realm undetected.

The new moon is a chance for you to get clear about your vision for the month ahead and to perform magick for whatever it is you're calling in. This means spiritual goal setting and using the energetic clean slate the universe is gifting you for what feels most aligned in the present. In this realm of emotional vulnerability, you can gaze at the reflective surface of your heart to see what's true. When you work with the new moon, you're working with your divine nature because you're able to create just as the universe does. You see the macrocosm to the microcosm; as the moon begins anew, so do you. As she creates, so do you. Embrace the occult, saying "As above, so below"; when the universe is still in the moment before conception, so are you. And you get to choose what to birth and bring in the light.

THE FIRST QUARTER OR WAXING MOON

Time for: checking in, readjusting, healing, trying new things, manifesting

If the new moon is a chance for you to get real, to embrace darkness, to see all your emotions in their truest state, then the first quarter moon, halfway between new and full, is a time to check in and see how you're *actually* feeling. This is when you can get off the train of your ambitions to take a look around. Are you going in the right direction? Do things still feel right? Are you in alignment? Listen, you're only human. This means you're going to fuck things up. Sometimes what you think you want isn't what you need, and what you need isn't what you want. When you're working with the energy of the first quarter moon, you can adjust all circumstances accordingly.

If I'm manifesting something, I'll usually start the spell on the new moon and work with it throughout the waxing moon until the full moon. You can practice manifestation magick at this time as well, or continue with whatever magick you started at the new moon if you feel you're on the right track. This is also a time to try new things: a new class, a new form of magick, a new restaurant, a new lover. During the first quarter moon you have the chance to expand your horizons, to think big, to embrace the beginnings and seeds you planted on the new moon—and then to continue tending to them. When the light of the moon begins to grow, you get to embrace your own growth. If you think of yourself as a plant, this is when you see the sprouts above the surface. You've germinated since you embraced the time it takes to nurture and water the seeds. Now you get to *grow*. You're not at full bloom yet (that is for the full moon) but you're witnessing your desires in action, evolving alongside you. Celebrate the hard work you've put in and your commitment to whatever it is you're nurturing. Or use this time to find some stillness and adjust accordingly; if something isn't working, change it.

At the very least, this moon phase is an opportunity to embrace your ability to start and flourish and learn, and start all over again. May the light of the moon guide you deeper into your truth and remind you that the goal isn't to be perfect but to grow.

THE FULL MOON

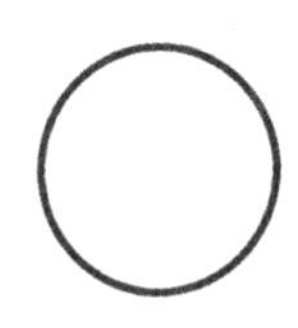

Time for: practicing divination, manifesting, healing, blessing a space, practicing sex magick, performing rituals of love and beauty, tapping into your power, ending a cycle

It's no coincidence that the moon is associated with magick and witchcraft, since witches adore a full moon, and for many reasons. The full moon is the most powerful time of the month and in her fullest and brightest state, she represents intuition, the subconscious mind, and the divine feminine. The moon reminds you of all you're capable of and when she is full, she is like a cosmic battery you can use to amp up your magical practice. This is the time of month where any sort of magick is supported (except banishing, which should be performed during the waning or new moon). The full moon is an excellent time to practice divination, manifestation work, healing, sex magick, love magick, beauty magick, or rituals of self-love, self-care, and devotion. Working with goddesses, spirit guides, animal spirits, and benevolent beings is also supported at this time. You can look at the current zodiac sign the moon is in to tailor your magick to this even more.

The full moon is also the ending of a cycle. It marks things coming to a close as the new moon marks a beginning. Later, as the moon wanes, you will have the opportunity to let go. But on the full moon you celebrate all its power.

The full moon is when you are supercharged with the intensity of the cosmos. And when greeted with a supermoon, when the moon is closest to the earth in its twenty-eight-day cycle (known as *perigee*) when it's full or new, you have the chance to embrace even more power. The full moon isn't necessarily the time to try something new or to do something that will drain your energy. Although some may choose to spend time with fewer people or instead practice magick to ride out the intensity of the full moon, others like to go out and celebrate. This can even change month to month. So honor what feels right for you in the moment—a lesson I will never stop reminding you of!

The two to three days before and after the full moon are also incredibly potent, and magick can be done then that you can't perform the day of the full moon. Sitting in meditation, doing breath work, creating an altar, taking a ritual bath, performing candle magick or sex magick, and spending time outside under the moon are easy ways to tap into its power. Honestly, the trope of the witch standing naked under the full moon in front of a bonfire in the middle of the woods isn't quite so off from what many practicing witches actually do, or want to do. I mean, that sounds like my kind of night, especially surrounded by my coven, as the full moon is an excellent time to perform magick with your community.

You can also charge crystals, talismans, and mementos under

the power of the full moon, for a few hours or all night. This will clear them of any negative energy and infuse your objects of choice with the fullest potential of this luminary body.

A note on covens

A coven is a group of witches that comes together for ritual, support, energy, love, raising hell, or community. Though the classic number of members in a coven is thirteen, I don't subscribe to this. I've been in covens with three people; the number doesn't matter as long as everyone is on the same page and there's a sense of balance. There is nothing wrong with practicing solitarily, so pick the path that makes the most sense for where you are physically, spiritually, and emotionally. Practicing with a group, however, is a valuable opportunity, and if you have the chance, I encourage trying it.

Some covens require an initiation, some don't. Some are groups of friends who practice together, some are witches who are friendly but only come together for the magick. Maybe you meet with your coven on Skype or Zoom for the full moon; things have to be tailored to the individual and what works for you. Thankfully, the Internet makes this easier than ever. So get creative, use social media and your local witch or occult shops (if you're lucky enough to have them) as a place to find a community. Embrace who you are and if you want to be a part of a coven, set the intention that you will find like-hearted people who will help you practice magick and evolve into your truest self. And so it is!

THE THIRD QUARTER OR WANING MOON

To do: banish, let go of things, close out cycles, address what patterns aren't serving you, protect

The third quarter moon happens the week after the full moon and a week before the new moon.

This is a time to shed your skin, let go of what's holding you down, and cut out things that aren't serving you. It is also an excellent time to do protection magick and banishing spells since you can release as the moon loses light. You can practice rituals of release like writing down what you want to let go of and burning it, and paired with meditation, you can begin undoing the energetic patterns that you've been clinging to.

The waning moon offers a chance to check in with the goals you set since the new moon and to do any maintenance on your spiritual, physical, or emotional life that you may have missed in the past few weeks. This is a time of introspection, when you can use tools like journaling and divination to process what you're feeling and why. As the light of the moon wanes, or lessens, you're led more into what you're calling to let go of, as the moon exposes the truth of the matter with more clarity. Whatever we were tending to has bloomed at the full moon, but at the waning moon we are enjoying the rewards of our harvest. Sometimes this means a lot of abundance, and sometimes it doesn't; take the time to honor this cycle of growth for what it is. This is a time for you to be honest with yourself and to release expectations of what things should look like. Sit with your work and honor it. The moon reminds you that we have the unyielding opportunity to change, that how you were doesn't determine what you'll be. Through the light of the waning moon you give yourself the chance to evolve.

A meditation on heart-centered love, to meet the garden of your heart

The way of water is the way of the heart, and you can explore what it means to live as a being of divine love by embracing your own emotional nature. One of the easiest ways to do this is through meditation, by tuning out the world and tuning into yourself and your soul. Meditation is a valuable tool for any mystic, but especially for any mystic who is journeying with the energy of the sacred heart.

You absorb so much of what you believe from the world around you. You take cues from media, friends, family, teachers, books, social media, and society that say you have to love a certain way, live a certain way, believe a certain thing, and behave a certain way to be deserving of happiness, freedom, and money. With the caveat that I don't condone hurting anyone and am a huge supporter of consent always, I do believe that you have the right to define what love means for you. Not what society tells you love should look like, not what your mom does, but what your heart says. What your soul says. When you take the time to do this sort of introspective work, you tune out the discord and approach your inner landscape to see what you believe. The goal for this meditation is to help you explore your inner world by embracing the energy of the sea and the rose, two icons of the heart and love that I'll be discussing in more detail through Venus and ritual.

To begin, set up your space, following the instructions on page 15.

You may wish to read over the meditation a few times so you're familiar with it, or record yourself reading it so you have a guided meditation of sorts.

Close your eyes. Take a few deep breaths in through your nose and out through your mouth. As you exhale, release any tension or anxieties. Allow yourself to get comfortable and present and then start doing the heart breath (see page 83). As you breathe in and out from your heart center, connect to the earth below, feeling supported and grounded. Then connect to the cosmos above, feeling its light move through your body to the earth below. Continue to inhale as you feel this connection, and imagine inhaling a warm, vibrant pink light that fills your lungs and spreads throughout your body. This is the energy of pure love, of divine consciousness, and you're held here as long as you need. Once you feel connected to this energy, imagine walking down the beach. Feel the waves and breeze as you walk along the shore. Feel your toes in the sand, your hair in the wind. Notice if it's overcast or sunny and what your heart is feeling, that same vibrant pink light from earlier surrounding you as you walk. As you walk, you notice a garden and begin walking over to it. Your heart skips a beat as you see that this garden is actually full of the most breathtaking roses. All the roses are tucked inside themselves, and you feel them waiting for you to talk to them so they'll unfold and bloom. This is the garden of your heart, and these roses are your soul and love and feelings. You notice one rose in particular and you kneel in front of it. Your lips almost graze it as you take in its intoxicating scent. Thank the rose for its beautiful perfume, and then whisper to it, thanking it for all the things you've learned, for all the love you've had and all the loss that's made you stronger. Tell the rose of your worries, of your hopes and dreams. Tell it how grateful you are for your strong and resilient heart. As you talk to this rose, it blooms, slowly showing you her true colors. What does she look like? Is she full and blossomed all the way? What color is she? Take it all in as you talk to her. Ask for any messages or wisdom she has for you, and when you're finished, kiss her and thank her once more.

You may wish to move on and perform the same ceremony with a different rose, or you may wish to finish your meditation. If you're done, take a moment to say thank you to the roses of your heart. They are always here to help you understand what you're feeling. As you feel ready, start walking back the way you came, the ocean to your side. Take a second to stand and face the sea as you thank her for all her love. Stay here as long as you need and then continue to walk back toward where you came from. Take a few deep breaths, thank the element of water, and slowly open your eyes.

You may wish to journal, take a bath, work with rose quartz, connect with the element of the rose, or do whatever else feels right in the moment. Repeat this meditation whenever you need to check out how your heart is doing. These roses will help you figure out how you need to nourish yourself.

Water in the tarot: the cups

The sacred container of the cups, or chalices, leads into the heart of the tarot. Here is where mysticism lies, where the heart is exalted, where you can honor the depths of your emotions and adoration and grief and love. The cups in the tarot are associated with the element of water and are the domain of what links us to the divine through love, pleasure, friendship, and depth. This suit asks you to be vulnerable, to honor where you are, and to gaze at the stillness in your heart with a solid and quiet contemplation.

The suit is tender, sensitive, psychic. This is where the mundane turns metaphysical, where your feelings grow into lessons, and where you're able to see what needs to be held onto and what needs to be let go.

The cups also represent the womb, the vortex from which life springs, the holy guardian of spiritual conception. This is an energy center you carry within you, regardless of whether you have a physical womb. This suit is the mystical beginning of all life, the emotional center that's conceived after the spark of fiery creation and the idea that came of it.

When you work with the cups, you're working with the most honest part of yourself: the part of yourself that can't pretend, can't run, can't hide. The cups are your emotional truth, your sense of soul, what you feel vibrating from the most ancient part of your being. Through this suit you can learn of the compassion necessary to create and sustain life.

When you ignore this suit, you're rejecting your own divinity, living life on the surface and not fully embracing what it is you're meant to embrace. And what fun is that?

THE ENERGY OF NEW LOVE—THE ACE OF CUPS

The aces represent the energy of things that are about to come into existence, and in the case of the Ace of Cups, these new beginnings are intricately tied to the emotional realm. This is when souls collide, when partnerships emerge, when friendships blossom, when chance happenings transpire, and when your heart feels seen, inspired, and supported. This is also a straight-up omen of love. But get this: that love isn't inherently romantic. The Ace of Cups isn't just here to tell you that you are going to find the love of your life. One of my favorite messages that this ace grants is the knowledge that the love of spirit and the universe doesn't

take just one form. Although our society likes to place a particular weight on romantic love, the truth is that platonic love, familial love, friendly love, and sexual and nonsexual love are just as valid and life-giving. And when the Ace of Cups appears, though it may mean a soulmate is around the corner, it can also be a reminder of the abundance of love that's already out there if you simply open your eyes. Expect connection, harmony, and new friendships, and love of all kinds. Likewise, remember the abundance of love you have, and appreciate the array of ways you're cared for, and remember that this includes how you care for yourself. The Ace of Cups can remind you what self-love and self-care actually look like, which can be starting a relationship with your feelings, investing in healing practices, or finally asking for help. When you recognize the love around you and value your own love, you end up attracting more love anyway, so it ends up being a win-win. There is no wrong way to dwell in the waters of love. This card is all the beautiful things about compassion, care, and desire for someone else in a nonegotistical way. When this ace shows up, she's blessing us with the fountain of soul youth—love—the eternal footnote on surviving and thriving in this life.

THE ENERGY OF GRIEF AND LETTING GO—THE FIVE OF CUPS

There's no way around this card; it just hurts. The Five of Cups depicts a cloaked figure facing a river, three discarded chalices in front of him and two standing behind him. This is a card of pain and trauma, of grief and of moving on even when it hurts so damn bad. In tarot, fives represent a split: a time for a decision, a make-or-break period, and often a period of letting things go. This card speaks to the nature of being human. Sometimes you're the one who loses and you have to keep going and living for those you've lost. This card can be the burden of sadness, of pain and depression and anxiety. It can be an omen of feeling overpowered and a time of struggle. But there is still hope. This card reminds you of your strength and your ability to navigate what the world is giving you. Sometimes you just have to ask for help or keep moving.

But sometimes you have to deal with what you're dealt head on. This card reminds me of something I often remind myself: "almost good enough" is not enough. If you're on a spiritual journey, then the work you're doing is to be in alignment with the universe, with your highest or most evolved state. And when you settle for things, people, and situations that aren't serving you but have the illusion of being "good enough," often the universe catches up and forces you to let that shit go, to accept your worth at its full price. It's never easy, but it's always worthy, and when you look at the entirety of this suit, you see not only the resilience of the heart but the necessity of the whole range of human emotions to be able to truly appreciate the sweet ones.

THE ENERGY OF LEADERSHIP FROM A HEART-CENTERED SPACE—THE QUEEN OF CUPS

In the tarot, each of the court cards is ruled by an element, and our gracious queens are ruled by the element of water. In her home as the Queen of Cups, this card exemplifies what it means to lead from a heart-centered space. Although the kings in the tarot get all mental and up in their heads, the queens demonstrate what it means to lead with compassion and love. The Queen of Cups is the most intuitive of her ilk, being led not only by her heart but by her third eye. It's not so much that she knows what will happen (which, let's be clear, she does) but that she feels what is right. And through this card you are able to do the same. The Queen of Cups sings of matriarchy, of societies built on collaboration and sharing where womxn and men are equal, of the ability to lead from a place of caring and connection. She declares that womxn *can* handle power, and they do so with grace and fortitude. And she also holds the key to the collective consciousness that permeates all beings. The Queen of Cups reminds you of the importance of community and collaboration, of the power of authentic relationship.

As the most psychic of the queens, she tells you that your emotions and intuition aren't a weakness but a strength and something that you can lean on when you are taking up positions of leadership in your own life. This card speaks to the nature of the human soul and human existence. This sings of the spiral journey that your healing takes, how honoring your heart can often feel impossible. This Queen reminds us your heart is a resilient beast who just wants you to listen to what it has to say. Being human means pain and grief as much as it does love, and the Queen of Cups remembers this and uses it to help empower those she leads.

When this queen comes up in a reading, you can be assured that the answer lies in your heart. Whatever you're feeling can guide you to the root of the matter. This can also be read as needing to be emotionally honest and vulnerable with yourself in the situation.

A TAROT SPREAD FOR HEALING PAIN WITH SELF-COMPASSION

When you're experiencing grief, pain, anxiety, or sadness, it can be hard to do anything, let alone think clearly. Even though you know that this shall pass, and that another cycle will eventually begin, it can be hard to see through the fog. This tarot spread can help you see more clearly, giving you an outside perspective of what you're going through. Let the calming nature of water carry you through this reading, giving your soul a chance to express itself in the way it feels at home; through symbols and archetypes, the language of tarot, and the element of water.

Before you do this spread, take a few minutes to breathe and relax as best as you can, visualizing a waterfall of healing light cascading around you. You may wish to work with amethyst and rose quartz by placing them near you as you read your cards. Journal on anything that comes up and give yourself space to process. Shuffle your cards, focus on your query, and pull as you're ready, pulling more cards for clarity if you need. Remember to be kind to yourself, and that whatever feelings you're experiencing are valid.

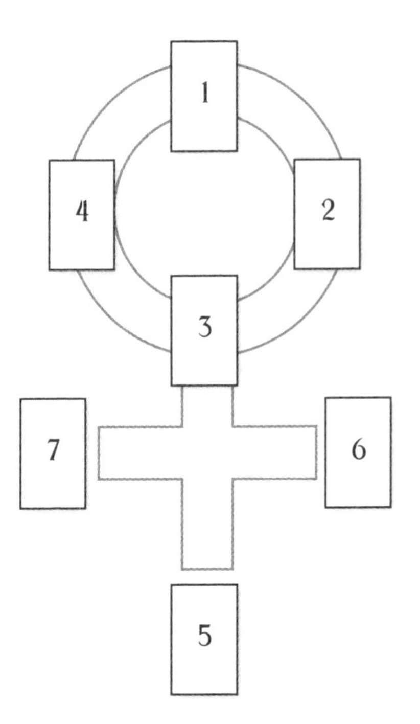

Card 1: *My emotional state at this time*
Card 2: *A message from the element of water*
Card 3: *The lesson my soul has learned*
Card 4: *What remains unseen*
Card 5: *What still needs to be healed*
Card 6: *What I need to remember*
Card 7: *My inner strength/emotional reserve*

Crystals for the element of water

You can connect to the element of water through the crystal realm. These stones help you unravel your emotions, transverse your depths, and get acquainted with your shadows and feelings. Take them into the bath and let them sit on your skin as you breathe into the healing properties of the water. Take them along when you visit a body of water like the ocean or a lake, baptizing them in this element. Let them charge under the rays of the full moon. Place them on your altar, dedicate them to your intentions. Charge them by meditating with them and inspiring them with your intention. Crystals can help you heal and protect your etheric body, also known as the aura. Let them whisper their healing messages to you in meditation or dreams.

TO TAP INTO THE ELEMENT OF WATER: AQUAMARINE

A crystal deeply connected to the element of water, aquamarine is associated with the throat and heart chakras and encourages you to align with the energy of love. Deeply purifying like water itself, aquamarine can release patterns of negativity, self-doubt, and criticism that you may have been holding on to. This stone acts as a mirror to your truth, allowing you to see where you are without shame and judgment. Said to be "the treasure of the mermaids," aquamarine was used by sailors for fearlessness and protection. This stone binds to your heart as energetic support as you process and untangle your feelings and emotions and is valuable for anyone who wants to heal from toxic patterns. Aquamarine is a gentle and present energy that gives you space to heal, like water that gently erodes away what's no longer necessary. Place this stone on your bedside table for tranquility, and hold it in your nondominant hand as you meditate for immediate connection to your heart.

TO TAP INTO WHEN YOU'RE OVERWHELMED WITH THE WATERY WORLD OF YOUR EMOTIONS: AMETHYST

Amethyst is one of the highest-vibrational stones we have and carries with it the calming and nurturing energy of water. The master healer of the crystal world, amethyst can help you let go of trauma and pain, aiding you in restoring the potency of your spiritual and energetic body. This stone is associated with the third eye, allowing you to see and explore the unseen in new ways, while also helping you open up to new paradigms and ways of being. This heart-centered and compassionate stone can help you live from a place in line with your truest and most evolved self since it helps open up your intuitive and psychic gifts. Amethyst can also help you with shadow work, transmuting grief and pain (your own and karmic or generational trauma) into stillness and wisdom and strength, and it can aid you when you're feeling overwhelmed by the immensity of your feelings. This stone can help you break patterns and overcome addictions, and it's said that if you carry amethyst when you're drinking you won't get drunk (though I have no personal experience with this!). Place an amethyst on your third eye or in your nondominant hand when you meditate to tap into your intuition and help you heal.

Venus: Roman goddess of love, sexuality, victory, beauty, and glamour

Through the goddess Venus, the Roman equivalent of the Greek Aphrodite, you begin to understand the depth of your heart. Love begins and ends with Venus, and this goddess of the sea can guide you in reclaiming your beauty, your sexuality, and your ability to receive.

It is said that Venus was born of sea foam after Saturn (the god of agriculture) castrated his father Uranus (god of the sky), whose blood fell into the sea, giving birth to this deity. Venus is the cosmic reflection you see when you stare in the mirror; she is love, and like her, your love is infinite. In the Roman pantheon, Venus is the goddess of love, sex, beauty, glamour, and fertility, as well as victory. She is the goddess of receiving. Like the chalice, and like the Queen of Cups, this goddess of love is intrinsically and unequivocally tied to the emotional range and depths of the most divine nature. Venus leads you to find the indulgent jungles of your inner world, and through her you can be guided deeper into your heart center.

Venus teaches you of the strength of the element of water, helping you to shed fear about the darkness that comes with the depth. Venus teaches you what it means to embody your divine essence through honoring your emotional nature and giving and receiving pleasure and love with ease, grace, and joy.

When you work with Venus, consider practicing rituals of beauty, glamour, and self-love. Ask for what you want and accept it with gratitude. Venus energy is the ability to receive abundance; sexually, emotionally, and monetarily. When you connect to her consciousness, intention is everything: treating yourself as divine, through adornment and pleasure, can help you embody your goddess essence. Beauty is a fluid concept, and you have the ability and the right to define it however you see fit. What does it mean for you to feel beautiful, to feel sacred? Venus asks you to embellish yourself, to love yourself, to please yourself as you would a deity. By treating yourself as a goddess and allowing yourself to receive, you arrive at the doorstep of her temple, and you have the chance to meet her directly. Carve out time to witness the beauty in your life. Take time to enjoy the ecstatic essence of dance and movement, of pleasure and romance. Indulge in the wet, flowing, and evolving energy of water and of Venus.

The ocean is a direct line to the heart of Venus, and you can visit or imagine yourself at her shore. Through the sea you witness her eternal beauty, and through the movement of her waves and tide you can connect to the heartbeat of the divine feminine. Whisper your secrets, or anxieties and fears, to the ocean and let them be released as the waves peel back from the shore.

AN ALTAR FOR VENUS

Venus is the goddess of beauty, so for her altar, don't be afraid to go for it! Think of each of the elements of this goddess to guide you. She is a goddess of the sea, so shells collected from the ocean and your travels, water from the sea, holy or blessed water, sand, pearls, and blue and green crystals (connected to the element of water and the heart chakra) all have a place. She is also the goddess of beauty and adornment, so you may place your red lipstick, perfume, oil, talismans, jewelry you cherish, and any precious stones you have on your altar as well. As the goddess of sexuality, Venus

would be down if you wanted to charge some lingerie, sex toys, lube, or condoms in her honor. Likewise, love letters, rose quartz, carnelian, and anything delicious that gets you connected to your heart center and sensuality has a home on this altar. As the goddess of victory, Venus may inspire you to place favorite items like a pen, journal, document, badge, or whatever else you have that reminds you of your glorious achievements here as well. Consider adding white, pink, red, or gold candles, as well as roses (especially white or red) and icons or statues of Venus or Aphrodite, or any of the following sacred symbols and offerings. As always, let your intuition guide you. And in this case, let Venus guide you! Maybe you have a red or pink candle you light to her every day; maybe you write her a prayer you read on Fridays, her sacred day. Trust in the process, and place anything on your altar that helps you connect to your heart. Remember, creating a ritual you can return to again and again is incredibly powerful. Let your love language guide you in dedicating a devotional act to Venus, listening to what feels in tune with your heart.

Colors: red, pink, silver, aquamarine, seafoam green, light blue, silver, gold, carnelian, bright red

Sacred objects and correspondences: Roses (especially red or white), snakes, doves, sparrows, and swans are all sacred to Venus, as are apples (especially golden apples), pearls, seashells, saltwater, and sea glass.

Crystals: opal, rose quartz, aquamarine, jade

Tarot card: the Lovers

Through the Lovers you meet one of the most ancient and powerful teachings of this goddess, that of unconditional love. Venus doesn't let boundaries or expectations keep her from loving; she loves others no matter where they are. In tarot, the Lovers teaches of this same energy, of harnessing the power of love for connection, creation, and growth between individuals. Venus creates and blesses the bridge you must cross to meet another person fully. And through the Lovers you see this cosmic state of love exemplified, a reminder that love in any form is worthy. Here you aren't worried about the potential of being upset or hurt; you're not invested in the negative *what ifs*. Here there is conscious connection, a union between partners or aspects of the self. Here Venus is in her purest form, shining the light of love in its essence: that which expects nothing and gives everything. Meditate on and journal about what this card and unconditional love mean to you. This is also a beautiful card in terms of self-love and asking yourself how you can give yourself the love you seek. The Lovers invites you into the realm of desire, into the land of love and lust. Explore and take stock. Make note of what speaks to you. Stay here as long as you'd like.

Offerings: wine, apples, rose water, honey, sweet cakes, sweets, roses, fruits, sexual fluids, devotions of love

A meditation to meet and embody Venus

This meditation uses breath, movement, massage, and glamour to tap into the sensuality and unconditional love of Venus. You'll be gazing into a mirror, calling on this goddess, breathing and touching yourself as you wrap yourself in a pink cocoon of light. If you want to add an element of sex magick, you may certainly do that as well. Sexuality and self-love are intensely personal things, and what matters most is not that you follow my instructions but that you find a ritual that unfolds organically and intuitively. Use this as a starting point.

You'll need: a mirror to gaze in, any lotion or massage oil that you have

Optional: sex toys, lube, rose quartz to keep beside you

Before you begin, set up your space following the instructions on page 15.

I suggest reading through this meditation a few times to get comfortable with the steps. You can also record yourself reading it to have a little guided meditation journey. If you wish to cast a circle as part of the ritual, do that before you begin.

Find a comfortable seat, either sitting up or laying down like in corpse pose. Close your eyes and practice the heart breath. Breathe in and out evenly as you connect to the earth below you and the cosmos above you. Feel the support from the universe around you as you melt deeper and deeper into your heart. Imagine a beam of warm, vibrant pink light moving from the cosmos, into the crown of your head, past your third eye and throat, down to your heart. This warm light grows brighter and brighter, and you know this is the energy of Venus Aphrodite. Continue to breathe into this warmth as you feel it radiate from your heart, through your chest and arms, down your spine and torso through your legs. When you feel cradled and in the arms of this loving energy, ask to connect with the energy of Venus. Let this unfold however it feels best. You may wish to ask for her blessing, messages, compassion, and light. You may wish to ask that you merge with her consciousness and the energy of unconditional love. Once you ask to connect with this goddess, continue to breathe and notice if anything changes. Stay here as long as you need to and then open your eyes and gaze at your nondominant eye in the mirror. Continue the heart breath, but inhale through your nose and exhale through your mouth. Make any sounds you like as you exhale, releasing any energy with hisses or moans or purrs. Know that your reflection is of the divine, that it is you who embodies Venus. Give yourself a massage, using oil or lotion as you connect with your body in the physical. Feel yourself continuously surrounded by this radiant pink light as you send this energy into your muscles and skin. Start at your feet and move up your legs, getting your inner thighs and torso, before moving from your hands toward your heart. Imagine that Venus is touching you and healing you with her pure and divine light. Continue breathing and embodying this energy of love, allowing whatever comes up to come up. When you're finished with your self-massage, close your eyes and feel the pink light once again. Take a moment to connect with Venus and ask her what messages she has for you. Stay here as long as you need, repeating the visualization of the pink light if it calls to you.

If you want to practice sex magick, continue this visualization as you masturbate, feeding into your pleasure. You're in charge of this experience and you can take it as slow or fast as you'd like. When you feel like the energy raising is complete and you're at your climax, picture an explosion of pink light that connects you to the universe. Send this energy out as an offering to Venus.

Regardless of whether you perform sex magick, when you're finished, thank Venus for her love and take a few deep breaths as you reenter your body. Slowly open your eyes, and press your forehead into the earth like in child's pose, exhaling any energy that you no longer need through your third eye into the ground. Record any messages Venus had for you in your journal, and make sure to drink water and eat something! You may wish to take a bath or go visit the ocean. Pay attention to your dreams and how your heart feels. Leave an offering of roses, honey, candy, wine, or sweets for Venus on your altar if you wish. Reconnect to this visualization whenever you need to feel the embrace of Venus.

Embodiment practice: how to make your bath or shower magickal

When I talk about embodying water, I mean a couple of things. One of them is working with glamour, using personal style as self-expression stemming from the soul, adorning yourself in a way that reflects this element. The other is embodying your emotions, your feelings, your heart, your depths; what water represents spiritually. But if you're already 60 percent water, how can you physically embody this element? By communing, cleansing, and surrounding yourself with it! Every culture has some kind of water cleansing ritual, from oceanside devotionals to the Roman baths to Jewish mikvahs. Water is sacred. And when you infuse intention into the way you bathe and shower, you are transforming these simple acts into acts of ritual, reverence, and healing.

WORKING WITH THE MOON PHASES

Don't forget that you have a chance to connect to the phases of the moon as you turn your baths and showers into rituals. Use the guide to working with the phases of the moon on pages 178–84 to help you decide when to perform/how to customize these rituals, and use the following cheat sheet for a quick reference.

New moon to full moon: *for manifesting, drawing in, starting something new, calling in something new*
Full moon to new moon: *for releasing, healing, letting go of, purifying, protecting, banishing, and cleansing*

HOW TO TURN YOUR SHOWER INTO A WATER RITUAL

Although I love a ritual bath, not all of us have the ability or time to take regular soaks. Showers, however, can be just as transformative. By working with herbs, visualization, and intention, you create a sensory experience that allows you to feel the refreshing and cleansing effects of water.

Set the space

Step 1 is always set the scene, following the instructions on page 15. Make sure you have everything you need in your shower, like nice shower gel (lavender, peppermint, eucalyptus, and rose are all good options) or soap. Grab a warm towel, leave your favorite postshower body lotion or oil out, and get to it!

Hang up eucalyptus

Tying eucalyptus to your showerhead has a healing and tranquil effect that may help you get into the flow and let go. This calming herb helps you unwind and destress and can be useful in releasing worry and anxiety.

Set an intention

Before you get into the shower, take a second to close your eyes and breathe. You may wish to do the threefold breath associated with the element of water on page 86. Take this time to ask yourself what you need, what you could use more of. A beautiful intention when working with water is to cleanse, heal, and release, or to connect with the element itself. Water can help you dissolve what you don't need, and it can help you tap into your heart. Water can heal and restore. It can bring your sensuality to the surface, intensify your intuition, or inspire your divine feminine side. Take a second and see what feels right, and when you're ready, set your intention.

Shower and visualize

Step into the shower (making sure it's at a comfortable temperature) and relax. *Enjoy.* Take the time to breathe and feel your skin come alive as the warmth from the water touches you. As you inhale, imagine the shower cascading down as a golden white light. As you exhale, imagine any worries, negative energies, or anxieties leaving your body. Continue to inhale the good and exhale the bad. Do this as long as you need to and then connect to your intention. Let the water surround you as you breathe into it and feel the white or golden light heal you of anything that's no longer serving you. Take the time to wash yourself and feel the soap cleanse you physically. Feel how the water glides over your body deliciously. Enjoy the connection to this element and allow yourself to dissolve into this and your intention. When you're cleansed, consecrated, and feeling your heart, exit the shower.

Close and ground

The shower may be done, but you still want to close the ritual. Take a few deep breaths as you thank the water for its healing, and take a second to come back to your intention. You may wish to use body oil or lotion, sending yourself gratitude as well. Take this time to

indulge in any beauty rituals you wish like using a face mask, dry brushing, painting your nails, or putting on your favorite moisturizer. When you're finished, take a second to say thank you, breathe in and out, and drink water. And so it is.

CREATING YOUR OWN RITUAL BATH

Although ritual showers can be as quick as you want them to, and thus easier and less time consuming to prepare, ritual baths require a little work, but the payoff is worth it. Give yourself at least thirty minutes to prepare and soak—I usually take at least an hour, even if I'm not in the tub for that long.

Before you begin, set up your space and grab your supplies. Check out the table of correspondences on page 89 to help you further define what herbs and supplies you should add to your tub. This is an outline that you may use to connect to whatever intention you want. Here are some ingredients to get you started.

A reminder: you don't need a lot of an herb to work with its properties. It's okay to add only a couple of pinches of herbs, or to make an herbal tea or infusion and pour that into the bath for easier cleanup. The colors are there to inspire your candles, what you wear, and how you decorate. They may also help with visualizations if you choose to meditate in the bath.

SALT

Epsom, Dead Sea, pink Himalayan*—all of these will help you ground, cleanse your etheric and energetic body, and heal your muscles since salt has purifying and healing properties. Salt is one of the smallest naturally forming crystals and can absorb excess energy, helping clear your auric body of psychic debris. I prefer Epsom salt as a base for my baths and I add a few handfuls before adding herbs or oils. I usually pick a lavender Epsom salt because I find it extremely* *relaxing, but you can use whatever salt you like, as long as it's non-iodized.*

FOR HEALING

Colors: *light blue, dark blue, white, lavender, gold*
Scents: *lavender, peppermint, eucalyptus*
Crystals: *amethyst, blue lace agate, clear quartz, rose quartz, charoite*
Herbs: *lavender, chamomile, pink rose, rosemary, butterfly pea*

FOR LOVE/SELF-LOVE

Colors: *pink, white, gold, red, scarlet, silver*
Scents: *rose, jasmine, lavender, cinnamon, honey*
Crystals: *rose quartz, rhodonite, carnelian, jade, peach moonstone rhodochrosite*
Herbs: *roses, lavender, damiana, deer's tongue, lavender, chamomile*

FOR CONFIDENCE

Colors: *yellow, orange, red, magenta—the colors of the sun*
Scents: *bright florals, cinnamon*
Crystals: *citrine, carnelian, tiger's eye*
Herbs: *chamomile, ginger, valerian, lemon balm, St. John's wort*

FOR CREATIVITY

Colors: *yellow, orange, red, deep purple, violet, royal blue, gold, white*
Scents: *citrus, cinnamon, honey, cloves, salt of the ocean*
Crystals: *clear quartz, carnelian, citrine, tiger's eye*
Herbs: *rosemary, peppermint, orange peel, mugwort, ashwaganda*

FOR GROUNDING

Colors: *white, gold, light blue, dark purple, earth tones*
Scents: *cedar, lavender, sage, copal, frankincense*

Crystals: *onyx, smoky quartz, tiger's eye, carnelian, pyrite*
Herbs: *roots, dandelion, rosemary, nettle*

FOR RELEASING

Colors: *black, silver, white, dark purple, dark blue*
Scents: *frankincense, sweetgrass, copal, cinnamon, tobacco*
Crystals: *black tourmaline, amethyst, smoky quartz*
Herbs: *nettle, devil's shoestring, rosemary, peppermint, thyme, St John's wort*

FOR PROTECTION

Colors: *white, gold*
Scents: *sweetgrass, lavender, copal, frankincense*
Crystals: *onyx, lapis lazuli, clear quartz black tourmaline, bloodstone*
Herbs: *cascarilla (powdered eggshell), yerba santa, juniper, basil, bay leaves, mugwort, hyssop, thyme, valerian, devil's shoe string*

FOR MANIFESTING

Colors: *yellow, gold, orange, scarlet, red, white*
Scents: *citrus, rose, honey, lavender, sandalwood, sweetgrass*
Crystals: *citrine, yellow topaz, moonstone, clear quartz*
Herbs: *dandelion, rosemary, pomegranate, ginseng, violet*

FOR CONNECTING WITH THE DIVINE FEMININE

Colors: *white, light purple, light blue, deep ocean blue, deep purple, violet, gold, silver*
Scents: *rose, jasmine, lavender, honey*
Crystals: *rose quartz, moonstone, angelite, angel aura quartz*
Herbs: *rose, lavender, mugwort, nettle, violet, damiana, butterfly pea*

FOR FOSTERING INTUITION

Colors: *white, silver, light pink, violet, light blue*

Scents: *mugwort, cannabis, frankincense, copal*
Crystals: *amethyst, clear quartz, moonstone, angel aura quartz, angelite, charoite, herkimer diamond*
Herbs: *mugwort, rosemary, dandelion, chamomile, skullcap, mint, nutmeg*

You can perform ritual baths on their own, as their own ritual, or to cleanse yourself before performing magick. Read over the steps to get familiar and to see what works for you, adapting as necessary.

Step 1: Set up the space and fill the bath

As with any ritual, set up the space and gather your supplies, following the instructions on page 15. Think about what you'll want to wear after the bath and lay it out for when you're done. Grab your fluffiest towels and then fill the bath. Add the salt when it's almost full and any herbs once it's full.

Step 2: Set an intention

Before you hop in, think of your intention. Since you picked out your correspondences and ingredients, you most likely already have one in mind. But take the time to honor this, to breathe into it. You may also wish to call on any deities or elemental guides you're working with: the element of water, or the goddess Venus, or your own heart.

Step 3: Connect and enjoy

Once your bath is set up and your intention is clear, get in the tub. Submerge yourself slowly, feeling the way the water surrounds you. Slide in as you breathe into these energies. Go at your own pace, closing your eyes when you feel ready. Once you're comfortably settled, you may do the clearing breath or fourfold breath on page 84. I enjoy taking ten breaths before I relax into the water.

The goal here is presence, melting into your intention. Let the herbs do the work of getting you there. Inhale a glowing white healing light and feel this spread through your body. As you exhale, release any worries or tension. Continue to connect to your intention and to the element of water for as long as feels right, aiming for at least ten to fifteen minutes to really feel the effects of the bath. Allow the act of the bath itself to be a meditation, letting yourself enjoy the process.

Step 4: Close

When you're ready to get out, take a few deep breaths to come back into your body. Remember your intention, sending and directing your energy toward that desire. Thank whatever deities or elements you worked with, sending them gratitude and love as you notice the effects of the bath. When you're ready, drain the tub, and step out. Go drink water, eat food, or perform magick, taking notes of any feelings or downloads that came up in your grimoire.

I always let the herbs I soaked with dry overnight, and then I clean them out of the tub the next day—this is easier than trying to clean when they're wet! Watch out for roses and other colored flowers staining your tub as they dry, though. You may also collect and use these herbs for a spell that correlates to your intention.

How to create charged healing water

Besides bathing in and drinking water, you can use it to cleanse and purify. Charge water with an intention under the full moon, with crystals and more, and then use this water in ritual to consecrate ritual items, to anoint yourself, to cleanse your space, or even as a way to add more magick to your bath.

Here are my favorite ways to charge water. If you can, use spring water or natural water, though spring water from the store or tap works as well. You can also collect water from the ocean. The more connected you are to where you find the water, the stronger the charge is going to be. It's not necessary, but it can help.

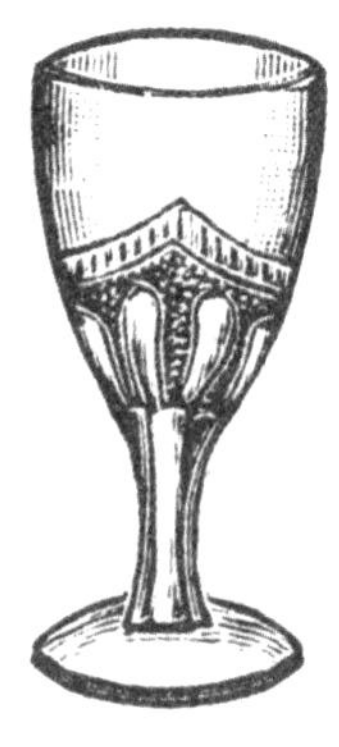

SALT

Add three pinches of salt to a jar or chalice of water, and then stir in multiples of three clockwise or deosil. Visualize white light from the heavens moving through you and out of your hands, infusing this holy water with divine light. Sprinkle it in corners and around the perimeter of a room to cleanse a space.

THE MOON

Leave water outside under the full moon to make moon water! You may do this for a few hours or all night. This infuses the water with the energy of the moon and can be added to baths, or used to consecrate ritual items, anoint energy centers like your third eye, and represent the Goddess (when poured into a chalice). Add crystals before leaving the water to charge under the full moon to enhance its energies, keeping in mind that some stones like selenite should not be submerged in water.

CRYSTALS

Adding quartz crystals to your water helps charge it. These are the safest crystals to leave in water for long periods, especially if you're doing this with drinking water. Choose stones depending on what you want the magical properties of the water to be. You may also charge the crystals and water under the light of the full moon. Use this in healing spells and ritual baths, and add drops of essential oils to create a room spray to cleanse a sacred space without smoke.

SUNLIGHT

Leave your water in the sunlight for an hour or two to charge it with fire. Fill up your jar or bowl with more water than you need, just in case it's warm outside. The sun will embed its strength, passion, and energy into the water. You may wish to bathe with this water, use it to dress candles for candle magick, or to consecrate new spaces or ritual tools.

VISUALIZATION

Place your water in front of you, palms face down over it. Take a second to ground and center, connecting to the earth below and the heavens above. Imagine a white light moving through the crown of your head, down your spine, through your hands, into the water. This white light surrounds you and funnels into the water. Breathe into it as you visualize the water starting to glow with energy. Send an intention to this water, whether it's for healing, clarity, purification, or devotion. When you're ready, slowly open your eyes. Use this water to drink, cleanse a space, in spells, in healing rituals, and in baths.

SOUND

Another way to purify water is through sound. Use tuning forks, gongs, sound bowls, or music to help cleanse and clear the energy of water. Try playing with different tones and frequencies until it feels right. Listen to healing music like binaural beats or solfeggio frequencies during your bath to really tap into this power.

The depths of the water: shadow work

Through water you witness your truest emotional nature. This is your wounding, your conditioning, your patterns. This is both what you see and what you don't see. Water is the inner world, the subtle realm, the part of who you are that affects everything else. This is the heart, the love, the shadows, the pain. It is through water that you hurt and it is through water that you heal.

When you are connected to this element, you are connected to your heart center. Everything becomes conscious communion. When you are out of balance, this may mean you take on other people's feelings and pain, which is also called being an empath. If you're sensitive and feel a lot and have an easy time tapping into the energies of others, this may be you! And although this can be a gift, it also means you need boundaries to be healthy. Although empathizing helps you hold compassion for someone else, you can't be responsible for other people's energy. You must have practices that allow you to stay protected and responsible for your own feelings, or you'll forever be picking people's shit up left and right (a great way to balance empathic tendencies is with grounding work). Shadow work can help you recognize the old programs that are keeping you operating in this space of taking on or giving too much.

Water is where the shadows dwell. Although there's a tendency in spiritual circles to focus on love and light, you must also deal with darkness and shadows. Life isn't one thing but many experiences interwoven. To feel fully alive, and fully in that intensity, you must open yourself up to all intense feelings, which include grief and disappointment and heartache.

This is where your shadow comes in. Shadow work is a complement to the work you do with your heart, with love, and light. Shadow work is when you witness the darker parts of yourself, the wounded aspect of yourself, the part of yourself that you feel is harder to love. Your shadow helps you understand the lessons and wisdom of your struggles. Through shadow work you can transmute some of this pain and integrate its lessons into your identity. You can't leave behind the parts of yourself that hurt. You can't ignore your shame or remove it. But you can learn its language, accept it, and talk to it. And that's the goal of shadow work.

So what is your shadow? Think of that person who annoys you the most. Who just makes you so uncomfortable, even if there's not a particularly good reason why. This is that person who grinds your gears, who gets under your skin. Make a list of the things that annoy you about this person (or people!). Be specific. Think of all the traits that make your skin crawl and your eyes roll, that make your stomach drop. When you're done, reread this list. Voilà, you have just met your shadow.

When you work with your shadow, you're working tenderly, with self-compassion. You are seeing yourself clearly without judgment. You can talk to the hurt child, the wounded teenager, the lonely adult. You can create practices and rituals that bring you to new parts of yourself. When you see the shadow for what it is, it doesn't have so much control over you. You're able to alter your tendencies and patterns. You see your fullest self without judgment. Your shadow self is integral. And if you want to be the most powerful, embodied, and potent witch you can be, it is vital that you know this part of yourself without shame or fear.

Something that is often thrown around in new age circles and some neopagan traditions is that white magick is good, that black magick is bad, and that white must equate good and black must equate evil. This is reductionist, and in terms of magick, wrong. White absorbs energy, black repels it. And in clothing the opposite is true, which is why you wear white in the desert. Black and white don't conform to the binary of good and bad. Magick is only what you judge it as. It is neither good nor bad; it just is. And so is your darkness. Your darkness and shadows will always exist alongside your light. It is how you work with this and channel this energy in a healthy way that matters. Having self-compassion is vital. I'll say it again—*having self-compassion is vital.* Give yourself permission to not be okay. Create a healthy space to feel that so it doesn't consume you, so you don't become a victim, but a survivor. Shadow work is soul work. Like water, it needs healthy boundaries—a container. You go to therapy at a specific time, in a specific place, right? Having a space and time dedicated to this deep processing of emotional shit that you can return to regularly is key for growth. You don't just water the soil and seeds once, you do it over and over. This is where ritual comes in, when you make a commitment to the universe to foster your evolution. Shadow work can be intensely transformational, like you're ascending and descending to and from the underworld.

The rituals in this chapter are meant to help you start to know your shadows. There is nothing to be scared of, but there is also nothing wrong with asking for help. I am a huge advocate of therapy and believe that taking care of your mental health is a vital part of a spiritual practice. If things become overwhelming and you feel like you need help, please seek it out! There is no shame in taking care of yourself.

SHADOW WORK: HEALING ANCESTRAL KARMA

You are affected by your family and their karma, whether you like to admit it or not. This doesn't mean that you are doomed to repeat whatever patterns in your lineage you don't like; it means that you have the chance to break this cycle. Shadow work extends from yourself to your family when you work to undo the trauma and pain you inherited from your family or picked up from them at a young age. Healing ancestral karma can mean undoing cycles of abuse, or releasing fears that have been passed down for generations, and it can mean learning traditional forms of magick and divination specific to your family or culture. It can mean recognizing how your family abused power through something like colonization or slavery, and then working to undo this dynamic in your magick and life. If you have any older relatives like grandparents or great-grandparents, take the time to ask them questions about their life growing up, their spiritual beliefs, any superstitions they grew up with. If you can, ask your parents, too—you inherit karma and trauma from your immediate family, too, and breaking these cycles and patterns through both spiritual work and practices like therapy is one of the most worthy things you can do. When you break cycles in this lifetime and on this timeline, you break cycles for future generations and also heal past generations. There is no future or past, so this work heals all those who were affected by it as well.

Ancestor work can mean calling on your benevolent and compassionate ancestors, especially those who are supporting you and fostering your spiritual practice. (Unfortunately, you have no way of knowing if all of your ancestors were kind and ethical, so you can ask for those who were when you call upon them during rituals for this kind of work.) Create an altar for them, with photos, trinkets, heirlooms, books, jewelry, or items you may have that connect you to your lineage. Dedicate a candle for your ancestors and leave them an offering. Spend time here, in meditation, in contemplation, in prayer. Talk to your ancestors and ask for their guidance. Learn their magick and practice it. Let them know when you see something that you connect with, mentally sharing with them. Your guides and ancestors are always around to help you and let you know you're going in the right direction; you just have to ask.

A ROSE RITUAL FOR HEALING WITH YOUR SHADOW

It's not that you're working against your shadow, or even that you're necessarily healing it. It's more that you're understanding its language and what it's trying to tell you, and that you create a healthy dynamic for this to happen. You're not trying to get rid of your darkness, instead you're trying to sit with it. Feel it. Explore it. Talk to it. Integrate it. Give it a set time and a space in which you can create a relationship with it. And then use the healing properties of water and roses to help you integrate these messages so eventually your darkness doesn't have as much power over you. Your shadow is a part of yourself you can choose to embrace, not a scary energy vampire that you don't consciously relate to.

This ritual uses journaling and meditation to help you reflect on and meet your shadows. Then you will be charging water with healing light and using a rose to cleanse yourself with this holy water.

The best time to do this ritual is at a full, new, or waning moon.

You'll need: a journal and pen, a bowl of water, a red or white rose (make sure to remove any thorns).

Optional: sacred herbs, a nonflammable container, a lighter.

Read through this ritual so you're familiar with the steps. You may wish to place it near you to help guide you.

Step 1: Ground

As always, the first step is setting up the space. Ask how you can create a healing environment, following the suggestions on page 15 for help. For shadow work especially, you want to make sure you create a conducive atmosphere for feeling emotionally and physically relaxed. Dim the lights. Light some candles. Gather your supplies and find a comfortable seat.

Close your eyes. Cast a circle physically or in meditation if it's in your practice. Then practice the heart breath, breathing in and out from your heart evenly. Ground, feeling the way your body is connected to the earth. Feel the base of your spine extend to the earth below as golden roots that dig deeper and deeper into the ground, sending white light up to your heart. The cosmos above sends white light to the crown of your head, which moves down your spine and meets at your heart. Breathe into this.

Now is the time to call upon any deities, ancestors, angels, spirit guides, or animal guides. You may wish to simply feel your heart, or the energies of love. Venus is a beautiful goddess to work with here, as she is a goddess of water, and red roses are sacred to her. Stay here as you share your intention to heal and soften with whomever you're inviting in, asking them to bring their compassion and light to the situation.

Step 2: Meditate and talk to your shadow

Once you feel grounded and tapped into your magick and are in a tranquil meditative state, it's time to make eye contact with your shadow and talk to it. Take a second to remember there's nothing about your shadow that can hurt you; you are in control. Any time you feel overwhelmed, breathe in the white light from above and below you and slowly open your eyes. Your shadow may simply look like a shadow, or like you, or like a silly monster. However you imagine this aspect of yourself, picture it sitting in front of you. Take a minute to feel it, notice what it's wearing, what its energy is like. Breathe with it, fostering this connection, knowing that the universe is always keeping you safe. When you feel ready, start talking to your shadow. Ask how it expresses itself, what it wants for you to learn. What is its message? Keep in mind that the answers you get may not be verbal; they may be a smell, or a feeling, or a sound, or a memory, or a color. In this way, you may wish to ask your shadow to share what it feels like in your body when it's present in your life. See what comes up in your mind, body, and third eye so when you feel this in the future, you know this is a message from your shadow so you can identify what brought it up. Allow yourself to feel into your shadow as much as feels right, and then when you're ready to close this part of the ritual, take a deep breath and ask your shadow for any last messages before thanking it for the conversation. Take a few deep breaths and when you're ready, open your eyes.

Step 3: Journal

Now reflect on your shadow. Go into as much depth as you want. Some questions to consider: What did my shadow feel like in my body? What is it telling me about what I'm going through right now? What did I learn about my shadow, about myself? What can I do to help balance out how I feel when this part of myself takes control? How can I accept this part of myself and love it?

Step 4: Charge the water

Now you're going to be using roses and charged water to cleanse yourself and help heal your energetic body.

Place your bowl of water somewhere you can sit or stand

comfortably with your hands above it, palms facing down. When you're ready, close your eyes and connect to the healing white light from above and below that meets at your heart. Breathe into this loving energy as you draw it down your crown and third eye, down your spine, down your arms, and out your palms, infusing the water with healing light. When you feel that the water is charged, open your eyes, grab your rose, and find a comfortable seat.

Step 5: Anoint yourself with the rose

Take the rose and take a moment to appreciate it. Smell it. Really take in its scent, letting your nose linger on the petals. Caress your body with the rose if you wish, feeling its silky leaves against your skin. Let the moment guide you, and when you're ready, dip the rose in the water you just charged.

Touch the top of your head with the rose and affirm that this energy center is balanced and blessed. Breathe into this. Then touch your third eye with the rose and affirm that this energy center is balanced and blessed. Breathe into this. Do this with each chakra, moving to your throat, your heart center, your solar plexus above your belly button, your sacral chakra below your belly button, and your root chakra at the base of your spine. Affirm to the universe that you're ready for what this next stage of your evolution offers. You may cleanse yourself with this rose and holy water along other points of your body, like your palms and feet, doing whatever resonates. Let the universe use you as a conduit to foster your own healing.

Step 6: Close the ritual

When you feel called to finish, put your rose aside and find a comfortable seat, find your breath, and find a steady breath. Take a moment to be here, connecting with the golden roots you planted before and the white light from above. Breathe into your heart space and take the time to notice how you feel. What's different? Is there more space for you? What did you learn from your shadow? Reflect and thank yourself and your shadow for the love and the journey. If you connected to any deities, like Venus, or any spirit guides, ancestors, or animal guides, thank them for their blessing and let them know the ritual is closed. Imagine the golden roots moving back up your spine as the white light from your heart returns to the cosmos above you. Take a few deep breaths as you slowly open your eyes. Press your forehead into the earth in child's pose, visualizing any excess energy or heaviness returning into the ground through your third eye. Close the circle if you cast one. Thank the cosmos, leave an offering on your altar, and then go drink water and eat something. If you're feeling heavy, try taking a bath with Epsom salt and doing something that makes you laugh. Drink some tea, spend time outside, spend time journaling, and give yourself time to adjust before reentering the real world.

One, two, three: banishing made easy

Banishing is the act of sending something away or, in this case, of freezing it in its tracks. You can't talk about water without thinking about the pure force of ice, of water in its densest and most concentrated state. You can use this power to stop energy from coming to you, to create a protective boundary, or to help you find distance from something unhealthy, toxic, or even abusive. It's important to remember that magick isn't the only operating force in this world, and that your timeline and that of the universe don't always match up. In the age of instant gratification, it's easy to forget that your spells don't run on Amazon Prime. Other forces at work may cause your spells to play out in unexpected manners. Although magick is a necessary and important supplement to your real life, taking other actions to remove whatever it is you're banishing is not only suggested but highly encouraged and in fact necessary. If you want the universe to meet you halfway, you have to do the other half! The following is a simple and powerful form of banishing, though, which I've also heard of as putting something or someone "in the void." This isn't negative, it's just distant from you; it's space.

Before you do any banishing work, make sure you have some distance from the issue at hand. Process it and take time to really understand how you feel. Sleep on it. You want your mind straight to perform magick, and magick like banishing shouldn't be performed willy-nilly. Let's say, however, that you recognize a toxic relationship, or a pattern that you've been attached to that you know is no longer serving you. Part of you probably still wants to hold on to it because it's easy and familiar, but you know you must find distance and separate yourself from it. Then you may wish to perform the following ritual.

Keep in mind that when you're banishing a person, you're pretty much just directing their energy away from you, sending it back to them. You're not sending them any negative energy, or making them do anything. Banishing is the energetic equivalent of a restraining order, giving you distance, space, and freedom.

Before you begin, set up the space, gathering any supplies you need, including a pen and something to write on. Then ground, cast your circle, call in the elements (using the ritual on pages 299–304) and draw a couple of tarot cards if you wish. Take time to meditate, reflect, or journal on what you're banishing and why. Make sure this feels in alignment, as you should before performing any kind of magick. Then write down what or whom you're banishing on a slip of paper and fold it up. Charge it with energy, through chanting, dancing, masturbating, spinning, drumming, or whatever else feels good. Send the energy into this piece of paper and into your intention of release. When you're ready, dismiss the elements, close the circle, and ground. *Now comes the fun part.*

Take this piece of paper with what you're banishing and put it in a cup of water (you can use a plastic cup), an ice cube tray, or a zip-lock bag filled with water, and then put it in the back corner of your freezer. You can also put the piece of paper in the freezer as is, straight up. Close the freezer door, forget about it, and enjoy your spell! If something shifts and for some reason you want to reverse the spell, just take the cup, ice cube, or plastic bag out of the freezer. And so it is!

Embodying water: the glamour of sensuality

Water is healing, it's mystical, it's the liminal, the sentient, the sensual. Although fire helps you connect to your sexuality and a sense of deep-rooted passion, power, and desire, it is through water that you reach your heart center, a place of deep surrender and truth. By embodying the energy of water you can embrace glamour that restores and revitalizes and allows you to access your heart center. When you think of embodying this element, you can think of what it means to connect to *romance*: a silk dress that feels delicious against your skin; perfume that smells like the beach; clothes that feel like summer crushes and warm spring days. This is the glamour of the woman adored, whose cheeks are flushed and lips are tinged with burgundy. What does it mean for you to be in love with the universe? What would you wear if you were romanced by the cosmos, turning the mundane into magick?

Let's start with the colors of the ocean. Think deep blues that

blend into the midnight sky, bright and brilliant turquoise, pearl white, and gold the color of sand in the sunlight. Think of the multidimensional blues of the ocean and sky, the ivory and soft pink of the clouds. Wear these colors to tap into the medicine of the ocean and to add a sense of tranquility to your day. Silver; holographic, opalescent whites; baby pink; and metallic are other options to consider when dressing up. And since the moon and water are intrinsically tied, white, eggshell, ivory, and all shades of the moon will bring you closer to this element. Brilliant fabrics like satin, silk, tulle, and crepe add a sense of easy amorousness that will leave you feeling dreamy. You may wear these colors, alongside pink and red to connect to your heart, in slips and dresses, in long flowing skirts or high-waisted trousers or blazers. You may also wear silver eye shadow and highlighter in luminescent gold and ivory, the colors of seashells—or even blue eye shadow if you dare.

Another way to deepen your relationship with glamour is by wearing pearls and shells. Make your own jewelry out of shells you find or buy, or buy it. Crystals associated with water, like moonstone, aquamarine, and amethyst may also be used as talismans. You can dedicate a necklace, earrings, rings, brooches, or whatever else as a talisman to water, the divine feminine, the moon, or a goddess of water or love (see page 67 for instructions). You may wish to do this under a full moon, leaving your piece out overnight to charge in her rays. You can consecrate this item to wear daily or dedicate it solely to when you're practicing magick in a ritual setting.

The key with glamour is to honor what feels right. Read back over this chapter and think about what water means to you. For me, it means honoring my shadow, connecting to the divine feminine, honoring my healing, and connecting to my heart. When I dress from this place, I may wear fishnets, a slip, my Doc Martens, my silver leather jacket, blue eyeliner, and rose water perfume: something that reminds me of my inner strength while also letting me feel romantic and sensual. Silhouettes can help us tap into different energies as well, and I find that longer pieces in flowy fabrics with lots of movement help me access water. Think about what you wear to spend time near water: big hats, oversized dresses, bathing suit cover-ups, lots of exposed skin. Perfumes that smell like the summer, like ocean, and the rain may also be worn as a way to connect with this element. You can even wear a vial of blessed or holy water as talisman to deepen this symbiotic relationship.

Think about what you want to feel before you get ready and let that guide you. Always listen to your intuition and let your heart share its needs.

Journal questions to connect with water

Your heart is a sensitive creature. You must return over and over again to understand its language, to live from a place of opening and of connection. To be in your power, you need your intuition. When you journal, you're allowed to be whatever you want to be: over the top, dramatic, messy, overwhelmed. Writing lets you access the depths because there's no judgment, no competition. Take advantage of this.

Let these questions lead you deeper into your healing. Get cozy with them. Grab some tea or water, turn off your phone, and set the vibe with candles, incense, music, and blankets. Then grab your pen and journal and dig in.

» What does the element of water represent to me?

» What's my truest emotional nature feel like?

» What is my soul saying to me right now?

» What does my shadow self feel like? Express itself as?

» What does it feel like to be living in the world when I'm connected to my heart?

» What practices can I turn to when I'm feeling overwhelmed, emotional, and like I need help?

» What are the parts of myself I am still learning to accept and love?

» What are ways I can nurture myself through this?

Water in astrology: Scorpio, Cancer, and Pisces

♏ ♋ ♓

Water signs are the intuitives of the zodiac. They feel and sense more than they see, and if they do see, they see things the rest of us cannot. Water signs are defined by their ability to transcend realms and travel to the darkest depths. They are sensualists, creatives, artists, reminding you of your ability to dream, to create, to love, to receive, to enjoy, to feel. Water signs lead you deeper into your magick, into your world of truth and self-expression. Through Scorpio (the scorpion), Cancer (the crab), and Pisces (the fish), you can learn to harness your creative truth, your heart, and your empathetic side. There is plenty to learn from these vulnerable and honest creatures, and each sign holds its own special medicine.

SCORPIO—THE SCORPION

The bad boy of the zodiac, Scorpios are polarizing. Love them or hate them, you can't deny that Scorpios are powerful. When they're centered in who they are and in their magick, Scorpios are transformation, sex, drugs, and rock 'n' roll. Scorpio is associated with death, magick, the erotic, and rebirth, and that's what they'll give you. Although they have fire sign vibes, Scorpio is actually a water sign, represented by a scorpion, which has an exoskeleton: a tough shell and a soft body, much like fellow water sign the crab. So although Scorpios offer plenty of depth, talking poetry and death and sex and kink all day, they do have a sensitive side, too. Scorpios at their lowest vibration can become attached to their shadow, feeling like their darkness defines them. They may cling to chaos to feel transformed, but if they're given a space to explore this, they're unstoppable. Scorpios teach of the power of sexuality, of passion, of darkness. They are the muses, the goths, the icons, and we have plenty to learn from their intensity.

CANCER—THE CRAB

Cancers are the nurturers of the zodiac, the friend who offers you a blanket, water, and food as soon as you enter their house. This is big Empress energy, the energy of being comfortable, of being received, of being home. This is the evolved and compassionate caretaker. Cancers are incredibly emotionally attuned and at their most evolved they are intuitive, sensitive, and empathic. At their least evolved, Cancer is overwhelmed with emotions and may not know how to channel them in a healthy manner. The crab, like the scorpion, may have a hard exterior, but they express a tender and soft center when they feel like they can be themselves. Cancer energy is expressive, and it's the healing energy of the ocean. When these signs love, they love with all their soul and are incredibly loyal. Home is important to the crab, and creating a soft and inviting environment can help them process their emotions with more ease. Cancers are considerate and gentle and can teach us the value of honoring how we're feeling. The crab reminds us of the value of creating spaces and relationships that not only support your growth but nurture it.

PISCES—THE FISH

Pisces is the last of the twelve signs of the zodiac and holds the wisdom of the signs before it. Represented by the fish, Pisces is the dreamer and the most intuitive of its cohort. Pisces teaches about the surreal and the language of the heart. Less vocal and more felt, Pisces's vision is a Technicolor daydream. This sign at its most evolved pushes limits while tapping into intuition and magick. Pisces is a very emotional sign, and in fact this is their superpower; when nurtured within the right boundaries, the feelings themselves become the art, the vision, the expression. In their least evolved state, Pisces can become immobile, caught up in too many emotions and *what if*s to actually start and complete anything. But when this sign is turned on and tuned in, expect creative, boundary-pushing magick.

IN THEIR LEAST EVOLVED STATE

In their least evolved state, water signs become a slave to their inner tides, their feelings. These signs can experience depression and anxiety when they're not getting the help or support they need. Water signs that don't have healthy boundaries or a healthy relationship to their emotions may feel overwhelmed by their feelings. This can turn into destruction, like a hurricane causing chaos without a second thought. Here water signs express their emotions through a lens of jealousy, anger, sadness, or even apathy and nihilism as they try to convince themselves that nothing matters anyway. Escapism through drugs and sex can also be an easy way out for water signs who feel and sense a lot but may not have the tools to understand this, especially in the case of naturally intuitive, psychic, or empathic folks. In its encumbered state, water sign energy can manifest as fantasy and future tripping, the mentality of being somewhere else and committing to believing that fully. By working with the other elements, especially earth, water signs can learn to harness their emotions to create and not destroy.

IN THEIR MOST EVOLVED STATE

In their most evolved state, water signs are in tune with their inner world. They feel it, know it, and accept it. They claim this as their magick and create, write, make art, transcend, and find freedom in the intensity of their emotions. These are the artists, creatives, poets, writers, nurses, doulas, and caretakers. Water signs are compassionate, divine love personified, the clear reflection of a body of water at its stillest. Water signs can delve into the subtle, into the sacred, and this is their work, their mission, their shadow, their job. When they honor this, water signs can tap into the ethereal with more ease than any of us. Water signs are the mediums, channels, and witches among us who have a natural connection to their psychic gifts.

When water signs have a supported container, they thrive. When they have healthy boundaries, they can do what they do best from a place of love, of art, of radical honesty and vulnerability. Water signs lead from the heart center, from the third eye, from a place of presence that has the potential to dissolve any barriers in front of it. Water signs teach us about what it means to love unconditionally, for the sake of the spiritual connection that comes from living in this way.

CHAPTER 5

Spirit: Embody It

You've taken the journey and come out the other side. You've moved through the grounded and physical energy of earth, through the expansive and present element of air, through the erotic and passionate reign of fire, and through the emotional and intuitive world of water. And now you enter the realm of the metaphysical, of the intangible, of that which connects each of the elements to each other; this is the domain of spirit.

You know that each element has the ability to teach you something of yourself, of the way you live, explore, dance, create, shapeshift, love, grieve. Each element supports you in a different manner, and yet it is the realm of spirit that transcends all, the ever-expanding direction of *up*. Spirit is the manifestation of earth, air, fire, and water at once, embodying the magick of all the elements. Spirit is the golden cord that keeps them together.

Spirit as connection to the elements

Embodiment, empowerment, and spiritual practice all have the same purpose: to connect you to your own power and spirit. In this way, spirit takes on two meanings. On one hand, spirit is that invisible web that unites everything. Spirit is the spark for the flame, the container for the water, the breath of the wind, and the rootedness of the forest. It is that which is invisible but felt. You can experience spirit through the way you connect to nature, the

energy you receive when you work in tandem with the universe, or the strength and passion that comes with owning your desires. There isn't one direct line to spirit, and thank goddess for that.

Although many patriarchal religions want you to believe that you must go through someone else to connect with the divine, witchcraft is of the belief that you are not only a direct connection to the divine and spirit but a reflection and an embodiment of it. You are of spirit, of the beating heart that comes from the center of the universe, of the unknowable darkness, of that which is awe-inspiring.

Yet spirit is also in you. We each have our own spirit or soul, or our own personal path that connects us to this cosmic energy. When I talk about spirit, I'm not only talking about this force that you can't truly comprehend, I'm also talking about the unyielding, undying, eternal part of your self that is of this nature. You feel this! If you've done the practices in this book, or really started on any sort of spiritual journey at all, then you know what I'm talking about, and you've probably already tapped into this expansive and numinous energy.

You can think of spirit connecting all the elements together when you think of a pentacle. A pentagram is an upright five-pointed star; the pentacle is this same star with a circle around it. The top point of the pentacle represents spirit; the other four points represent the other elements. Spirit encloses the pentagram, and in this way spirit unites earth, air, fire, and water. When you think spirit, think of prana, kundalini, love, of the energy of your spiritual practice, of the energy of the universe. This is what keeps the water moving, the fire burning. Spirit is the catalyst, the transformer, the emotions that take the elements from something you simply know of to something you connect with in your own life. Spirit provides you space and time to examine what you can learn from the natural world. Spirit is the language of nature.

Spirit as connection to the self

Working with spirit means recognizing that the divinity found in nature and around you is also reflected within you. Connection to spirit is connection to self. When you connect with your spirit, you connect with the highest and most evolved version of who you want to be; this is the *spirit* in *spirit*ual practice. This is your higher self! Spirit can speak loudly or subtly. Sometimes it feels like the breeze against your skin, sometimes it's as clear as someone whispering in your ear. Spirit speaks in a unique language to you: What makes you feel alive? What inspired you on this path anyway? It is spirit that guides you now, taking the shape of the elements and archetypes to bring you its messages.

Spirit as a connection to yourself means giving yourself permission to own every part of who you are. It means embodying all of your dimensions, and it means doing so with pride. Connection to spirit means owning your boundaries, your thoughts, your shadow, your anger, your sexuality. Connection to spirit means you recognize the responsibility of living a spiritual life, and it means accepting it. It means gratitude for the ability you have to heal, not only for yourself but for your family, for the future generations to come. Like air, spirit is intangible, but you feel it, and you need it to survive or you wouldn't be on this mystical path.

Spirit as intuition

One of the most valuable gifts of starting on any self-healing or spiritual journey is the ability you gain in listening to your intuition. Your intuition is that sudden flash of knowing, the gut feeling you get that manages to never guide you wrong. Intuition takes many different shapes and voices, but it usually lets you know when something is out of alignment, when something isn't right. Depending on mental health and factors like trauma, it can be really difficult to distinguish this gut feeling from the feeling of panic or anxiety. The only way to learn this distinction is to work with your intuition. Although your intuition can speak to you without prompting (like in moments where you just *know something*), your intuition is always there and always accessible whenever you need it.

Your intuition is your body's inner GPS, a radio communicator from your higher self that asks you to listen and respond accordingly. This is one way spirit communicates with you. Intuition is multidimensional and will evolve over time. All you can do is listen, and know that if it's telling you something, there's a reason.

You can learn this language by taking the time to ask your gut and intuition questions. Start with low-pressure situations in mundane settings for mundane things, like whether you should go get vegan or Thai food. Close your eyes and envision each option. See what feels right, what feels like an expansion, an opening. Whatever feels like a contraction or a closing is a no! Do this when you're driving, or when you're taking a walk. Let your intuition be your backseat driver sometimes. Ask your intuition for guidance and trust it. Keep doing this, even in moments where you may have stress or anxiety. Continue having this conversation with your gut so that when an intuitive hit comes up naturally, you can differentiate it from anxiety or recognize it as a messenger for what's going on in the present. Intuition is one of the gifts you get to fine-tune through magick, so paying attention to what your body is telling you during spells and rituals is another way to understand spirit's message.

Ways to connect with spirit

You can connect to spirit, source energy, the Goddess, and your higher self in endless ways. You can do this through dance, through spending time in nature, and by working with the elements. You may choose to use a specific element as a vehicle into spirit, choosing earth, air, fire, or water depending on how you want this connection to feel or what you want this experience to look like. Connection to spirit is intensely personal, as is all magick, and there isn't a "one size fits all" approach for what this feels like.

If you've worked with the practices in this book, you may use them to reflect on what is and isn't working. Maybe you know you love creating altars and practicing breath work and sex magick, but you struggle with shadow work. You may wish to use the practices that come more naturally to you (that correlate to air and fire) to help guide you deeper into where you feel resistance (the element of water). Working with spirit in this case may mean breath work and sex magick in the bathtub followed by some meditation outside the tub to work through this aversion, to see what your shadow is trying to tell you. You may also call on your higher self for wisdom or guidance.

Spirit urges you into new territories and terrains. This is the initiation, the path of the alchemist, mystic, and shaman. This is fire, exalted and of the gods, blessed and purified. Spirit is the energy of the Tower card in tarot, asking you to face growth and transformation head-on, even when you want to shy away, when it's too hard and scary and sharp. In this way, even the pain contains the medicine of this element. In occultism, this is the principle of polarity, which states that everything has poles, that everything is dual. But this duality is actually just two extremes of the same thing. Pain and pleasure are just two extremes along the same spectrum, as are love and hate, good and evil, and all the rest of whatever other polarities you witness.

To say you connect to spirit is missing the point in many ways. You are always connected to spirit. You are always experiencing karmic cycles of life, death, and rebirth. You are already going on the fool's journey. You are plugged into the energetic matrix of the cosmos whether you realize it or not. It's not so much that you connect to this energy but that you remember. You reconnect. You recharge. You return. Here are some more ways to connect to Spirit in case you need some inspiration:

» Spend time in nature, near a body of water on a sunny day if possible so you can connect to all the elements.

» Dance! Dance ecstatically, shaking and moaning and breathing. You can often get into a trance or altered state through dance, especially by spinning in circles and listening to drumming. Give your body permission to move without shame or judgment.

» Sing or chant. Sound is an incredible healer, and chanting mantras or singing can connect you to the universe as well as heal your energetic field. Hindu, Buddhist, and Tibetan mantras are all powerful ways to channel and connect with source energy.

» Pray. The old gods are bored! And missed! Really, though, prayer doesn't have to be stuffy, and it doesn't have to look a certain way. I love talking to the Goddess and spirit like my friends; I share and connect and sometimes I even beg. I tell them about my day, thank them, or ask for guidance and protection, or share, or let them know a message is received.

» Be receptive. If you want to connect to the subtle realm, acknowledge that. If you want to connect to spirit, expect it! Look out for it and when you receive it, say thank you! Acknowledging omens, messages, feelings, and vibes lets the universe know that you're aware, grateful, and receptive, which keeps the circuit flowing and leads to the next practice . . .

» Be grateful. Take time to connect to that which fills up your soul. Your body, the earth, the sun, your friends, your family, that book you love, music, whatever it is. Fostering a sense of gratitude is such potent magick that it is a direct line to the sustenance of spirit.

» Perform rituals. Hello! Magick is the gateway to the subconscious, to the realm of spirit. When you access these altered states and connect to these archetypes that have been charged for thousands and thousands of years, you're in the realm of the divine, of spirit, of the collective unconscious.

» Work with the tarot, energy healing, crystals, goddesses, and the elements. All of the practices in this book put the *spirit* in *spiritual.*

» Have sex or masturbate; spend time kissing. Romance and seduce yourself, or a lover, since spending time in pleasure will get you in an altered state of mind.

» Work with storms to embody different combinations of the elements. Storms are their own magick, and you can meditate and embody the energy of a storm when it's near you, or when you want to channel its power. Spend time in meditation as a storm approaches, making sure you're somewhere safe, as you breathe and draw this energy into your body. You can try this even in the absence of a storm, using lights, sounds, and videos to help channel this energy. Use this as a way to raise energy during ritual, or to understand the elements with more clarity. You can also meditate and call in an element like water through rain, asking the water spirits and elementals to help; this is a potent meditation if there's ever a wildfire nearby.

A pentagram meditation to embody the elements

As spirit embodies the qualities of each element, the pentagram is the physical and metaphysical map you can use to experience this. In this guided meditation you will be visualizing the pentagram, connecting to the element associated with each point and finishing at the top of the star at Spirit, where you'll visualize white light cleansing and aligning you with the highest vibration and energy possible, that of the cosmos, of source, of the divine.

Find a comfortable position lying down or sitting up, and take a moment to notice your breath. Inhale into any part of your body where you may feel tension, and as you exhale allow this tension to leave and dissipate. Once you feel in your body, visualize drawing the pentagram, starting at the top point. See this or feel this happening like a warm golden light that is both powerful and protective. Visualize tracing the pentagram from the top point (spirit, which you will close with) to the bottom right of the pentacle, the element of fire. Start to feel this warmth in your body. You may visualize the cool violet flames of Saint Germain that cleanse and clear away what's no longer serving you, and fortify what does. You may wish to feel warm lava moving through your body, or you may wish to feel the energy of sexual passion and lust. Breathe into what the element of fire means to you and notice how this feels in your body.

Once you feel ready, return to the visualization of the pentagram in front of you, seeing its golden shining light. Trace from the bottom right corner to the left middle, where you meet the element of air. Start to connect with this element, either through breath or by visualization. You may feel the edges of your body dissolve, as if your spirit were suddenly expanding, like the element itself. You may feel the air hit your face, the wind on your cheeks. Allow the feeling of presence and freedom and expansion to unfold in whatever way feels best.

Once you feel ready, return to the pentagram visualization, moving from air straight over to the right, to the element of water. Start to feel the element of water in your body. Maybe you visualize yourself at a body of water outside, or with your feet in the sand at the shore of the beach. Perhaps you feel the energy of love, of the flow of water throughout your body, like all your emotions are enveloping you as if you were in a warm bath. Take the time to connect with this element and breathe into what this feels like in your body, allowing whatever comes up to come up.

Once you feel ready, return to the visualization of the pentagram in front of you, seeing its golden shining light and moving from the middle right to the bottom left, the element of earth. Start to feel the element of earth, breathing into the ground beneath you. You may feel the element through a sense of stillness and deep peace, or through a rooted and grounded quality. Feel yourself melt into Gaia, connecting with her wisdom and stillness. Allow yourself to experience this strength, maybe feeling the energy of flowers blooming in your body, or a sense of warmth and blossoming.

Once you feel ready, return to visualizing the pentagram. You'll be moving from the bottom left point straight to the top, the realm of spirit. Start to breathe into the white light of the heavens above you, breathing into the space at the crown of your head. You may visualize or feel a vibrant, warm white light moving from the cosmos to the crown of your head, down and around your spine and body, through every part of you, connecting to the earth beneath you. Feel this white light healing you, allowing you to release what's no longer serving you. Give space to whatever spirit feels like or means to you, how it feels for you to connect with each of the elements' messages. Allow yourself to feel this space of divine presence and light and balance.

When you're ready, return to the golden pentagram in front of you. Feel each point vibrating with the love and intention you connected with when exploring the elements. When you feel like the meditation is complete, say thank you to the universe and visualize the pentagram dissolving and open your eyes. And so it is!

Ritual practice: scrying—seeing spirit through the elements

If spirit is intuition, then scrying is one of the ways you can tap into and call upon it. Spirit is the psychic sense that lives in you, and you can work with methods of divination to unlock it. You've already learned about some of the tarot cards, and now you'll be learning another ancient method of fortune-telling.

Scrying is the art of gazing at a surface for divinatory purposes. This is classically a crystal ball or a scrying mirror, but you can work with all of the elements to scry. Some experience visions while scrying; you may hear something or smell something or feel something, tapping into one of your *clair-* senses. Clairvoyance is when you see things, clairaudience is when you hear things, clairsentience is when you sense things, and claircognizance is when you know things. We all have the ability for all of these psychic gifts to be unlocked, but some of us come more tuned in with gifts than others. Like any other part of magick, this isn't good or bad, it just is! You have your own karma, your own gifts to pursue, and you can work with scrying to help you connect to your psychic gifts in a new way.

Scrying can help you go beneath the surface of a feeling, too. So if you're feeling particularly overwhelmed by one elemental energy, you may wish to scry with that element to see what may be under the surface or to see what this energy may wish to share with you at that time.

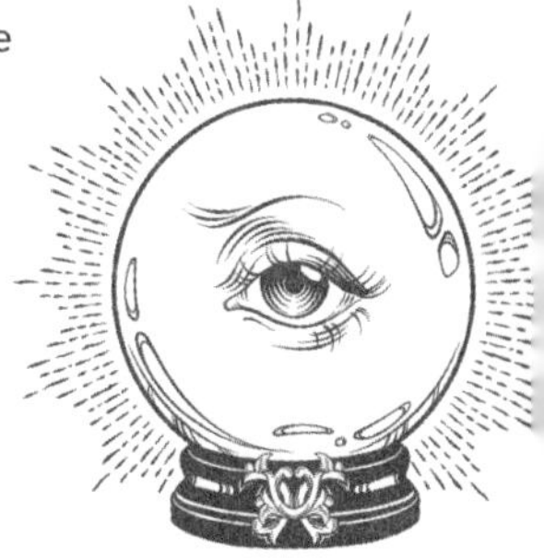

Before you begin: Scrying can be its own ritual, or it can be part of a larger ritual, like for the new moon or one of the witches' holidays like Samhain. Either way, you'll want to set up your space and get everything ready. You may wish to set a timer for five or ten minutes the first time you scry if you think that will help you be more present.

If you're scrying with earth, like a crystal ball or a black obsidian mirror, you'll want to charge these objects before you use them. You can charge these items during a full moon, and you may wish to charge these objects over multiple full moons before you use them for best effects.

EARTH

A crystal ball, a black obsidian mirror, concave black mirrors

Although many crystal balls are actually glass, this is still from the element of earth, and these orbs can still be scryed with, as can regular concave mirrors that have been painted black. The black obsidian scrying mirror is incredibly powerful but is not necessary in the ability to scry. You may wish to light a white candle and place it near your crystal ball or mirror before you begin.

How to: Ground and come back to your body, finding presence as you start to inhale and exhale effortlessly, feeling the grounded element of earth melt into your energy field. When you're ready, start to gaze at the mirror or the crystal ball. As you do so, do your best to clear your mind of all thoughts, worries, and anxieties, feeling all of them leave with each exhale. Visualize your third eye opening as you ask the universe and the element of earth to allow you to receive messages meant for your highest good at this moment. Gaze at the surface of your crystal ball or mirror, making sure to blink as you continue gazing into its surface. Breathe and notice if anything comes up, whether it's a taste, smell, feeling, color, vision, or voice. Stay here as long as you need to, and when you're done make sure to record your experience.

AIR

Smoke

To some, smoke scrying may seem difficult because smoke moves and expands, carrying the eye with it. This also may be why it's easier to go in a meditative state, allowing the gaze to trace where the smoke dances. You may wish to burn incense, herbs, or resin based on what you're feeling and what your ritual is, working with correspondences like scents and herbs to help you further connect to the smoke. Having a solid background while you smoke scry will also make the exercise easier.

How to: Ground and come back to your body, finding presence as you start to inhale and exhale effortlessly, feeling oxygen swirling through your lungs as you breathe into the element of air. Exhale any thoughts, worries, and anxieties, feeling all of them empty out of your lungs with each exhale. When you're ready, light the herbs or incense and start to gaze at the smoke, visualizing your third eye opening. You may ask to receive visions and messages from the universe at this time as well. Allow your eyes to do what feels best, whether that's staying in one spot or tracing the way the smoke dances. Breathe and notice if anything comes up, whether it's a taste, smell, feeling, color, vision, or voice. Stay here as long as you need to, and when you're done make sure to record your experience.

FIRE

Candles, a fireplace or fire pit, paper

Fire seems to captivate unlike any other element, begging us to watch the way the flames lick and leap. You can scry with fire to connect to your passion, sexuality, desires, and confidence. You can scry with candles, at a fireplace or fire pit, or with paper you've used for spell work and are now burning.

How to: Make sure you have a safe and contained space for your fire. Start to breathe, coming back into your body and present as you start to visualize and connect with fire. Start to feel a warmth in your belly as you inhale and as you exhale, releasing any worries, anxiety, and tension. Visualize your third eye opening as you take a second to connect with the universe and the element of fire, asking to receive any messages meant for you at this time. Light your flame and find a comfortable gaze, making sure to blink, as you let the fire bring you into a trance, allowing yourself to merge into this enchanting element. Breathe and notice if anything comes up, whether it's a taste, smell, feeling, color, vision, or voice. Stay here as long as you need to, and when you're done make sure to record your experience.

WATER

A bowl of water (holy water or moon water can work), the ocean, a natural body of water outside, a bath or pool

Technically, there's nothing stopping you from scrying the next time you're at your best friend's pool or when you're in the bath. You can scry with whatever form of water you want, including water you've blessed (see pages 210–13). A bowl of water placed against a dark surface and a candle works well too, as do oceans and natural bodies of water.

How to: Start to connect to your breath as you come back into your body. Start to feel the fluid and emotional energy of water in your body as you connect to the element. Visualize your third eye opening as you take a second to connect with the universe and the element of water, asking to receive any messages meant for you at this time. Then start to gaze at whatever surface you're scrying with, feeling the water blend into your soul. Breathe and notice if anything comes up, whether it's a taste, smell, feeling, color, vision, or voice. Stay here as long as you need to, and when you're done make sure to record your experience.

Spirit in tarot

The spirit in tarot is represented through the major arcana, the twenty-two cards that tell the story of the Fool's journey. This is

the story of the individual evolution of the soul, of individualization and of the spiritual journey that you go through that connects you with the collective unconscious. In the tarot's major arcana, you witness the journey of the spirit, of what it means to grow and learn and evolve and die.

You see the Fool take the risk and start the voyage, finding the courage to do it even if it's scary, sprinkling it all with a bit of naïveté. The Fool learns and evolves their skills as the Magician, who uses each suit of the tarot, reminding you that you are master manifestor. You can consciously work with the elements and the tools you have to create whatever life you want. You enter more deeply into this realm of the magick through the High Priestess, where you're led into the subconscious, where you learn to balance the receptive and active parts of yourself, symbolized by the Empress and Emperor and the Lovers. This starts the process of self-actualization, where you start reclaiming your power, driving your own Chariot, eventually seeking out inner wisdom through the Hermit. Soon enough though you realize you are only in control of your own world, that the "as above" really doesn't belong to you. The Hanged Man speaks to us of dissolving this idea of individuality for the sake of connecting to spirit, of dissolving the ego, or the self, and preparing for Death, which is actually a door for transformation. This door just happens to open to the Tower, which is near crumbling to the ground. But what you don't see is that the Tower falling leads to a solid foundation, a new sense of clarity and grounding, directly followed by the Star and its celestial siblings, omens of strength and intuitive wisdom and fate. You are not just you, you are a part of the spirit, of the universe, of the All. Judgment is the flag of karma, letting you know you're ready for what's next as you approach the World, the celestial prophecy that lets you know you've reached the end of the cycle. Now you must start again, the same journey, but as the Magician, going through the cycles with all the knowledge of having done it before.

Since I don't have space to talk about all of the major arcana cards, I decided to share a few key cards that relate to each of the elements, as well as a couple of cards that connect to spirit in its fullest duality. If you feel called to study and explore tarot further, you should follow the calling. You can use the further reading list at the end of this book for more suggestions as well.

EARTH: THE EMPRESS AND THE EMPEROR

The earth in its richest, most abundant form is full of life. It is constantly dying on one level and birthing and blooming on another. The energy of earth is that of compassionate nurturing, of care and safety. You find this in its purest, most distilled state through the rule of the Empress. The Empress is Mother Earth personified, the womb from which all life springs. You don't have to gender this card to understand its message of growth, birth, commitment to oneself, and long-term pleasure. This is the energy of balance, of receptivity and action that allows life to grow. This is the energy of spirit, of spring, of loyalty. The Empress is the water that flows through the fields, allowing the crops to grow and bloom. Her consort is the following card in the deck, the Emperor, who is the riverbank that allows the river to flow, the boundaries that allow the Empress to grow and thrive. The Emperor is the structure to the Empress's intuition, both of which are necessary to feel safe and loved, and also fulfilled and validated. You can't just rely on your knowledge or just rely on your intuition. You need both to build a solid foundation that serves your evolution in all facets.

These cards teach you balance, knowing when to listen to your gut or to your brain. It's the structures you have that support you and it's the balance of the feminine or masculine qualities you see in yourself, since regardless of your gender expression, you have both energetically within you. The Emperor and Empress are duality expressed—they are the extremes of the same spectrum. Through them you can embody what it means to be both active and receptive, flexible and rooted. They teach you of intuition and knowledge, and you can work with them for guidance and to find a sense of structure and support in your life.

How to: Meditate on both cards, or spend time noticing them and taking them in. Then make a list of all the qualities in yourself that are more Emperor oriented—all those that are more action oriented, more structured, more masculine. Now make a list of all the qualities in yourself that are more Empress oriented—all those that are more feeling, more receptive, more feminine. Compare the two and see what you could use more or less of; this will help you figure out where you need balance and support for your foundation, or earth.

AIR: THE HIGH PRIESTESS

Although multiple cards correspond strongly to certain elements (each card also has its own astrological associations), I feel called to share the High Priestess as the card for air. Air is the suit of the mind and of intellect. It is both how you think and what you think, ruling over all pursuits of the mind. It's also the element of freedom and growth, of the ethereal, and of course the unseen. This mystic, etheric, energetic, expansive realm is that of the High Priestess. And there's plenty she wants you to know.

The High Priestess is a card of the occult, of magick, of secrecy. She is the hidden wisdom, the secret teachings, that which has been kept alive by being passed from mouth to ear, to keep things sub rosa, or "beneath the rose" (or surface). The High Priestess is a reminder of your own magick, of your own ability to express and banish and invoke. She is the ritual, the energy, the action, the intention. She is every part of the spell. Like air, she cannot be tied down. Like air, she transcends. The High Priestess guards the veil, so only those she deems worthy can slip behind it. The High Priestess speaks of air in its exalted state, of its ability to pierce as the sword does, dissecting and cutting. The High Priestess, like air, is the truth. The High Priestess is the old Snake Goddess of Crete, of the mysteries, of the cycles, of the shedding and rebirth that comes with life. She, like air, can never be boxed in. To experience her is to know her; calling on the High Priestess will help you get into your own power like nearly anything else.

How to: Create an altar dedicated to this card and to your inner priestess. Reading tarot, studying divination, practicing ritual, and learning about a new magickal path are all ways to connect with her as well. Smoking or burning sacred herbs like cannabis, chamomile, damiana, and lavender is also a portal for both this card and the element of air.

FIRE: STRENGTH

The image on the Strength card is an inspiring one: a woman holds open the jaws of a lion, a serene smile on her face as the infinity sign floats above her head. Like the element of fire itself, this card is one of confidence and a deep-seated resolve. Fire isn't shy, nor does it apologize for what it is. This card reminds you that this inner strength exists within you always, just as the infinity sign reminds you of this, floating above her head like a crown. Fire speaks of your desires, but it also speaks of anger and ego. It tells you of that which hurts so bad, that absolutely almost kills you, yet somehow you manage to pull through and be stronger because of it.

Strength is an omen of comfort because it reminds you of your inner reserves, but it's not a comfortable card. This indicates change, leveling up, evolution; this is the fortification that comes from the descent into the underworld and the renewal that comes from the return. Strength, like fire, speaks of rebirth.

When you work with this card, you work on releasing old fears. You're stuck with old stories and narratives that look like the scariest lion you've ever seen. You feel too weak, too small, unable to cope with the massiveness of it. But then you remember who the hell you are. Like fire, you recognize your ability to surrender what no longer serves you while feeding what does. The Strength card reminds you that the lion really doesn't have sharp teeth and that you're much tougher than you seem. If you face your ego and your fears even when you're scared, you will pass through the alchemical fire and rise through the ashes like the phoenix you are.

How to: Make a list of all the times you've ever been proud of yourself for being strong. Carve the alchemical symbol for fire (a triangle) on a red candle, alongside your name. Place the strength card on the altar with your candle. Light the candle and read off your list of things you're proud of. Let the candle burn all the way down. Hang up this list for a month and read it to yourself whenever you need to be reminded of how capable you are.

WATER: THE MOON

Through the Moon you engage with the subtle. Singing over the subconscious, the intuitive, the mysterious and foggy, this is a card of what you feel. The card for psychic water sign Pisces, the Moon is the celestial body that rules over the ocean and her tides, tying it directly to the element of water, of your own internal world of moodiness and the metaphysical.

Through the stillness, through the clear reflection of the ocean against a midnight sky, through the portal of the Moon's light, you find a path back into yourself, your truth. This card is one of intensity, even amid the calm. Although the moon is the more passive energy to the sun's action, it is still one of earnest depth. The element of water allows you freedom and flow, and it guides you back into your fullest emotional expression. So too, does this card.

The Moon is the path that the High Priestess walks. It is here that the Priestess practices her magick. Through the Moon you get to witness all of your dimensions, all of your feelings, all of your shadows and wounds. The Moon's light illuminates, allows you to process and witness this. It gives space to the whole array of experiences you emote and project and internalize. Through this card and through water, you can heal and work through the trauma, and see where the healing and trauma are in the first place.

This card also reminds you of creativity, of your own inner hierophant and priestess. This is the magick that you know, that you feel. It is your inner connection to spirit, to source, to the god/dess. This can also, however, be a card of nightmares, of pitch-black darkness, of the veil of confusion hanging in front of your eyes like the new moon. But the moon is never in one phase for long, and if you accept that the pendulum will swing the other way soon, toward mystical illumination, then the spiral path isn't so scary.

How to: Meditate or "moon-bathe" by spending time under the full moon. Make a full moon altar. Use moon water in a bath to further soak up the moon's energies. Add rose petals, lavender, white and silver candles, and Epsom salt for a healing self-love lunar bath.

SPIRIT IN THE STRUGGLE: THE TOWER

Spirit doesn't exist in a low or high vibration because it just is. The way in which we humans, with limited senses and capabilities, experience spirit is what's low or high vibration. But in this life we struggle. There are moments when you feel like the rug is being ripped out from under you, when things feel heavy and grief hangs in the air. These are the shadows, the ocean crevices so deep the light can't hit. This is what the Tower can feel like.

This card is that of endings and transformation to the *n*th degree. This is the energy of foundational structures in your life, or relationships or work or beliefs, breaking down and crumbling. This is endings, chaos, revolution. This is uncomfortable, but in this card is one of the most potent messages of spirit and the tarot: things must end to begin.

When you see the Tower, you see something breaking, something ending, structural damage that has to be fixed at the foundation. That which isn't serving you is clearing away, being leveled so you can rebuild from the ground up, with safety and sturdiness and a base that's actually going to allow you to grow.

Sometimes spirit takes the form of a cleanup crew; after the bad thing ends or something happens, you get to the other side and see just how much better it is or how much you learned. Sometimes you have to break it to fix it. Sometimes you just don't know that yet.

How to: To work with the energy of the Tower, work with the idea of surrender. Of letting go. Of allowing what needs to be done to be done. Give yourself space to process and give yourself permission to make mistakes. Take it one day at a time as you remind yourself you'll come out the other side. Create an altar for new beginnings with white flowers and white candles and a white altar cloth. Choose to experience your experience.

AT OUR MOST ALIGNED AND CONNECTED WITH SPIRIT: THE MAGICIAN

The Magician stands with their feet planted, one hand pointed to the heavens above, one to the earth below. Before them are the four suits of the tarot: the pentacle, cup, sword, and wand. Above their head is the infinity sign. The Magician is a culmination of the elements' power, the strength of all the suits of the tarot intensified by the energy of the major arcana. This is a card of the balance of earth, air, fire, and water that creates the environment necessary for growth and rebirth. It is the Magician's magick that speaks of spirit, the last piece of the pentacle.

The Magician is also the occultist, the one who studies the subtle, who refines the energetic realm and causes shifts to happen on the physical. This is someone who knows that this life is a reflection of the cosmos and heavens above. As above, so below. As within, so without. This card reminds you of your own strength and ability to create, banish, rebirth, destroy, and love. This card speaks to your array of experiences as a spiritual being experiencing human things. It is the card of your unyielding connection, reflection, and channel to spirit.

It's irrational to expect yourself to be balanced all the time; in fact, that would probably kill you! You need to constantly be finding balance in whatever situation you're in, depending on how you're feeling, what will keep you safe, and what you need. You still go through the shit, no matter how magickal you are. But the Magician tells you that all the tools, all the lessons of the elements, are right there on the altar beside you. They're yours for the taking. Regardless of when you use these allies, they're there for you, as is spirit—the insight and intuition to know when and what to connect to.

How to: You can embody the energy of the Magician by working with the elements, by cultivating and caring for an altar, by working in rituals that ask you to transcend and go deep. You can work with this archetype by *being it*. You are already on this path; allow your curiosities and whatever language that speaks to guide you. The tarot, crystals, the elements, ritual, astrology, goddess worship, glamour, journaling—these are all ways for you to become the Magician.

A TAROT SPREAD FOR GUIDANCE FROM EACH OF THE ELEMENTS

The tarot is the perfect pathway to learning about the elements because each of the suits can help you relate earth, air, fire, and water to your own human experience. You can be guided through your own journey by seeing your reflection in the tarot and by carrying this wisdom throughout your life.

One of my favorite spreads uses the pentacle and the elements to help you examine where you're feeling supported, where you're feeling safe and fulfilled, and where you need to step it up or ask for help. By now, you've learned about the lessons, language, and messages of each of the elements. This spread will help you take this deeper, and when read with intention and presence, it can help guide you into the energy of spirit, of connection and balance between nature and all her children.

What are you craving to learn from Earth? Air? Fire? Water? Spirit? Let this spread help you experience this wisdom in a new way. Journal anything that comes up, and invite the elements into your space before you begin. Light some candles; light some incense or herbs; fill a chalice with some wine, moon or holy water, or another offering; grab your cards; and take some deep breaths to connect to your body. Call to the elements if this feels right, and ask for their guidance and compassion. Whenever you're ready, shuffle the cards and let the path unwind for you as it will.

Card 1: *Spirit—Where am I being asked to witness the abundance and miracles in my life?*
Card 2: *Water—What are my emotions trying to tell me right now?*
Card 3: *Fire—What is keeping me fueled and passionate?*
Card 4: *Earth—Where am I supported and safe?*
Card 5: *Air—Where am I able to be my fullest self, to be present?*
Card 6: *Where am I living in alignment?*
Card 7: *Where am I being called to live more in alignment?*
Card 8: *What element can I call more into my life to help me find balance?*
Card 9: *What wisdom should I carry with me moving forward?*

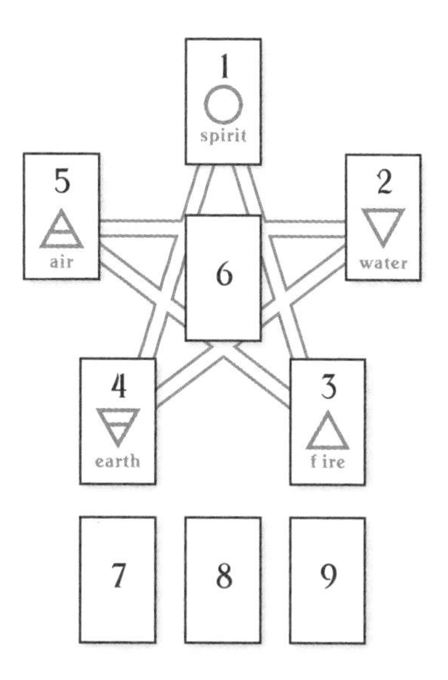

An elemental blessing ritual for protecting and cleansing a space

The elements speak of balance, of what you need to find grounding, to do more than just survive, but to thrive, to be abundant. Through the elements you can transform a space into a home, inviting in the spirit of earth, air, fire, and water to help you charge your new space. And when your own spirit is nurtured, when you feel safe enough in your home to let your glamour down, then spirit comes into the mix. You are the connection between the elements, though you can also see your home as spirit itself as well. Regardless, adapt this ritual as you see appropriate!

This is a great ritual to do during the new or waxing moon, but it can be performed whenever your space is begging for some energetic maintenance. I love to do a space cleansing like this on Sundays after I clean my room and bathroom.

This ritual works with holy water, candle magick, visualization, intention, and some crystal work to help you cultivate a relationship with the elements in your home.

You'll need: a bowl of water, salt, a white candle and candleholder, matches or a lighter, honey (to dress the candle), herbs like mugwort or lavender or sweetgrass, or resins like copal or frankincense.

Optional: herbs to dress the candle (check the correspondences on page 89), an athame, angelite.

Angelite is a light blue stone that can help you access insight, wisdom, and messages from angelic beings, spirit guides, and the universe. This stone inspires a sense of compassion and can help you find surrender and acceptance as you continue evolving along your spiritual path. This stone can help you feel the subtle messages, downloads, and intuitive hints the universe is sharing with you and can be worked with in this ritual as a way to help you tap into your own psychic gifts with patience and love.

STEP 1: GATHER SUPPLIES

Gather your supplies and take some time to read through the ritual, noting anything that doesn't feel right and adapting as necessary. You can also write this in your grimoire and use that if you don't want to carry around this book. Then set up your space, following the instructions on page 15.

STEP 2: GROUND

It doesn't matter where you start your ritual as long as you're near your supplies. You'll be walking around your space, but you want to begin near your bowl of water. Once you're set, close your eyes and start to breathe. You can ground in any way you wish: breathing in white, healing light from the cosmos above you, visualizing it moving through the crown of your head, down your spine, all the way into the earth. This white healing light cleanses you of any worries, of any energies that aren't working 100 percent in your highest favor. Feel this warm, cleansing, bright energy moving through all the energetic meridians of your body.

STEP 3: INVITE IN THE ELEMENTS AND LIGHT THE CANDLE

Once grounded, you're going to invite in the elements for their blessing and protection. You may also invite in any spirit guides, angelic beings, deities, ancestors, or ascended masters and beings who work in 100 percent light to this ritual as well. If you're inviting in the elements, you can say something like the following as you invite them:

Element of earth (tracing the alchemical symbol for earth)
Element of air (tracing the alchemical symbol for air)
Element of fire (tracing the alchemical symbol for fire)
Element of water (tracing the alchemical symbol for water)

> *May you cleanse, consecrate, and bless this space, in your fullest embodiment and most exalted state. I trust in the god/goddess/spirit/universe, in the spirit and myself, and from this space I banish any energy that doesn't serve me well.*

STEP 3: BLESS WITH HOLY WATER

Take your bowl of water and add three pinches of salt to it, representing the merging of earth and water. Use your finger or an athame to stir it clockwise, or deosil, in increments of three. As you do this, visualizing the white light moving from the cosmos through your body and out of your hands. Once you're done mixing, hold your palms over the water, visualizing this healing white light moving into the water, removing any energetic impurities, and instilling it with love and healing.

Once you feel the water is charged, take it with you and sprinkle it at each corner of the front entrance of your space. Then move clockwise around your space, sprinkling the holy water in all the corners of the room. Once you've done this, set the water down with all your supplies.

STEP 4: BURN THE SACRED SMOKE

Now take your sacred herbs and light them so their smoke dances and expands. Start at the front entrance of your space and move clockwise once again, fanning the smoke into all the corners and around the perimeter of your space as you continue connecting to your breath and the healing light of the universe.

STEP 5: VISUALIZE, SET THE INTENTION, AND LIGHT THE CANDLE

Go to where all your supplies are, set the herbs down, and grab your candle. If you want to work with angelite, now is the time to charge it. Hold your candle in your hands as you send the energy of the cosmos from above you through your arms, hands, and palms into the candle. Take a second to set an intention for your space: how safe you want it to be, or how you want it to feel, or what sort of relationship you want it to nurture. You may hold your angelite in your hand as you charge it with your intention, visualizing this stone absorbing your incantation. Then you may wish to say something like the following:

Earth, air, fire, water, I call on your fullest power.
I am the spirit that weaves the thread, and through the elements I have cleansed and blessed.
This space is protected on all planes and in all ways.

Now rub the honey on the candle, from the middle to the ends (to banish any negative energy). Then light the candle as you connect to earth, feeling its energy beneath you through your feet and in your body. Connect to air as you feel your breath moving in you, anchoring you in the present. Then connect to fire as you feel the flames surround and embody you with fierce protection. And finally, feel water move its way into you after this, supporting you emotionally with a sense of peace in your newly cleansed space.

STEP 6: CLOSE THE RITUAL

Once the candle is dedicated, move back to your front door. Draw the banishing pentagram (a pentagram starting and ending in the left bottom corner) and as you do so, visualize a golden version of the pentacle left behind. You can also imagine white light from above acting like an energetic shield or waterfall of protection at your front door.

When you're finished, say something like the following:

In the name of the elements, in the name of (my highest self, the cosmos, the Goddess), it is done. This is a sacred space consecrated in the name of the highest good of all involved. And so it is.

When you're done, take a second to breathe back into your body. You may wish to visualize the white light from the cosmos moving up your spine back into the sky above you. You may also press your forehead into the earth in child's pose, exhaling any excess energy into the earth through your third eye.

Place your angelite near your front door or on an altar in your home for further protection and guidance from angelic beings.

Tips: Save your holy water in a jar for cleansing your space, and leave it out under a full moon to really charge it. Leave your candle to burn all the way, leaving it in a sink or bowl of water when you're gone. If you have to put it out, fan or snuff it out—don't blow it out! Then relight it each day, connecting to your intention and the elements as you do. If there's excess wax, throw it out in a garbage can at an intersection.

Crystals to connect with the element of spirit

Crystals are portals to the realm of the earth, and they're also a portal to the realm of spirit. Spirit is the oxygen floating around you, the connective tissue, the nebulous, and it is also the healing, the shift, the magick that allows you to collaborate with the crystal kingdom. Although the stones themselves are connected to spirit, it is the stones' affects and their ability to shift things that are *of* spirit. The way a stone helps you cross the bridge to a trance, or shows you insight you didn't see before, or acts as a talisman of strength, guiding you with compassion: these are all the languages of spirit.

However, certain stones are more attuned to the high vibrational energy that we perceive as this element. Clear stones like quartz and selenite are also effective and powerful conduits for spirit and have the advantage of being especially easy to program with intention or desires. Other stones like charoite, turquoise, and labradorite can help you attune to the highest vibration you can and also protect and ground your energy while you do it.

TO EMBODY SPIRIT: CHAROITE

A rich and opaque purple hue, charoite is an incredibly psychic stone that allows you to tap into and experience energies in new ways. By allowing you amped-up access to your intuition and your third eye and crown chakras, you're able to receive divine guidance in the form of downloads, synchronicities, and messages. Charoite helps clear the path for this to happen while acting with a gentle and compassionate strength that guides you deeper into your own wisdom and truth. Charoite's calming and elevated presence is both soothing and encouraging, making it a great holistic and spiritual healer.

Charoite can serve as a catalyst for embracing your subtle and perceptive powers more. It can also help you awaken to your own inner knowing so you can stop relying on other people for validation or direction. Instead, this stone allows you to see the mirror of your own truth with more clarity. This stone can also help you release old fears and wounds that are playing out as patterns over and over again, aiding in your karmic evolution. Place this on your third eye when meditating to help stimulate this chakra and to connect with your psychic senses and intuition.

TO HEAL WITH SPIRIT: TURQUOISE

A stone of balance and harmony, turquoise is said to unite the earth and sky, the masculine and feminine parts of yourself. Often worn as an amulet of protection, turquoise is a rich blue stone that helps to shield the auric body, protecting you from any energetic pollution, while also helping to align and balance your chakra system. This is an uplifting stone, with specific connection to the higher chakras, that allows you to claim your fate by accessing your intuition, clearing away old beliefs and inhibitions, and recognizing what karmic cycles need to end. Turquoise transcends realms, offering you guidance through other worlds while also offering up protection and keeping you from harm. This stone is also great for abundance, helping you feel safe in all ways. Place this stone on your third eye while meditating to gain deeper awareness of your intuition and any psychic messages. Place it on your throat to help you shed old beliefs and patterns, and wear it or keep it on you for protection physically and energetically.

TO GROUND AND PROTECT WITH SPIRIT: LABRADORITE

Associated with all of the chakras, labradorite is a powerful protector and ally for any witch, magician, or occultist. This iridescent stone comes in shades of blue, green, yellow, and purple and is mesmerizing to gaze at, shining pearlescent. A true stone of spirit, labradorite also helps your intuitive gifts, fostering synchronicities and messages from the universe that you're able to dissect and understand. Labradorite helps to balance the physical and etheric bodies, helping you access universal wisdom or messages from dreams. This is an incredibly useful tool for ritual and magick, for dream work, and for connection to the subconscious.

This stone also helps shield and protect the aura, while also helping to balance all of the chakras. Like an energetic detox, this stone also helps you shed what you don't need while helping to stop energy leakages from happening. This stone has a strong, gentle, and grounding quality to it that can help you dissolve what's keeping you from reaching the next stage in your evolution. To work with this crystal, try meditating with it in your nondominant hand or along any chakra that needs it when you're lying down. You can also have this stone on your desk while you work for inspiration and presence, or on your nightstand to help remember your dreams for dream work.

Inviting in the Goddess: the divine feminine as spirit

You've probably recognized that the Goddess speaks in many languages. She speaks to you in subtle tongues that send shivers of recognition up your spine. It is the ancient language of the wind hitting the leaves of the trees. The Goddess speaks to us in dreams, in visions, in poetry. She is the lightning bolt and the destruction left behind. The Goddess, no matter what her name is, what element rules her, or who worships her, is bigger than it all. There is no goddess for spirit, because the Goddess *is* spirit.

In Hinduism, the energy and principle of the divine feminine is known as Shakti, the Mother Goddess, whose name means "power" or "energy." She is the dynamic force that also resides at the base of your spine—Kundalini. It is she who birthed other Hindu goddesses like Kali, Parvati, and Durga, and since Shakti is the energy of life energy, it is said that even gods have Shakti, or Shakti energy.

Shakti is everywhere. Life force is everywhere. The Goddess is everywhere. What do you remember? Your own divinity. How do you call this back in? Through magick, devotion, and claiming your power.

Honoring spirit, the Great Goddess

There are infinite expressions of the divine feminine, of the Goddess, of spirit. You could go your whole life and never dedicate yourself to one deity, or you could spend your entire life dedicated to a particular goddess, and one doesn't make you a more valuable feminist or goddess worshipper or witch. There's never been and never will be one "right" way to worship, and at this point in the toxic patriarchy, we need as many goddess worshippers as possible.

However, you may not feel called to worship a particular goddess. Maybe you feel more connected to the energy of the divine feminine when she doesn't have a face. Perhaps you worship her through the cycles of the moon, or as the Great Goddess who dies and is reborn as we go through the Wheel of the Year. While I lay out rituals and meditations for you to connect with different facets of this divinity, what matters most is your connection, what speaks to you, whatever magick you feel like bringing to the table. What matters is whatever language you find yourself and the divine both fluent in.

You can connect to the Goddess through the elements, using these aspects of the natural world to create faces for her. Maybe instead of worshipping Venus, you worship bodies of water. Instead of Gaia, you worship the mountains that surround your family home. Instead of Kali, you worship the sun, and instead of Nut you worship the sky and wind. Goddess worship is worship of the natural world, of the earth in all her fullest glory. It doesn't matter if you don't call her name as long as you feel it.

If you don't want to devote yourself to a specific goddess, and perhaps instead want to work with an all-encompassing energy like Shakti or spirit or the moon, you can still work with individual goddesses through meditation and specific spells and rituals. You can also create an all-white altar to Shakti or the moon, complete with perfumed candles and blooming white roses. Or you can dedicate an altar to all the goddesses and goddess energy you have in your life.

Goddess energy isn't only cultivated by goddesses; as all of us are reflections of this divine nature, you can also honor people who have the qualities that you admire and want to foster in yourself, including ancestors, deities, and pop stars alike. There's nothing and no one stopping you from putting photos of your mom or Lana Del Rey or Ruth Bader Ginsburg on your goddess altar. If you admire qualities in a person, it is important to remember that these are just people, that they may not live up to your standards or be who you expect them to be. But you can still find your inner goddess by following the spark and the light these people shared with you.

Working with a Matron Goddess

Even among celestial beings, drama is drama. Each deity comes with their own baggage, their own point of view, their own voice. When you work with goddesses, you're seeing spirit in a container; you're seeing one manifestation out of endless ones. This means you're seeing one side to something that has an infinite number of sides. The truth is that gods and goddesses come with their own agendas. The celestial and divine beings that are Venus and Nut and

Kali and Gaia come with their own intention. Kali and other dark goddesses like Hecate, Lilith, Babalon, and the Morrigan who dwell in the realm of death and transformation and decay can ask a lot of us, sometimes in a scary way. Yet these goddesses hold potent wisdom and can help you face your fears and demons head on. I love working with dark goddesses and have had some of my most transformative and potent experiences in this realm. If you decide to approach or are approached by a dark goddess, you can ask to connect with them with compassion and with love. Cast a circle if you feel like it would help you feel more comfortable; talk to the goddess of your worries. But know that if you're entering the sphere of this potent feminine wisdom, you're surrendering to the Goddess. And sometimes the Goddess can be that bitch, and do something you think is unfair, something that hurt you in the moment. Yet, in one way or another, these manifestations of divinity teach a lesson, helping you on your path of unfolding karma, and that's why you come back.

When you work with a goddess, you're getting spirit distilled into whatever this goddess rules over. Venus is the distillation of love, as Kali is the distillation of transformation. These archetypes are specific aspects of the divine. You can work with different goddesses at different points of your life, connecting to archetypes that embody the cycles and experiences you're going through. Whether you need healing, transformation, abundance, love, to grieve, to create, or whatever else, there's a goddess for that.

A Matron Goddess is a goddess you dedicate yourself to, one that you mainly work with and are devoted to. Personally, I am a devotee of Venus, although I also work with other goddesses, including Kali and Hecate, the Goddess of the Witches. I have a daily meditation practice that includes a devotional aspect to Venus, and I also create art for and inspired by her. I meditate and perform rituals dedicated to her, I invoke her, and I see myself as a reflection of her. Each person's relationship to a Matron Goddess (or Patron

God, which is the same relationship with a god) will be unique and a reflection of that person's own unfolding and evolution.

FINDING YOUR MATRON GODDESS

It is said that the Goddess shows herself, that she chooses the witch, and this is true. Very often the Goddess will come to you. But for many, myself included, the invitation has to be sent. The ritual has to be performed. If you're looking to open the portal to the divine, here are some ways you can do that:

» Create an altar to the Goddess and make space for her in your life by connecting with and talking to her regularly.

» Leave offerings and share words of gratitude with her.

» Create art and poetry in dedication of the goddess, as a way of affirming your relationship with her.

» Write a letter or petition asking to meet and connect with the Goddess, place it under your pillow, and ask for her to connect with you in your dreams.

» Charge an angelite or clear quartz crystal with this intention and meditate with it.

» Meditate and ask the Goddess to reveal her face to you, spending time in nature, ritual, or ceremony to help foster this.

» Create a ritual in which you tell the Goddess your intention, reaffirming the connection you're looking to create.

» Research different goddesses and see who speaks to you, who makes you feel something.

» Look into your own ancestry and family to see what goddesses were honored and see if one speaks to you.

Creating a devotional practice

You devote yourself to things you care about: your work, your relationships, your health. And you can also devote yourself to a relationship with the cosmic. You can take the time to think of the Goddess like a friend you want to keep a healthy relationship with. What do you do to nurture bonds? You spend time together, you reaffirm, you listen, you hold reverence for it. Through working with the Goddess, you ask how you can dedicate energy into honoring the divine outside (and inside) yourself.

My suggestion for any devotional or ritual practice is to start small and then build. In the next chapter you'll be connecting all the elements and spirit with a guide that will help you create your own ritual practice. Working with the Goddess can be a part of this, evolving naturally with a devotional practice.

Regardless of your daily rituals, my suggestion for creating a consistent, solid, and loving relationship with the Goddess is to pick one thing you can absolutely commit to every day (or more days than not), and commit to it!

Some examples of devotional rituals to the Goddess that can be practiced daily include the following:

» Lighting an anointed and dedicated candle

» Burning sacred herbs

- Meditation on connecting with the Goddess
- Working with crystals dedicated to the Goddess
- Leaving offerings
- Masturbation or sex magick
- Chanting or meditating with prayer beads
- Saying a prayer
- Creating art like music, writing, painting, photography
- Interpreting your dreams
- Wearing a ritually charged talisman
- Free writing or journaling
- Repeating affirmations or mantras
- Dancing, stretching, movement

A ritual for drawing down the Goddess

This rite can be performed on its own, during another ritual to invoke the Goddess, or to draw down the energy of the moon. You may invoke specific goddesses through this method, or choose to work with the divine feminine in her fullest expression. Through this ritual, you will be inviting goddess energy into your body through your crown chakra and working with an offering and the sacred symbol of the chalice to tap into this wisdom.

You may wish to invoke the Goddess for many reasons: as a part of a devotional ritual dedicated to her, to further connect and receive messages, as a part of a working for sex magick (solo or partnered), or to further find guidance for your own path of magick.

You'll need: a chalice, an offering of wine, blessed water, or juice in it (but don't fill it too much because you're going to be holding it).

BEFORE YOU BEGIN: GROUND/SET THE RITUAL

If you're doing this as its own ritual, you'll want to make sure to set the space, cast a circle, and go through a grounding technique or do some breath work and visualization. If you're doing this as part of a ritual, then make sure you have your chalice and an offering of wine or juice on the altar.

STEP 1: BREATHE AND CONNECT WITH THE CHALICE

Grab the chalice full of an offering of wine, holy water, or juice in both hands and hold it near your heart center. Start breathing white light into the crown of your head, down your spine, through your arms and palms, and into the cup. Start connecting with goddess energy already, feeling this healing light illuminating the offering and chalice.

STEP 2: STAND IN THE POSITION OF THE GODDESS

If you can, stand with your legs shoulder distance apart while holding the chalice carefully in one hand. You're going to be making a snow angel with your arms, only from the bottom of the wings to the top.

Starting with your arms straight, hands down near your hips and palms out, feel your chest expand and your shoulders move down your back. Rest in this power.

Then move your arms up, elbows straight, being careful to not spill the contents of the chalice, so your body forms a star with your elbows near your ears. Stand here as you continue connecting with the energy of the Goddess, infusing the chalice in your hand with white, purifying light.

STEP 3: INVOKE THE GODDESS

Then grasp the chalice with both hands, so your arms and the chalice are in a straight line with your third eye and spine. You form a column, a pillar, that the universe's healing light can move through. This is also when you can invoke the Goddess, saying something like the following or taking the time to write your invocation before the ritual to read aloud.

I draw down [the name of the Goddess or just "the Goddess"].
I invoke you into me, with perfect love and trust. I merge consciousness with thee.

Repeat this three times as you connect to your crown chakra, drawing down the Goddess through each of your chakras, feeling her fill up your body.

Take the chalice and touch it to your third eye.

Now take the chalice and touch it to your lips, taking a sip of the drink if you wish, as you invite the Goddess into the ritual. Stay here until you feel the invocation has been completed. It may not happen right away. Keep trying and know for future reference that you may have to adapt your words and bring offerings specific to your goddess if you feel that this ritual wasn't what you needed it to be.

STEP 4: FINISH WHATEVER RITUAL YOU'RE PERFORMING

If you're drawing down the Goddess and then performing another ritual, now is the time to do that ritual, or divination, or art, or sex magick, or whatever else.

STEP 5: CLOSE THE RITUAL AND DISMISS THE GODDESS

Once you're done, you'll have to let the Goddess know the ritual is complete. Stand with your hands clasping the chalice above your head as you say something like the following:

> *Through perfect love and perfect trust, this ritual is complete. Thank you, Goddess, for your blessing; now you may leave my being. So it is, so it shall be.*

Then move your hands out to either side of your head like the star from before, and then straight down to your sides. Take a second to connect with the Goddess, to thank her, to share anything you want her to know. Visualize the white light moving from around you back into the universe, where it still surrounds, listens, and supports you.

STEP 6: GROUND AND LEAVE AN OFFERING

Once you're done with this ritual, clap or ring some bells to come back into your body. You may choose to leave another offering or to fill up the chalice with more juice, holy water, or wine. Press your forehead into the ground as in child's pose as you exhale and visualize any excess energy moving back into the crystal core of the earth. Eat some food, drink some water, record any experiences in your grimoire, and enjoy.

A NOTE ON INVOKING

Traditionally, when you draw down the moon you're invoking the Goddess, letting her know that you consent to being a vessel for the great and divine mother. You accept the Goddess into yourself, through your crown chakra, through the chalice you sip from, through your breath and incantation.

Many think of invoking the Goddess as becoming a channel, which is one aspect of it. I have also been taught that when you invoke the Goddess or God, you're not so much fitting these giant and divine beings into your tiny human body, but more so that you are plugging yourself, your consciousness, and your soul into that god or goddess. You are becoming part of their energetic makeup.

If you've never worked with a goddess before, you may follow the preceding ritual and invite the Goddess into your space instead of invoking, changing the language so it feels right for you. See how this feels; continue cultivating this relationship. Then when you feel ready, you may wish to invoke the Goddess, to connect with her on a physical level by merging yourself with her. Magick is real, and this is the real deal! Although nothing serious is likely to happen, when you mess with universal forces, it *is* a possibility.

So know this before you invoke the Goddess; know who it is you're invoking and why. Be clear with your intention and incantation.

Goddess worship as invoking the matriarchy

The toxic paradigm we're living in is killing our planet. We're out of balance, and with man at the top of the food chain, there's no reverence or care for Mother Earth and how we're depleting her and robbing her of what *we* need to survive. This is the patriarchy; womxn, femmes, nonbinary individuals, queer people, POC, trans people, indigenous people, disabled people, anyone who isn't The Man is marginalized, pushed further into the cracks because they're not seen as people or as fully sovereign individuals. With patriarchy, we see man and corporation and profit at the top of the pyramid; this isn't a conscious or sustainable cycle. Once we started making the switch to agriculture some twelve thousand years ago, we started going from hunter-gatherer societies where we collaborated and shared to societies where there was competition, where it was each man and family for himself. Now, in the new millennium, in what's called the Age of Aquarius, we're being called to think of the whole again. The sign of the humanitarian, this is the age of matriarchy, of goddess worship, of coming together and of ushering in a new paradigm. Although the Mayan calendar cycle ended in 2012, this wasn't the end times they were predicting, but a new way of being, a new era, a new paradigm.

Many of us believe, myself included, that 2012 was a mass awakening where we returned to knowledge we've been holding deep in our soul, in our bones. This is one part of the witch awakening happening right now, where many of us are returning to the earth to heal her, ourselves, and the collective. We are advocates for her, protecting her, calling out unfair treatment when we see it. We are of the earth, not separate from her.

The year 2012 was hopefully the beginning of the end of patriarchy. Those of you who work with the Goddess, who work intimately with the elements, who wander in the subconscious and wax and wane with the moon, are already ushering in this new paradigm. By giving a voice and space to the Goddess, you're calling in balance. We're ushering in the matriarchy.

Matriarchy isn't the equivalent of patriarchy because in matriarchal societies, womxn aren't more powerful than men; in these societies, men and womxn are equal. Womxn are the heads of the household, revered and honored for their wisdom. There's collaboration and sharing, not competition and capitalism. There's an intimate understanding of the earth, of the power that comes from when we bleed, of working alongside and not against those you care about. This is what you're working toward, part of why we do this work: to usher in a world that is more compassionate, more accepting, and more supportive of different expressions of what the soul can look like.

The elementals: working with the nature spirits of the elements

When you start walking the witches' path, or along any path that honors nature in all her vastness, something shifts. Everything seems to come alive. Suddenly the trees have spirits and the flowers seem to talk to you. Rocks have their own distinct vibration and so do bugs. The sun seems to laugh with you and the wind seems to wink. All the energies around you start becoming tangible and perceptible in new ways. Animism isn't something that only witches believe in, and it's not a belief that every witch holds either. You don't have to believe that everything has a spirit to understand how the elemental world can take shape as energetic entities.

The elements themselves are manifest in the astral realm as the faeries, an umbrella term for magickal beings and nature's ancestors, who help keep the natural world in balance. There are stories of little people and faeries from all corners of the globe, all with their own mythology, but there are plenty of overlaps. Faery mythology is rich and extensive, and you can look to the faeries that embody the elements to work with and understand these energies in new ways. You can also form personal relationships with the elements through working with the faery, or fey. They are the guardians of the earth, and this is one spiral path of knowing Gaia in a totally different way. Also, keep in mind that when you make contact with these beings it's usually on the astral plane. You can access this realm through meditation or trance, and at the solstice, equinox, and cross quarter days (the days that fall between the solstices and equinoxes) the veil between our realm and that of the faery is extra thin. The faery exist in a liminal space, neither here nor there, somewhere between the physical and intangible. These sacred holidays that make up the Wheel of the Year are the energetic equivalent of these liminal spaces, hanging in the fog of the shifting seasons. Working with the faery realm is easier and more supported during any of the Sabbats.

When you work with faeries, it's best to remember that, like deities, these are beings with their own feelings, and they are also protective of the earth. When working with elementals outside, make sure to leave a space cleaner than how you found it. You'll also want to leave an offering like milk, honey, bread, sweet cake, sweets, sugar, berries, or fruit.

EARTH: GNOMES

The elemental energy of the earth is well represented by the gnome, the thousand-year-old creature who doesn't look too far off from the classic garden gnome. Said to live deep in the roots of old trees, gnomes are the patrons of animals, are vastly protective of the earth, and can be called upon for rituals of healing, especially for pets and animals. Gnomes can assist in raising energy and may be invited to participate during rituals of protection, for help with divination, and with understanding systems of energy. You can connect to the elementals of earth by meditating and moving through the root system of an ancient tree, down to where the gnomes live, deep in the earth where there's no light. You may connect and ask the gnomes for a specific request or for their wisdom on a certain topic. When you're done, don't forget to leave an offering; milk and honey is always a safe choice.

AIR: SYLPHS

The embodiment of the weightlessness and lightness of air, the sylphs are delicate and small winged beings who often appear as whispers of light or as gossamer illusions. These faeries are inspired creatures who remind you of the never-ending power of your dreams and joy. Like the wind personified, sylphs can teach you to see things differently, to follow what's calling your heart and find the support to feel safe in your growth. Sylphs are said to fly through the wind with joy, unless there's a storm, in which case they can turn aggressive and destructive, becoming channels for the storm's energy. You can call on the sylphs to help you find inspiration and also to help you create the changes you've been longing for. You can connect to the sylphs by burning sacred smoke or meditating outside or near a fan as you connect to your breath. You can visualize and connect by flying through the wind, meditating on the energy of a storm, and asking the sylphs for inspiration. You can also create art as a ritual to the sylphs. When you're done, leave an offering of milk, honey, or sweets; you can also blow bubbles as an offering to air elementals.

FIRE: SALAMANDERS

Salamanders look like red or yellow lizards that live in flames and hide deep in the hottest parts of the earth, and these elementals have the same untouchable quality of fire: an intense heat. These beings can be dangerous and difficult to work with, but they can be called upon when intense protection or banishing is needed. If you choose to work with salamanders, make sure to banish them when your ritual is finished. You can more safely work with these elementals through meditation, or by scrying to understand their energy more. These beings can lead you into realms of intensity, both in the astral realm and in your emotional body. I suggest inviting the salamander only at the boundary of a circle, or working with them in meditation. If you do invite them in, burn an offering of incense after you banish them.

WATER: UNDINES

The elemental energies of water are best captured by the undines, the umbrella term for water spirits that include mermaids, nereids, and sea nymphs. Connected to all bodies of water like oceans, lakes, and streams, the undines can teach you about your emotions and spiritual body, and they can nurture your inner artist. When you're in the bath or outside in water, you can ask to connect to the undines in all their compassion and love. You can call upon them to help support you when you're in emotional turmoil or to help you heal. This is the realm of the subconscious, and you can connect to these water faeries to process and understand your dreams and subconscious. The undines bless you with an ability to heal, and you can meditate with them when in a body of water or by visualizing it. Imagine a white healing light emanating from the water, surrounding you, holding you. You may call out to the undines at this time, asking for healing or understanding. Allow yourself to melt into their support, and when you're finished come back to your body and leave an offering of honey, milk, mead, wine, or sweets.

Embodying spirit: creating your own glamour

You don't have to pull together a whole look to work with glamour in a meaningful way, but there is power in intention. When it comes to creating a look for yourself that speaks of what you're trying to call in, embody, or work with, there is power in a signature, there is power in clothing, and there is power in allure. What would it take for you to feel divine? To feel like a god/dess among mortals? Having certain items or rituals to which you can return in order to embrace and work with this divine energy can be transformational. It can also be a practice of self-care, a physical anchor you can use to help you shapeshift or connect to the element of spirit in a different way.

To connect with what *spirit* means in terms of glamour, take a second to think of your favorite outfit you've ever worn. It doesn't matter what it was for or what you looked like. All that matters is

how you felt. Take a second to visualize the outfit, noticing all the details, the way it fit and fell against your body. Notice the color and the silhouette. And now breathe into your body. How does this look make you feel? Note this and take a second to reflect on what was so special about this outfit. Hopefully this outfit inspires you, makes you feel something: sexy, capable, glamorous, unstoppable, beautiful, handsome, otherworldly. *This* is spirit.

Creating a personalized glamour is really just creating a personalized style with a twist. The twist is that the elements are the cornerstones of this.

Before you begin, go into your closet and see what you like.

Give stuff away and donate what you don't wear. Make space to receive what it is you want! I also suggest making a Pinterest board or starting a collage of outfits, colors, makeup, accessories, and things you like. That way you have a place for all your inspiration and you can also see the patterns and trends you're drawn to.

If you're not even sure where to start, ask yourself the following questions, which you may choose to write down or to use as inspiration for collages and mood boards. Use Instagram, Twitter, magazines, Tumblr, thrift shops, runways, old movies, and the universe around you to inspire you.

What colors do I love?
What silhouettes do I like?
What inspires me (visually, artistically, historically) right now?
Fave celebrities/musicians/models . . . and so on with style I like?
What am I looking to feel more of in my day-to-day life?

Then ask yourself what you want to cultivate more of. You can use the qualities and glamour of the elements to guide you deeper into the realm of spirit. You can also use the tarot, goddesses, and planets to help inspire your glamour, turning to your daily card pull, or what zodiac sign the moon or sun is in for inspiration. Use the following questions for some clarity. You can also work with the individual elements' glamour in their respective chapters and the color correspondence chart in the next chapter. But more than anything, listen to your intuition! If you know you're way too comfortable with your look (very earth) and want to experiment, you may wish to channel the creativity of air, or the fearlessness of fire. If you're starting a new job and have to dress a bit more professionally, you can channel more of earth through crisp silhouettes and clean tailoring, or water's ease with comfortable and flowing lines that allow you to be confident and relaxed.

Earth: What grounds me? What helps me feel safe?
Style: Grounded, professional, chic, classic, comfortable, layered, structured, effortless
Air: What inspires me? What has me feeling present and confident?
Style: Eccentric, colorful, sheer, flowy, creative, elegant, sharp
Water: What makes me feel loving and beautiful? What makes me feel comfortable?
Style: Loose, soft, silky, expressive, intentional, divine, flowing
Fire: What helps me feel influential and capable? What makes me feel sexy?
Style: Powerful, bold, fierce, sexy, sultry, loud, daring

Use these questions and your collage or Pinterest as tools for experimenting with your look! This is more than clothing; it's talismans, scents, makeup, colors. It's your intuition. It's your cloak, your costume, your armor. It's your style, your sense of self-expression and the freak flag you get to wear every day so you can share yourself fully with other people. It's also seeing the clothing you have in a new way, being creative with your closet. Maybe you do a clothing trade with friends, or go to your favorite thrift shop for a couple new hero pieces. You don't have to spend a lot of money, or any at all, to connect with glamour on a personal level. Allow your glamour to be your own and remember that as you and your magick grow and evolve, so will it.

Journal questions for spirit

Intuition is a witch's most important companion, a voice that you can learn to listen to by *listening*. You can work with journaling about each of the elements to dive deeper into what your intuition is telling you about different aspects of your life. Spirit, the golden thread weaving it all together, can also act as a bridge with journaling, helping you process and wrap your mind around the divine. Use these journal questions for spirit as a starting point for reflection, answering whatever questions speak to you. Then dive in deeper by following where the elements guide you.

As always, you may wish to set your space before you begin, turning to page 15 for instructions. Prepare the space in a way that helps you connect with spirit and begin to journal whenever you're ready.

Spirit: What am I grateful for right now? What does my intuition feel like? What does it feel like to be aligned with the divine? How does the divine speak to me? What spiritual experiences have been important to me? What am I still longing for? Why is it important for me to find connection to something larger than myself?

Earth: What's keeping me grounded and in my body right now? What's helping me feel safe? Where could I use more structure and support in my life? What am I growing, nourishing, and tending? How am I being nourished and tended to?

Air: What am I inspired to learn more about? Where in my life am I craving expansion? What does freedom and space mean to me right now? Where am I present? Where am I lacking presence? Where do I need to soften and be less sharp?

Fire: What's my sexuality telling me at this time? Where am I feeling love and lust and eroticism in my body? What am I feeling passionate and invigorated by? What am I feeling inspired by? What am I feeling inspired to let go of? Where am I looking for more intensity? Less?

Water: What are my emotions telling me at this time? Where am I feeling this in my body? Is my spiritual practice supporting me in the right ways? What does my spirit need more of? What is my heart telling me? Where am I healing? Where am I ignoring my healing?

Spirit in astrology: understanding the planets

☉ ☿ ♀ ☽ ⊕ ♂

♃ ♄ ♅ ♆ ⯓

Astrology has an infinite number of uses. You can use it to ask questions about a specific event (horary astrology); you can use it to understand the events that a group of people are going through collectively; and, of course, you can use the birth chart to understand your own life and being with more clarity. Ultimately, astrology is a tool you can use to help understand and guide your soul in its evolution, much like tarot. In a chart, which you can cast for a question, for an event, or for a person, there are three main components; the planets, the houses, and the signs. If the planet is the actor, then the house is the scene and the sign is the costume or glamour they wear. The relationship between the houses and signs and planets is what an astrologer will interpret, alongside their transits, or what's currently going on in the cosmos. Learning about how these individual pieces of your birth chart work together can help you understand why you operate the way you do, as well as share what lessons you're meant to learn and overcome in this incarnation.

If the planets themselves are the characters in the play, then they can be seen as the element of spirit personified in the zodiac. The planets can also be seen as archetypes since they have their own correspondences, their own lessons, their own baggage, and their own deity that the Romans named them for. The seven classical planets (sun, moon, Jupiter, Venus, Saturn, Mars, and Mercury) as well as the newer additions (Uranus, Neptune, and Pluto) are all powerful energies that you can choose to work with in your rituals and spell work. Regardless of whether you choose to follow the path of planetary magick, knowing the correspondences for the planets, what they mean, what day they rule, and what happens when they are retrograde will only help you further develop your magick.

THE SUN

Creator of all, sustainer of life, in astrology the sun represents your light, your radiance, and your identity. This is how you see yourself and how you move through the world. It is through this celestial body that you shine, take up space, and form a sense of self. The sun represents and governs your will and your personality, as well as the way you express yourself. The sun is the active counterpart to the moon's receptive energy, and through it you can learn what it means to be confident, rooted in your power, dynamic, and consistent in your actions. Think of fire when it's contained safely and beautifully, hot wax, sun on bare skin, new ideas, bright yellow, gold jewelry, creating for the sake of it.

Deity: *Sol (Roman)/Helios (Greek)*
Sign(s): *Leo*
Day: *Sunday*

THE MOON

The moon rules the realm of the subtle, connected to that which whispers or crawls or feels its way up into the crevice of your subconscious. This is not the same analytical realm of the sun, but one of the energy body. You enter this space from the heart, not the brain. The moon represents your inner emotional world, often a more accurate representation of how you feel, of your true internal nature. The moon reflects your cycles through her wax and wane, and through her you learn what you need to be taken care of and how you like to be nurtured. It is also through the moon that you witness your shadow. In this way, the moon bares all and shows you what's hiding under the surface, away from the light from the sun. The moon is your intuition, your perception, and through her you learn of your softness.

Deity: *Luna or Diana (Roman)/Selene or Artemis (Greek)*
Sign(s): *Cancer*
Day: *Monday*

MERCURY

The patron of communication and ruler over thoughts, knowledge, travel, and intellect, Mercury is a planet that asks you to expand and evolve. Mercury wields the sword of wisdom, taking knowledge and mixing it with discernment. This planet aims for truth for truth's sake. Mercury rules over the way you express yourself verbally, how you think, calculate decisions, and analyze. Although many know their sun/moon/rising sign, Mercury tells you how you share all the different facets of yourself: online, offline, and everywhere in between. Mercury, the Greek god Hermes, and the Egyptian god Thoth, god of writing and occult knowledge, are all the same, and are said to be incarnations of Hermes Trismegistus.

"Hermes thrice great" was one of the most famous occultists and philosophers of the old world who is credited with writing famous Hermetic texts back around the first century CE. This planet isn't as tied to the occult as planets like Pluto, but the knowledge and mastery of thought and self for evolution and growth and enlightenment is of the spirit of this planet.

Deity: *Mercury (Roman)/Hermes (Greek)*
Sign(s): *Gemini, Virgo*
Day: *Wednesday*
Retrograde message: *When a planet stations retrograde (which is when retrograde begins), it appears to be moving backward from our view here on Earth. This isn't actually happening, but energetically it sort of is, which means that during retrograde whatever things the planet rules over have the tendency to go haywire, or misalign. Mercury retrograde happens three to four times a year, for a few weeks at a time. During this period, you're advised to travel as little as possible and avoid signing contracts; communication can become more difficult than usual; exes pop back up. But in every retrograde there is a lesson. In Mercury, it reminds us to slow down, to plan ahead, to read the fine print twice and then again. Mercury retrograde can be a fiercely loving reminder of where we need more presence, patience, and clarity.*

VENUS

The lover, the pursuer of pleasure, the planet of wealth, abundance, sensuality, and beauty, Venus is the hedonist of the planets. This planet teaches you how you love, how you want to be loved, how you receive wealth, what inspires you and your desires. Happiest when she's pursued, Venus teaches you receiving, seduction, what it means for you to be sexually and emotionally fulfilled. This is also the planet of glamour, affluence, and self-expression, and through Venus you can learn about yourself in relationship to others, to power, to money, and to the Goddess. This planet rules over the relationship with the self, guiding you into self-love and self-compassion as does the goddess of the same name. Venus is passion and the muse of the Muses. She is romance personified, asking you to connect to your heart and to whisper to it to see what resides there. Love is her language and she never tires of its sweet song.

Deity: *Venus (Roman)/Aphrodite (Greek)*
Sign(s): *Taurus, Libra*
Day: *Friday*
Retrograde message: *When retrograde, Venus can bring patterns to the surface that you haven't had the energy or attention to witness and break. Venus retrograde happens about every year and a half and lasts six weeks. During this time, old lovers may come back, you may be faced with heartache or miscommunication, and creative juices and money may be flowing slower than normal. This period asks you to honor wherever you are in your emotional journey, to take time to not say things in the heat of the moment but instead to process them as they need to be processed. Although this can be a taxing period monetarily, it's also a chance for you to trust and release fear about money and abundance. This period can help lead you deeper into the eternal truth and spaciousness of your heart center if you give it the container to do so, through art, poetry, ritual, sex magick, working with rose quartz, glamour, or whatever else.*

MARS

If Venus is the hunted, then Mars is the hunter. This planet speaks of action, of dominance, of power. This planet loves the chase.

Although this energy can feel overwhelming and forceful, Mars does best when these energies are tamed and directed, alchemized for a purpose or goal. Mars rules over power, aggression, sex, war, and how you fight for what you want. You can learn about what force and direction mean to you through this planet, as well as how you can best work with them. This planet speaks in sharp tongues about how you act and the narratives that drive you, since Mars himself is the god of war. What are you willing to battle over, to not compromise on? This is what this fiery and passionate planet asks you to ponder.

Deity: *Mars (Roman) / Ares (Greek)*
Sign(s): *Aries, Scorpio*
Day: *Tuesday*
Retrograde message: *The least common of all planetary retrogrades, Mars retrograde happens every twenty-four months and lasts for two to two and a half months. When this planet is retrograde, you're left facing parts of yourself that you may wish to avoid. Plans fall through, and all the action from before may seem to slow down. A sense of aggression or power imbalance may be in the air, and moods may be sharp. During this time, you have the opportunity to witness your shadow self from a new perspective, seeing what unsettled trauma and stories are coming to the surface. You notice what this retrograde is asking you to settle and rewrite, using your anger as a tool for clearing pain from the past and rewiring it for the future.*

THE OUTER PLANETS

Jupiter is the first of the outer planets in astrology, alongside Saturn, Uranus, Neptune, and Pluto. These planets shift away from exposing the personal to representing generations and parts of the collective conscious. So while the inner planets of the sun, the moon, Venus, Mercury, and Mars represent influences on the individual in the birth chart, the outer planets represent influence on groups of people born during each planet's transits. Since the outer planets have a slower orbit, they transit through each zodiac sign for years at a time, even decades and more, which is why these are seen as less personal and more for the collective.

Jupiter

When you walk lucky, feel lucky, and get lucky, you are in the domain of Jupiter. King of the gods, who goes by Zeus to the Greeks, Jupiter speaks of your generosity and how you manifest. Through Jupiter, you see where you're being called to step up into a new and more prosperous way of being, relating, and living. This planet pushes you out of your comfort zone, asking you to embrace your gifts and share them with others. A planet of optimism and one that asks you to see all possibilities, Jupiter brings you fortune and the ability to expand your horizons with its bigger-than-life energy, since it is associated with philosophy and spiritual studies. You can work with this planet to enrich your life with more abundance, purpose, and positivity.

Deity: *Jupiter (Roman)/Zeus (Greek)*
Sign(s): *Pisces, Sagittarius*
Day: *Thursday*
Retrograde message: *Jupiter retrograde happens pretty frequently, every nine months for about four months at a time. When this happens, you have a window of time to turn inward and to reflect. Trips may have detours, opportunities may pan out differently than expected, and you may end up on a new spiritual path during this retrograde. This is a chance to course correct, to honor whatever path you're on and to find a new one if necessary.*

Saturn

Father Time has a bad reputation as being strict, mean, and all about the deadlines. And although this is partially true of Saturn, this planet can also teach you about the structure you need to be certain in your groundwork and rooted in your practice. The ruler of karma and discipline, Saturn tells you of the foundations you've built and asks that they be firm and supportive. This is tough love, growing pains, the edge of "hurts so good" and "hurts too much." But Saturn does it all from a place of compassion, of wanting what's most sustainable for you. This is the planet that reminds you that you become the strongest witch, magician, mystic, occultist you can be when you work with your problems, facing them head on. Saturn loathes escapism or avoidance of things that will only help you grow.

Deity: *Saturn (Roman)/Cronus (Greek)*
Sign(s): *Capricorn, Aquarius*
Day: *Saturday*
Retrograde message: *With Saturn retrograde, you can expect anything karmic you may have hidden beneath the bed to come back. Saturn retrograde happens once a year for about four months, giving you a chance to deal with anything you may have been avoiding. If the habits in your life aren't sustainable, this is a period of time that can make that glaringly clear. However, if you're the one who's receiving a check from karma, then this retrograde period can bring you your just deserts. This is an ideal time to revisit boundaries and routines in your life, and this planet's tight grip on time and boundaries minimizes while retrograde, giving this period a malleable feel.*

Uranus

Through Uranus, god of the sky, you enter the energy of awakening, sudden change, invention, and revolution. Not one of the seven classical planets, Uranus was discovered in the late 1780s, during the Industrial Revolution when the world was changing at an incredibly rapid rate. Uranus reflects the power of the human will, the limitless possibilities that come with following your intuition and knowing that you can do whatever your third eye guides you toward. This is exciting and dangerous, earth-shattering and totally drastic and different from anything before. Uranus causes transformation and metamorphosis, forcing you to see things in a different way. This planet reflects the unyielding power of human potential, as well as the power of the spiritual to revolutionize the way you see the world.

Deity: *Caelus (Roman)/Uranus (Greek)*
Sign(s): *Aquarius*
Retrograde message: *When Uranus is retrograde once a year for about five months, you can expect things to slow down a little bit. You're able to see the shifts you've been asked to make in your life with more objectivity, and you're able to dive into the root of your newfound ideologies with a more level head instead of one obsessed with rebellion and revolution. You can use this time to reexamine the things that are stirring at your core, making sure they align with your values and beliefs. This retrograde offers you an opportunity to be present amid all the transformation, to really see where you're going with a newfound sense of appreciation, clarity, and compassion.*

Neptune

Neptune is glamour, an illusion of dreams and senses that pulls you in, catching you in unexpected depths. If Venus rules over how you relate to love and glamour on a personal level, then Neptune is the collective version of this. This planet rules your fantasies, your spiritual studies, your connection to unconditional love as a state of being. This is the planet of cosmic consciousness. This is the realm of the subconscious that craves the shadow, the darkest crevices of the ocean. The realm and ruler of mysteries, Neptune energy pulls you into the deep sea of feeling, pulling a cotton candy veil of rose pink over your eyes and then distracting you with promises of riches. Neptune wants you to grow, but it also wants you to explore what lurks beneath the surface of your dreams.

Sign(s): *Pisces*
Deity: *Neptune (Roman)/Poseidon (Greek)*
Retrograde message: *Like the other outer planets, Neptune is retrograde often for a long period of time, once a year for about five months. Neptune retrograde can actually help you see clearly past the veil of the planet's glamour, softening its hold on your rose-colored glasses. Sometimes this can be harsh, sometimes it can bring clarity, and it's often subtle. You can work with this energy by embracing the artistic and spiritual inspiration this time brings you and by resisting the temptation for escapism by working with a spiritual or ritual practice.*

Pluto

The god of the underworld and ruler of sex, death, and transformation, Pluto thrives when there's something shapeshifting, changing, bubbling to the surface. A planet that prospers in metamorphosis, Pluto speaks of a generation's ability to analyze, feel, perceive, create, and react. Pluto is the realm of what you fear, of what keeps you small and in your own underworld. This is the kernel of light that lies beneath all else; to transform you must be willing to face what you fear most, and Pluto is the mirror that reflects that back at you. Pluto's power is unexpected and potent, and it will leave you evolving whether you want to or not. This is the sex, drugs, and rock 'n' roll, the power of radical vulnerability, the transformative power of death and magick. This celestial body is the farthest from the sun and teaches you to slow down and look inward to see what must be dissolved and reborn.

Deity: *Pluto (Roman)/Hades (Greek)*
Sign(s): *Scorpio*
Retrograde message: *During Pluto retrograde, you may feel as though you have the chance to examine your subconscious and psyche with extra clarity. Pluto is retrograde once a year for five to six months, giving you the chance to recalibrate, release, and prepare for rebirth. During this time, you have a chance to examine what changes have taken place in your life and which still need to. Issues concerning death, sexuality, and magick may surface, but it's all intended for your highest good. Leaning into the mystery and volatility of Pluto, or the lack thereof, can help you experience this ego death in a more compassionate way.*

WHY THE PLANETS

The planets all have higher intelligence, a kernel of some cosmic truth to share with you. The planets speak even more clearly through the signs they wear, and with their transits through your birth chart they tell you the lessons you need to learn at this moment in your evolution. The planets are aspects of spirit, fractals or reflections of the gods and goddesses they're named for. In this way, they speak of our collective relationship to these icons and deities, and to the correspondences each of the planets rule over. They connect each person's individual spirit with that of big-S Spirit, of god, of the collective spirit.

CHAPTER 6

In Connection

Having journeyed the pentacle, you return transformed. Touched by the light and shadows and darkness, by the rivers and mountains and fire. Held by the oceans and wind and the Goddess. You have planted the roots, tended the seeds, watered the soil, and been blessed with rain. Through the ethereal, you see that all is connected and the poem unfolds. The spell you have cast is one that calls on all directions, on the elements in all their power. And after you've been led through each point of the star, you stand at the boundary of the circle, your ritual complete. By bewitching the elements, you return empowered and embodied.

In this chapter, with the elements as your guide, you'll be led through creating your own rituals and moments of sacred unfolding. Though you can learn from the individual characteristics of earth, air, fire, water, and spirit, it's in the way they relate, communicate, and connect that you can really bring their medicine into your life.

The elements guide you back into your multifaceted nature. You see this through the way the elements mingle. You see this in steam, which embraces water and fire, sensuality and feelings. You see this in ice: water and air, emotions and distance, the piercing cold. And you see this in smoke: fire, air, and earth; expansion, grounding, and clearing. You can also see this in a storm, in the way tornadoes and hurricanes and lightning strikes leave their mark, their ferocious intensity magnified by each element in the mix. Although the elements can exist in their own separate environments, this isn't often the case. You too are constantly embodying different elements, depending on what that moment in time calls for.

The elements can act as archetypes to help you identify what you're feeling in the moment. You know that earth is associated

with the physical, the body, and home. Air is the mind, presence, your thoughts and ability to process. Water is your subconscious, your intuition, your dreams and feelings. Fire is your passion, your need to take action, your sexuality and power. Spirit is your ability to give thanks, to connect to energies and other realms, the divine.

Some days you may wake up grounded, relaxed, and in your body. Heavy. Rooted. The domain of earth. Some days you may wake up emotional, raw, sensitive. In the land of water. Other times you may feel energized, buzzing, ready to work hard to bring your passions to life. Fire has taken you. Or you may wake up inspired with a million ideas in your head that you must manifest. The realm of air.

Some days you may feel like you're out of balance, like you need more of a certain element's energy. By working with the elements you feel disconnected from (and the breath work, crystals, cards, journal questions, corresponding energy centers, and goddesses that come with that) you can bring more of this element's magick into your life, creating more of a balance, more equilibrium.

How to invite the elements, elementals, and watchtowers to your ritual

As a witch, you cast your circle and made a boundary for yourself. You stand unapologetically, your feet planted into the earth. You create a sacred space in which you raise, charge, and direct energy.

And you can invite the elements, the elementals, and the directions (known as watchtowers) to your ritual, to join you at the boundary of your circle to help you celebrate and raise energy. You may wish to invite only one of these energies (the elements, elementals, or watchtowers) into your ritual, or you may invite all three. As always you can invite and invoke goddesses, spirit guides, ascended masters, or other divine beings into your ritual as well.

You can invite the elements and elementals to any ritual you wish, with Sabbats and the full and new moon being especially auspicious times to work with the natural realm in this way.

A note on inviting the salamanders and elementals of fire: Salamanders can be intense energies, and if you choose to invite them to your circle, just take extra precaution. Invite these beings who work with compassion, and when you dismiss them back to their realm, you can "banish them" and order them back to their realm for safety, which is written in this ritual. If you don't feel comfortable, skip inviting the salamanders and just call upon elemental fire (the energy of this element personified) instead.

STEP 1: SET UP THE SPACE

Prepare for whatever ritual you'll be performing following the steps on page 15 so you can arrive to the circle with presence, love, and trust.

STEP 2: GROUND

When you feel called to begin the ritual, take time to ground. You can do this sitting, lying down, or standing up. Breathe into your body, feeling any tension disappear with each exhale. Feel yourself supported by the earth beneath you as you visualize roots moving from the base of your spine into the ground below you, all the way through the floor and concrete and dirt, through the dark damp soil of the earth, all the way into the core of Gaia. These roots send you vibrant, healing golden light that moves up your spine and nourishes you. Breathe into this for as long as you need.

STEP 3: CAST THE CIRCLE

Starting at north, use your pointer finger or a wand and walk deosil, or clockwise, around your space as you cast your circle, envisioning violet-blue flames creating a boundary around you as you walk. Follow the directions on page 28.

STEP 4: INVITE IN THE ELEMENTALS AND DIRECTIONS

You should finish casting your circle facing north, where you will begin by inviting the elementals and quarters from this direction. You may say something like the following as you connect to the element of earth in all its grounded presence:

> *Guardians of the watchtower of the north, element of earth. I call upon the gnomes, earth elementals, and ancestors to join me at this [ritual/the name of your working]. Welcome, and blessed be.*

Turn to your right so you're facing east and say something like the following as you connect to the element of air in all its expansion and freedom:

> *Guardians of the watchtower of the east, element of air. I call upon the sylphs and air elementals to join me at this [ritual/name of your working]. Welcome, and blessed be.*

Turn to your right so you're facing south and say something like the following as you connect to the element of fire in all its fierce and powerful energy:

> *Guardians of the watchtower of the south, element of fire. I call upon the (salamanders and) fire elementals who work with compassion to join me at this [ritual/name of your working]. Welcome, and blessed be.*

Turn to your right so you're facing west and say something like the following as you connect to the emotional and psychic energy of water:

> *Guardians of the watchtower of the west, element of water: I call upon the undines and water elementals to join me at this [ritual/name of your working]. Welcome, and blessed be.*

Take a second to breathe and feel the faeries surrounding you, the ancestors and directions making themselves known.

STEP 5: PERFORM THE RITUAL OR WORKING

Whether you're practicing full moon sex magick, reading your tarot at the summer solstice, or writing poetry in honor of your Matron Goddess, now is the time to enact your ritual.

STEP 6: DISMISS THE ELEMENTS AND DIRECTIONS

When you're done with your working, you'll want to close the ritual. Start facing west. You'll be moving widdershins, or counterclockwise, to dismiss the directions, ending with north.

Face west and say:

Guardians of the watchtower of the west, element of water. Undines and water elementals, I thank you for joining me at this [ritual/name of your working]. The ritual is closed and the boundary is dissolved. So it is.

Turn to the left, facing south, and say:

Guardians of the watchtower of the south, element of fire. Salamanders and fire elementals, I thank you for joining me at this [ritual/name of your working]. The ritual is closed and the boundary is dissolved. You are banished back to your realm. So it is.

Turn to the left, facing east, and say:

Guardians of the watchtower of the east, element of air. Sylphs and air elementals, I thank you for joining me at this [ritual/name of your working]. The ritual is closed and the boundary is dissolved. So it is.

Turn to the left, facing north, and say:

Guardians of the watchtower of the north, element of earth. Gnomes, earth elementals, and ancestors, I thank you for joining me at this [ritual/name of your working]. The ritual is closed and the boundary is dissolved. So it is.

If you invited any other deities, spirit guides, or ascended masters, now is the time to thank and dismiss them as well.

STEP 7: CLOSE THE CIRCLE

Now you're going to be closing your circle, using a finger or wand as you did before. You'll be walking widdershins or counterclockwise to close the circle, feeling the blue violet flame move up your arm, down your spine, and through your feet, back into the earth below you. Find the full instructions on page 30.

STEP 8: FINISH AND GROUND THE RITUAL

When you're ready to close the ritual, find a comfortable seat sitting up or lying down. Return to your breath and once again, feel roots connecting you to the earth. Feel them move back into your spine, bringing a sense of serenity and warmth with them. You may wish to press your forehead into the ground as in child's pose, sending any excess energy back into the earth. Leave an offering, get some water and some food, and celebrate your hard work. You are done!

A quiz for learning your current elemental makeup

Sometimes it can be hard to figure out what you're experiencing both physically and psychologically. Our emotions and life can feel like they're getting the best of us, and we may feel out of balance but unsure of how to return to equilibrium. So to make this introspection easier, I'm sharing a quiz that will help you see your current elemental balance, or what elements you're currently channeling the most of. You may wish to look at your birth chart as well, noting what sign and element each of the planets are in. This can help you understand how best to nourish and understand yourself holistically, acting as a map to your energetic being.

Although your birth chart can tell you your personal nonshifting elemental makeup (since it's like a photograph in time), the way you relate to the elements shifts day to day, just like your aura. Depending on all the factors of your life, like your health, work, home, sexuality, and spiritual practice, you may oscillate between channeling different elements each day. This quiz is designed to help you see which elements you're relating to the most and the least at the present moment. This way, you know what elements may need to be brought into balance, and you can work with those respective practices, and the suggestions at the end of this quiz, to help make that happen.

During the quiz, if you feel like two answers are true, mark them both. This isn't a pass/fail quiz but one that's intended to help you relate to your spirit in a new way.

1. **Right now I am currently feeling:**

   a. *In my body—I feel grounded, capable, and centered. I feel confident of getting what I need done, even if there's occasional anxiety in my body.*

   b. *In my head—Thinking a lot. Going over things mentally, really getting all of it clear in my head, even though this can feel difficult sometimes.*

   c. *In my feels—I'm in my feelings, and even though it can be challenging to concentrate, my emotions are my fuel.*

   d. *In my passions—I'm feeling inspired, lit up, and excited. My main mode of working and thinking is through my passions, and it can be difficult to work on things I don't care about.*

e. *In the flow—I am feeling grateful, aligned, and balanced. I know I have what it takes to accomplish all I need to. I'm not stressed or worried about it.*

2. **I am currently craving more of this in my life:**

a. *Freedom—I want to travel, see more, experience more, learn more.*

b. *Stability—I want to feel a sense of peace, abundance, and comfort. I want to feel at harmony in my surroundings and in my life!*

c. *Expansion—I want something to ignite my desires, to give me something to be inspired by.*

d. *Love—I want to feel my heart, my feelings, the divine. I am aching for some connection.*

e. *Transformation—I'm not sure what I crave, but I want it to be different than what I'm experiencing now. I crave change on a cellular level.*

3. **This area of my life is flourishing right now:**

a. *My self—My mind, body, and spirit are feeling balanced and healthy and cared for. I've been taking good care of my spiritual, physical, and mental health.*

b. *Work and home—My job is supporting me and I come home feeling fulfilled and like what I'm doing matters.*

c. *My heart—I live with compassion and with love. My heart is so happy, and I'm surrounded by so many relationships that honor, respect, and feed me.*

d. *My sexuality and desires—I feel so fed with my erotic side and what turns my body and soul on. I am passionate about everything.*

e. *My inspiration and magick—My mind is racing with ideas and I've been inspired to create as a form of devotion, art, and magick.*

4. This is something I'm actively working on right now:

a. *Quieting my mind. I'm learning to work with my thoughts and not against them.*

b. *Using my spiritual gifts to help others. I'm learning and healing so I can pass it on one day.*

c. *Getting healthy, finding stability. Exercising, stretching, eating better, meditating; I'm here to step it up.*

d. *Understanding and connecting to my feelings; anxiety, love, jealousy. All of it. I'm always working on knowing what my emotional present and equilibrium is.*

e. *Finding healthy ways to express my anger and intensity. I'm learning how to channel my feelings of rage, passion, and desire through art, creation, breath, and movement.*

5. Where would I rather be right now?

a. *Nowhere. I'm happy being right here, right now.*

b. *Flying through the clouds, with total freedom like a bird, in a plane or hot-air balloon.*

c. *In a jungle or rain forest, somewhere far away surrounded by nature and trees and animals.*

d. *On the shore of a tropical beach or near a body of water as the sun shines, relaxing and sipping on a drink.*

e. *Hiking a volcano or doing something totally adventurous and extreme in a totally different climate than I'm used to.*

6. When people describe me, they usually say I'm:

a. *Perceptive—I feel a lot, and I'm intuitive and emotionally intelligent.*

b. *Passionate—If I believe in something, I go for it full force.*

c. *Inspired—I'm always thinking, always plotting, and my mind is my biggest asset.*

d. *Mystical AF—Everything I do is intentional, conscious, and plugged in.*

e. *Loyal—I am loyal, chill as hell, and dependable, and I really value what it means to be a good friend.*

7. I love to spend my free time:

a. *In nature, outside exploring, or inside decorating my space, going shopping, cleaning, organizing.*

b. *Learning, taking classes, reading books, going to museums, watching documentaries, doing something new.*

c. *Creating, making art, writing poetry, kissing, doing things that are taboo, learning and fostering my passions and hobbies.*

d. *Relaxing with friends and lovers, expressing myself, taking baths, practicing rituals of self-care, making art inspired by my feelings and healing.*

e. *Meditating, journaling, reading tarot, working with goddesses, studying spiritual texts, practicing spells and rituals, doing anything esoteric.*

8. One of the things I love about myself is:

a. *My ability to communicate effectively, to share my thoughts with clarity, charisma, and honesty.*

b. *My empathy, my ability to feel and to connect to whomever I'm talking to.*

c. *My spirit; I am bold, passionate and unapologetic with my beliefs and who I am.*

d. *My magick, my belief in the divine, my commitment to spiritual growth and healing my soul on all timelines.*

e. *My body, the fact that I never stop exploring, dancing, and touching, and my ability to create healthy boundaries that serve me.*

9. If I had more hours in the day, I would spend them:

a. *Having sex, kissing, exploring erotic possibilities, and creating art inspired by it, traveling.*

b. *Saving the world, learning, thinking, growing, inventing, creating, and envisioning new ways of being.*

c. *Outside in nature, surrounded by animals, eating delicious food, shopping.*

d. *Making art, writing poetry, watching old movies, going on dates, swimming, learning a new form of art.*

e. *Meditating, going on retreats, learning new systems of magick, studying tarot or crystals or the occult, obtaining enlightenment.*

10. **When I am stressed out and overwhelmed, I experience this as:**

a. *Emotional turmoil, sadness, pain, like I'm drowning and can't get out.*

b. *Cycles of thoughts, obsessive thinking, being extremely self-critical and harsh.*

c. *Anxiety, tension and tightness in my body, difficulty breathing, like all I want to do is sleep.*

d. *Panic, tension, like I'm spinning out of control, like I'm a runaway train; I feel burned out, manic like I can't stop.*

e. *Numbness, a distorted version of peace; finding a way to go inward with it.*

11. **What inspires me to live my best life?**

a. *All the things there are to learn and experience that I haven't had the chance to see or do yet; books and all the stories out there that haven't been told yet.*

b. *The earth, flowers, having a home, safety, abundance, being able to support those I care about and the ability to pay it forward.*

c. *Sex, subversion, revolution, art, rock 'n' roll, the occult, destruction, creation, transformation, action, and adventure.*

d. *Magick, witchcraft, the cosmos, enlightenment, growing and healing so I can dedicate time to helping other beings do the same.*

e. *Love in all its forms, the heart, my ability to connect so deeply with others, art, the beauty of the world around me.*

KEY

Earth: *a, b, b, c, c, e, a, e, c, c, b*
Air: *b, a, e, a, b, c, b, a, b, b, a*
Water: *c, d, c, d, d, a, d, b, d, a, e*
Fire: *d, c, d, e, e, b, c, c, a, d, c*
Spirit: *e, e, a, b, a, d, e, d, e, e, d*

IF YOU ANSWERED WITH MOSTLY EARTH

Dearest witch, you are firm in your convictions, present in your body, and planted in your truth. If you're mostly an earthy babe, then you're probably incredibly devoted to nature and inspired by this transcendent power. You have solid boundaries and know what you need to be supported and cared for. You embody the steadiness of Gaia alongside her reliability, and you have the gift of helping living things grow.

When this energy is out of balance, however, it can manifest as anxiety, depression, and the feeling of being stuck. In its less extreme forms, this may come up as fatigue, laziness, or a lack of motivation or confidence. If you're too attached to your beliefs and your current situation, you lack the ability to bloom, which earth wants so badly of you. To balance this energy, make sure you're engaging your mind by learning something, honoring your emotions by actually feeling them in your body (and then processing them), connecting to your sexuality and passion by masturbating or doing something you love, and feeding your spirit through ecstatic motion, dance, rituals, and gratitude.

If you need more earth energy:
When you lack this element, you feel disconnected from the physical. You may feel scattered, unable to settle down, unable to anchor yourself. You can return to the body, your soul's home, by spending time in nature, feeling her support, lying on the ground, and inviting in Gaia's messages. You can also invite more earth into your life by moving your body through dance, working out, stretching, or yoga, as well as by taking care of your health and eating well. Spending time practicing grounding visualizations can help you come back to earth, and so can physically changing or redecorating your environment. Making your home welcoming and beautiful is a grounding ritual in itself.

IF YOU ANSWERED WITH MOSTLY AIR

With a sharp wit and an ability to pierce like the sword, you're able to morph, transform, and shapeshift, defining your limits for yourself. Your mind is your superpower, allowing you to analyze, process, and communicate with conviction and ease. Know thyself indeed, and you do. With your mental power comes a need to create and share your knowledge with others, and you thrive when you are both student and teacher. Like the sword, you know the authority of your tongue, and you know when to reveal or impale without shame. The power of air is presence; it's mirrorlike clarity, the life force of the breath. Even though you can't see air, you still notice its effects.

Air, however, tends to disappear or float away, and this can happen if you're very "in" this element. When out of balance, air can become detached, distant, and caught up in patterns of its own making. This mental anguish and anxiety can cause you to seek escapism through unhealthy habits or to cycle through patterns and thoughts that don't serve you. To balance this energy, practice breath work and grounding meditations to connect with your body, take a bath or journal about your feelings to process your emotions, spend time doing something you're passionate about, and spend time in ritual releasing what no longer serves you to keep your soul healthy.

If you need more air energy:
When you lack air energy, you feel stagnant, uninspired, and too rooted in where you are. You're missing the sense of freedom and growth that this element offers you. You can invite air into your life by working with sacred smoke and using it to cleanse yourself and your space. You can also foster your curiosity and your need for knowledge by taking a class, researching a topic you care about, or by starting something new; anything that inspires the mind is the domain of air. And, of course, you can be guided into this element by working with your breath, by connecting to the present moment, and by working with your thoughts (and not against them).

IF YOU ANSWERED WITH MOSTLY FIRE

You're one hot babe, plugged in and inspired by life popping off all around you. You're sensual, deep feeling, and magical and fiery as hell. You move through this world with a shine and magnetism that attracts others to you, and your commitment to being your own person makes others feel safe in your presence. By working with sexuality as a mode of self-expression, you channel the energy of this element, and you transmute it through creation. When you know this element intimately, you are one with your desires, owning them and not being ashamed of what you feel. You feel safe to live with your fullest expression of self, even if it defies the norms and patriarchal standards you're living with.

Fire's warmth calls you into your fullest manifestation, but when you're too much in this element, you can get burned out, disconnected from what your soul needs, feeding what your ego desires. When you're too much in this realm, you may become detached from your compassion or you may be consumed with lust as its own form of escapism. To balance this element you can ask yourself what you need to be able to find emotional clarity in the present, work with boundaries as a means of self-care, breathe into any discomfort you feel, and heal by releasing any shame around your sexual expression.

If you need more fire energy:
The energy of power and seduction, fire invites you into the realm of sensual transformation. You can summon it into your life by surrounding yourself with this element and its colors. By working with candles and wearing red, gold, yellow, and orange, you can embody the commanding presence of this element. If you want to embrace what this element has to teach you, spend time honoring your own sexuality through masturbation, spending time naked, dancing, making love, and touching and seducing yourself. Sex magick, spending time under the sun, fostering your passions, doing what makes you tick, going on adventures, traveling, eating citrus and spicy foods, and wearing what makes you feel like a sex goddess are all other ways in which you can fan your inner flame to feed your soul's pyre as well.

IF YOU ANSWERED WITH MOSTLY WATER

You're a natural psychic and intuitive, aren't you, dear watery one? This is the element of the heart, of the gracious and divine feminine. Of the subtle. Of unconditional love. You feel things, sensing them in your bones and heart. You have your own relationship to the subtle, talking to the universe in your own way. You are the psychic, the medium, the channel. And you know this already. People often mistake your tenderness and kindness as weakness. But water is strong, even in its softness. Just a drop of water over and over again can carve into rock. Water is gentle, but it can be fierce, the most lethal storm, or the darkest depths of the ocean where not even the light can touch.

Too much water, however, and you can lose sight of which direction is *up*. You become pulled by the current, as if your feelings or emotions are rocks keeping you beneath the surface. With too much water, you become consumed by your story, your pain, the pattern: a victim. Water can also be volatile and unapologetic, taking the form of hurricanes and monsoons and all types of natural disasters. You become these storms when you don't provide space to feel the full range of your emotions. You can find balance by coming back into the physical by grounding, by working with your breath, or through meditation to process and find presence. You can spend time with your passions and turn-ons and by finding gratitude for the emotions and experiences before you release them to the universe.

If you need more water energy:
When you shut yourself off from experiencing one emotion, you shut yourself off from experiencing other emotions as well. To feel all the most delicious, pleasurable, joyous, ecstatic feelings possible, you have to be willing to feel the pain, heartbreak, darkness, and shadows. When you disconnect from water, you lose your center, your intuition, your understanding of what your emotions are telling you. You lose your connection to the feminine and to your dreams. You can spend time submerged in water, in a shower or bath or outside in nature, to welcome this energy into your life. By spending time with your feelings through practices such as therapy, meditation, art, or journaling, you can connect to this

element. Channel water by finding self-compassion, creating based on your feelings, listening and honing your intuition, spending time under the moon, watching sad or moving movies, listening to romantic music, and crying.

IF YOU ANSWERED WITH MOSTLY SPIRIT

Hello, seeker, mystic, old soul. Hello, witch—I see you. You'd much rather be in the forest, or in the ancient temple upon the altar with your soul laid bare. Sipping out of the chalice of the Goddess. Chanting naked under the full moon as you raise energy with your coven. Learning ancient rituals and studying the tarot. When you are working with spirit, you're learning a new way of being that asks you to center your magick and then spread it. Spirit is your connection to the divine, of course, but also your connection to all beings on this earth. We are all spirit manifest, and when you're in the vortex of the magician in your personal life, you also work as a healer and channel for the collective's evolution. Living with spirit means you're attuned to your inner wisdom, accessing inner guidance with ease. Well done! When you live with spirit energy, you see yourself reflected in the divine and you honor this by treating yourself as divine.

Spirit is a little bit of all the elements, the exalted states of earth, air, fire, and water combined. In this way, spirit doesn't have a low vibration, but it can become something that can make you feel alienated. Whether this is real or imaginary doesn't matter; you can use spirituality as a way to bypass all the shit life throws at you. Sometimes it would be easier to lock yourself in a convent or in a cave and meditate, dedicating your life to ritual and disconnecting from the physical, leaving the body. But witchcraft asks for embodiment, bringing divine wisdom into the physical so you can pay it forward and transform the world around you. If you feel like spirit is pulling you away from your life, you can spend time making your home beautiful and inviting over loved ones, being social. You can practice breaths like the fourfold breath to help you physically engage with your body, and you can work with sex magick to further this as well. You can also practice shadow work to make sure you're not spiritually bypassing or ignoring your actual emotions, by exploring what your psyche is really trying to tell you.

If you need more spirit energy:
You can connect to spirit through magick, through what asks you to see past the veil of this reality. Practicing ritual, studying and practicing divination, spending time under the moon, working with crystals, honoring the God/dess, chanting, meditating: all of these mystical practices are meant to lead you to spirit. Try dancing, spinning in circles, practicing rituals of beauty and self-love, honoring your own inner god/dess in whatever way feels best. Find spirit by kissing, making art, lighting candles, gazing at fire, spending time in the ocean, praying at the altar of the elements, crying, re-inventing yourself, having a crush, driving with the windows down. Spirit is the realm of the esoteric, of the spiritual, of the metaphysical. Spirit is also the realm of the miracle of the everyday.

A worksheet to create your own ritual practice with the elements

Witchcraft is many things: A way to reclaim your wild sacredness. A return to the earth, to Gaia, to the Goddess. A way to enchant yourself and the world around you. Witchcraft is also hands-on, tended to with care, with fleshy palms and eyes open wide at every possibility. Witchcraft is ritual, commitment, devotion. Witchcraft is communion with the collective. Witchcraft is claiming your magick.

The elements have (hopefully) already bewitched you. They've courted you, made themselves known, become a familiar presence and perhaps flirted a bit with you. And now you want to take the relationship to the next level. So what do you do? You commit, of course; and you do this through a ritual practice.

In each chapter of this book, there have been rituals, embodiment practices, and magick to help guide you into earth, air, fire,

water, and spirit's spell. Now you are taking these golden threads and weaving them together, customizing a ritual that honors where you are and what you need. Use the following as a guide, and change it up as often as you'd like. Take what works and leave what doesn't. Listen to your intuition, ask the universe for guidance, and don't forget to trust yourself.

As always, before you begin a ritual, set up the space and make sure your environment is conducive to the work you'll be doing. Keep in mind that a ritual usually consists of a beginning and an ending, something to mark the start of the ritual like grounding or lighting a candle, and ending with something like clapping or doing another grounding visualization. You can work with the elements in this worksheet in any order you wish, so don't feel like this is a rigid structure you can't adapt. Add to this list whenever feels right, keeping a copy in your grimoire so you have a list of the rituals you practice, what works for you and what doesn't.

Pick at least one activity from each element to create a balanced ritual practice.

1. EARTH—THE PHYSICAL

a. *Ground—Visualize golden cords moving into the earth, feeding you healing energy and light (grounding meditation on page 25)*

b. *Cast a circle, creating a boundary of protection (page 28)*

c. *Work with crystals—These can be from the earth or associated with any other element*

d. *Practice a tea ritual, choosing herbs based on correspondences or your intuition/how you're feeling that day (page 53)*

e. *Practice earthing or a walking meditation to connect to nature (page 56)*

f. *Meditate with Gaia, connecting to Mother Earth (page 63)*

g. *Embody the earth through slow movement (like the ritual on page 48)*

h. *Spend time in nature, unplugged, being present and taking in its wisdom*

i. *Dance, spin, come back to your body through yoga or exercise*

2. AIR—THE MENTAL

a. *Practice breath work using the guide on page 82 to figure out what breath to work with*

b. *Work with sacred smoke to cleanse you or your space, or try the smoke cleansing ritual on page 104*

c. *Meditate—can be a goddess meditation, guided meditation, silent meditation, or whatever resonates with you*

d. *Meditate with color and breath using the chart on page 89 to help*

e. *Practice letting go of old patterns and relationships through etheric cording (page 102)*

f. *Free write or journal, letting everything out of your mind; you can also use the journal questions on page 112 as a guide*

g. *Spend time in a gratitude practice (page 79)*

3. FIRE—THE SENSUAL

a. *Light a devotional candle on your altar*

b. *Work with mantras and affirmations (page 126) to invigorate your spirit*

c. *Embody fire through working with Kali (page 146) or through feeling it like in a lava meditation (page 132)*

d. *Practice sex magick (page 147) to embody this heat*

e. *Write out what you want to release and burn it up, writing a letter to the person, pattern, or thing you want to let go of*

f. *Find your feral and wild feminine side with breath work and movement, like in the exercise on page 122*

4. WATER—THE EMOTIONAL

a. *Work with the moon, knowing what phase and sign it's in, taking time to connect and reflect with it through meditation or visualization (see page 178 to learn about moon phases)*

b. *Take a ritual bath or shower to cleanse and center (page 203)*

c. *Work with your shadow by meditating, free writing, creating, or connecting to your shadow in another way (page 213)*

d. *Cleanse yourself with holy water or moon water (page 210)*

e. *Connect to your intuition by working with divination or scrying with water*

f. *Realign with your heart center and check in with your emotions through meditation (try the rose meditation on page 217), visualization, or working with Venus and practicing her meditation (page 200)*

g. *Work with roses to help you to heal and integrate your shadow with love and compassion (page 217)*

5. SPIRIT—THE SPIRITUAL

a. *Pull tarot cards at the start of your day, journaling what this means to you*

b. *Create an altar with an intention, whether it's for the elements, the moon, healing, a holiday, or a specific goddess*

c. *Work with goddesses, using the elements to guide you to a good match (see page 270 for how to create a devotional goddess practice)*

d. *Connect with each of the elements through meditation (page 239)*

e. *Invite the elements to help protect and cleanse your space (page 277)*

f. *Invoke or invite in the Goddess (page 271)*

g. *Work with the elementals or a specific elemental (page 299) or invite them into your ritual*

h. *Pick a glamour for the day that embodies the energy you want to carry with you. Base this off your tarot card, the phase and sign the moon is in, what your intuition is telling you, what guidance you received from your meditation, or whatever else speaks to you*

Taking the elements with you

We've come to the end of our journey, but that doesn't mean the journey is over. It only means that your road continues to spiral, and you are meant to follow it. Let the elements guide you wherever you're going. May your magick cradle you in the palm of the universe, reminding you of all your infinite wisdom. You have every right to live the life you have always dreamed of. You have every right to live a life that is full of deep and divine love, mind-blowing and transformational experiences, abundance, and true friendships. You have every right to submerge in the waters of the mystical, to burn with sexuality and eroticism, to expand in moments of freedom, to find a home that you can ground in. Look around; the elements are everywhere. And when you bewitch them, they bewitch the world around you.

Witches choose to see a different world, one in which there's balance, where you strive for your healing alongside the healing of all beings, and the healing of Gaia, the planet, and Mother Earth. When you choose to work with the elements to help you experience karmic evolution, you're weaving a new paradigm that puts the earth back in the center of it all. When you work with and live along any path outside the "acceptable" model and start to take this path seriously, when you consciously connect to the earth and nature, you're returning to the ancestral, to the natural, to that which you inherently remember in the most ancient parts of your soul. You're healing yourself, but you're also healing Gaia.

Dear witch, my hope for you is that you continue to be enchanted by the elements. I hope that you continue exploring with a sense of curiosity, with a sense of wonder, with a sense of hope and optimism. Even when things feel dark, I hope you remember that magick gives you a new set of tools to imagine a different world, a world in which anything is possible. I hope that you choose to see a new paradigm, one in which there's balance, where you strive for your healing alongside the healing of all beings, and the healing of Gaia and the collective. May you take these elemental tools—the pentacle, the sword, the wand, the cup, and the secret ingredient of yourself, spirit—and use them to invoke a better world, for all future generations. It has been an honor sharing this magick with you. With love, compassion, and perseverance, it shall be! And so it is.

APPENDIX 1

Elemental Correspondences

Element	Direction	Archangel	Sense	Herbs
Earth	North	Uriel/ Ariel	Touch	Rosemary, frankincense, bay leaves, oak, daisies, clovers
Air	East	Raphael	Smell	Lavender, eucalyptus, rosemary, dandelion, mugwort, honeysuckle, nettle, thyme, sandalwood
Fire	South	Michael	Sight	Cinnamon, basil, carnation, clove, vanilla, vervain, tobacco, cumin, devil's shoestring, cayenne, mandrake, dragonsblood, St. John's wort, deer's tongue
Water	West	Gabriel	Taste	Rosemary, apple, chamomile, catnip, poppy, ginseng, rose, gardenia, jasmine, birch, watercress
Spirit	Up	Metranon		This one doesn't have as clear associations: aphrodisiacs; herbs like pomegranate, butterfly pea, rose, nettle, ashwaganda

	Crystals	Colors	Magick	Astrological signs
	Black tourmaline, onyx, hematite, obsidian, all crystals since they come from the earth	Green, black, brown, gray, the colors of the earth, neutrals	Wealth, abundance, prosperity, boundaries, protection, grounding, commitment, loyalty, home	Capricorn, Taurus, Virgo
	Selenite, clear quartz, smoky quartz, sodalite, celestite, fluorite, lapis lazuli, lepidolite	Yellow, white, silver, iridescent, gossamer	Business, legal problems, communication, travel, inspiration, knowledge, breath work, astral travel, divination	Aquarius, Gemini, Libra
	Carnelian, citrine, orange calcite, pyrite, tiger's eye, bloodstone, garnet, ruby, peridot	Red, orange, yellow, gold	Transformation, initiation, sexuality, passion, confidence, release, adventure, banishment	Aries, Leo, Sagittarius
	Amethyst, blue lace agate, jade, moonstone, pearl, topaz, malachite, rhodonite	Blue, purple, indigo, silver, white, light pink	Divination, shadow work, love, healing, self-love, karmic and ancestral healing, pleasure, intuition and psychic work, dream work	Pisces, Cancer, Scorpio
	Clear quartz, labradorite, charoite, herkimer diamond, selenite	Silver, gold, the rainbow, all colors	Spiritual development, connecting to your intuition, karmic untangling, past life work, enlightenment, channeling and working with deities	

APPENDIX 2

Correspondences of Herbs

Properties	Herbs
Love	Herbs of Venus, acacia flowers, jasmine, lavender, mistletoe, myrtle, valerian, vervain, violet, rose, gardenia, apple, and cinnamon
Protection	Basil, feverfew, hyssop, laurel, motherwort, nettles, juniper, yerba santa, mullein, cascarilla (powdered eggshells), patchouli, rosemary, rowan, sandalwood, frankincense, myrrh, cinnamon, and vervain
Healing	Lavender, carnation, rosemary, gardenia, garlic, ginseng, hops, mint, saffron, rowan, rue, eucalyptus, and peppermint
Psychic work	Dragonwort, mugwort, ginseng, laurel leaves, saffron, chamomile, dandelion, skullcap, catnip, clover, mint, and nutmeg
Manifesting	Bamboo, beech, dandelion, ginseng, pomegranate, mint, rosemary, sandalwood, violet, and walnut
Creativity	Laurel, lavender, cinnamon, myrtle, valerian, and orange
Banishing/binding	Cascarilla, nettle, devil's shoestring, bamboo, benzoin, cayenne, rosemary, frankincense, mandrake, and peppermint
Wealth	Balm, High John the Conqueror root, lavender, mandrake, oak leaves, saffron, valerian, mint, cinnamon, and citrus

APPENDIX 3

Correspondences of Color

Color	Meaning
Red	Passion, sexual love, vitality, heat, health, attraction, fire
Pink	Love, femininity, nurturing, protection of children and healing, the heart, tenderness, feeling, bliss
Orange	Encouragement, creativity, stimulation, warmth, attraction, power
Yellow	Confidence, inner strength, power, vitality, vigor, self-awareness, happiness, energy, masculinity
Green	Finance, luck, wealth, prosperity, abundance, healing, heart opening, the energy of the earth, fertility
Blue	Tranquility, patience, healing, the ocean, the subconscious, dreams, femininity, relaxation
Purple	Royalty, magick, power, ambition, business progress, spirituality, connection to your third eye and higher self
Black	Absorbs negativity, darkness, night, shadow work, banishing
White	Attracts positivity, healing, light, purity, the energy of the cosmos. Cleansing and clearing as well as protective.
Silver	Celestial energy, the moon, protection, the unconscious, the heavens, the divine
Gold	Wealth, abundance, radiance, victory, money, power

FURTHER READING

Armady, Naha. *Everyday Crystal Rituals: Healing Practices for Love, Wealth, Career, and Home.* Emeryville, CA: Althea Press, 2018.

Ashley-Farrand, Thomas. *Shakti Mantras: Tapping into the Great Goddess Energy Within.* New York: Ballantine Books, 2003.

Basile, Lisa Marie. *Light Magic for Dark Times: 100 Spells, Rituals, and Practices for Coping in a Crisis.* Beverly, MA: Four Winds Press, 2018.

Beyerl, Paul V. *A Compendium of Herbal Magick.* Custer, WA: Phoenix, 1998.

Conway, D. J., *Elemental Magic.* Newburyport, MA: Weiser, 2005.

Crowley, Aleister, and Israel Regardie. *777 and Other Qabalistic Writings of Aleister Crowley: Including Gematria & Sepher Sephiroth.* York Beach, ME: Weiser Books, 1996.

Cunningham, Scott. *Magical Herbalism: The Secret Craft of the Wise.* St. Paul, MN: Llewellyn, 2003.

Dale, Cyndi. *The Subtle Body: An Encyclopedia of Your Energetic Anatomy.* Boulder, CO: Sounds True, 2009.

Driessen, Tamara. *The Crystal Code: Balance Your Energy, Transform Your Life.* New York: Ballantine Books, 2018.

Echols, Damien. *High Magick: A Guide to the Spiritual Practices That Saved My Life on Death Row.* Boulder, CO: Sounds True, 2018.

Farrar, Stewart, and Janet Farrar. *A Witches' Bible: The Complete Witches' Handbook.* Custer, WA: Phoenix, 1996.

Faulkner, Carolyne. *Signs: Decode the Stars, Reframe Your Life.* New York: Random House, 2018.

Garcia, Amanda Yates. *Initiated: Memoir of a Witch.* New York: Grand Central, 2019.

George, Demetra, and Douglas Bloch. *Asteroid Goddesses: The Mythology, Psychology and Astrology of the Re-emerging Feminine.* Berwick, ME: Ibis Press, 2003.

Gillett, Roy. *The Secret Language of Astrology: The Illustrated Key to Unlocking the Secrets of the Stars.* London: Watkins, 2012.

Grossman, Pam. *Waking the Witch: Reflections on Women, Magic, and Power.* New York: Gallery Books, 2019.

Herstik, Gabriela. *Inner Witch: A Modern Guide to the Ancient Craft.* New York: TarcherPerigee, 2018.

Horowitz, Mitch. *The Miracle Club: How Thoughts Become Reality.* Rochester, VT: Inner Traditions, 2018.

McCoy, Edain. *A Witch's Guide to Faery Folk: Reclaiming Our Working Relationship with Invisible Helpers.* St. Paul, MN: Llewelyn, 2003.

Pollack, Rachel. *Seventy-Eight Degrees of Wisdom: A Tarot Journey to Self-Awareness (A New Edition of the Tarot Classic).* Newburyport, MA: Weiser Books, 2019.

Reed, Theresa. *The Tarot Coloring Book.* Boulder, CO: Sounds True, 2016.

Ryan, Christopher, and Cacilda Jethá. *Sex at Dawn: How We Mate, Why We Stray, and What It Means for Modern Relationships.* New York: HarperPerennial, 2012.

Sollée, Kristen J. *Witches, Sluts, Feminists: Conjuring the Sex Positive.* Berkeley, CA: ThreeL Media, 2017.

Starhawk. *The Spiral Dance: A Rebirth of the Ancient Religion of the Great Goddess.* New York: HarperOne, 1999.

Wintner, Bakara. *WTF Is Tarot? & How Do I Do It?* Salem, MA: Page Street, 2017.

LIST OF SPELLS

EARTH

AIR

FIRE

WATER

SPIRIT

IN CONNECTION

ACKNOWLEDGMENTS

This book is dedicated to Gaia, to Mother Earth. To Venus. To the Goddess in all her faces. This is for the witches who have come before me and allowed me to be here. Thank you to the cosmos, for the privilege of being a priestess and oracle for its magick.

Infinite thank-yous to my literary agent, Jill Marr, at Sandra Dijkstra Literary Agency; to my editors Nina Shield and Lauren Appleton; and to Roshe Anderson, Marlena Brown, and my whole team at TarcherPerigee.

To my family, who have always supported me in all my witchiness and subversion. To my mother for being my first introduction to the divine feminine and glamour magick, for being my first face of the goddess, and for always being there with support y besos. To my twin sister for having my back like no one, for her unconditional love always, for being my Yaya and for shooting the beautiful photos in this book. To my father, for his loving kindness and for fostering my love for the unknown, the twilight zone, and the divine, and for being a shining example of the embodied and divine masculine. To my grandma, my Tita, for being another one of my first glamour icons, and for her belief and support in my vision always. To my Grandma Rose, for being one of my angels and guides, for her resilience, for her poetry, and for passing her love of life and words down to me. To my Grandpas—Tito, Joseph, and Harry—for being the best guides and angels, for their humor and support and blessings. To the womxn and men in my ancestry who have aligned with me to get me here, who have my best interest and compassion in mind. To my cousins, *mi tio y tia*, my aunties, my second moms, my LA crew, and all of you who have been a part of my path. I love you all.

To Alexandra Roxo for teaching me about claiming my fullest, wildest, most sacred feminine potential and for the touching foreword to this book. To Suzanne Tatoy for the striking and powerful crystals I babysat that took the photos for this book to the next level. To Konrad and Jenn Ribeiro for sharing the sacred secrets of Topanga with me through these photos, as well as for the new friendship. To all my editors who have fostered my voice to help me get here; at *Nylon*, *HelloGiggles*, *The Numinous*, *The Hoodwitch*, *High Times*, *i-D*, *Allure* . . .

To my coven: Marissa Patrick, my human forever whose support keeps me in gratitude, joy, and alignment. To Ashley Laderer for being the best support system, and the best coworking buddy. To Kristina, Kelsea, Cory, Miranda, Hayley, VV, Amelia, Ivory, Zanya, Jennifer, Brent, and all the other magickal, inspiring, divine, mystic, and talented beings whom I call my coven. To all the Internet witches out there who have seen me and held space for me. To all the witches I get to call my friends and teachers. To my therapist. To Naha Armady, 22 Teachings, Mitch Horowitz, Theresa and Terry Reed, the UPR, Los Angeles, Thoth, and all my other guides, patrons, and mentors on this path—I am so thankful, grateful, and humbled to have your support.

ABOUT THE AUTHOR

Gabriela Herstik is a writer, fashion alchemist, and witch living in Los Angeles, and is the author of *Inner Witch: A Modern Guide to the Ancient Craft*. She is a columnist for *Nylon*, *High Times*, and *Chakrubs*, and writes for publications like *Dazed Beauty*, *Allure*, *Glamour*, *i-D*, and more on witchcraft, fashion, cannabis, and sexuality. Gabriela publishes ritual guides for the full moon, new moon, and holidays of the witch and has been practicing ritual and witchcraft for more than thirteen years. She is a devotee of Venus and believes that magick is for everyone. You can keep up with her magick on Twitter and Instagram at @gabyherstik and find her online at gabrielaherstik.com